The main theme of this book is religion and identity, not only national identity, but also regional and local identities. It is an attempt to penetrate to the heart of vigorous religious and political cultures, both elite and popular, in the long eighteenth and nineteenth centuries. David Hempton deals with all parts of the British Isles at some point in their histories, and brings to life a diverse and variegated spectrum of religious communities, from Argyll to Armagh, from Cornwall to Clare, from the Welsh valleys to the Scottish Highlands and from Birmingham to Belfast. With so much new British history really an extended version of old English history, Hempton has devoted more attention to the Celtic fringes, especially Ireland. It is an exercise in comparative history, but on another level, it attempts to show how richly coloured is the religious history of these islands. It demonstrates also that even in their cultural distinctiveness, the various religious traditions in Britain and Ireland have had more in common than is sometimes imagined.

This book arises from the 1993 Cadbury Lectures at the University of Birmingham.

# RELIGION AND
# POLITICAL CULTURE IN
# BRITAIN AND IRELAND

# RELIGION AND POLITICAL CULTURE IN BRITAIN AND IRELAND

*From the Glorious Revolution to the decline of empire*

DAVID HEMPTON

*Professor of Modern History,*
*The Queen's University of Belfast*

CAMBRIDGE
UNIVERSITY PRESS

Published by the Press Syndicate of the University of Cambridge
The Pitt Building, Trumpington Street, Cambridge CB2 1RP
40 West 20th Street, New York, NY 10011–4211, USA
10 Stamford Road, Oakleigh, Melbourne 3166, Australia

First published 1996

Printed in Great Britain at the University Press, Cambridge

*A catalogue record for this book is available from the British Library*

*Library of Congress cataloguing in publication data*

Hempton, David.
Religion and political culture in Britain and Ireland : from the Glorious Revolution to the
decline of Empire / David Hempton.
p.      cm.
'This book had its origin in the eight Cadbury lectures delivered
in the University of Birmingham in 1993' – Pref.
Includes bibliographical references and index.
ISBN 0 521 47375 6 (hardback). – ISBN 0 521 47925 8 (paperback)
1. British Isles – Religion – 18th century.   2. British Isles –
Religion – 19th century.   3. British Isles – Religion – 20th century.
4. Identification (Religion)   5. Group identity – British Isles.
I. Title.   II. Title: Cadbury lectures
BR758.H46   1996
274.1'07–dc20   95–16854 CIP

ISBN 0 521 47375 6 hardback
ISBN 0 521 47925 8 paperback

C E

*For*
*Louanne, Stephen and Jonathan*

I was born in Belfast between the mountains and the gantries . . .

World is crazier and more of it than we think,
Incorrigibly plural. I feel and portion
A tangerine and spit the pips and feel
The drunkenness of things being various.

Louis MacNeice

# Contents

# *Preface*

The subject of this book is religion and identity; not only national identity in the way that Professor Colley has dealt with it in her recent study of the *Britons*, but also regional and local identities. Within that framework my interest is in trying to penetrate to the heart of vigorous religious and political cultures, both elite and popular. My chronological boundaries, in the main, will be the long eighteenth and nineteenth centuries when the interaction of religion and identity was a vital ingredient in the religious, social and political history of the British Isles, but I shall also say something about how that pattern was eroded in the twentieth century. Foolishly, perhaps, I intend to deal with all parts of these islands at some point in their history, and to try to bring to life a diverse and variegated spectrum of religious communities from Argyll to Armagh, from County Cornwall to County Clare, from the Welsh valleys to the Scottish highlands, and from Birmingham to Belfast. Much is based on my own research over the past decade, but much more is dependent on a great number of distinguished historians of the four nations and beyond whose work can only gain from being brought into a closer relationship with one another than has customarily been the case. I am glad to record my debt to them right at the beginning as well as in the conventional way through the notes, which, for the sake of accessibility, will be kept to a decent minimum. They nevertheless reflect, in a small way, the healthy state of the writing of religious history in these islands.

This book had its origin in the eight Cadbury lectures delivered in the University of Birmingham in 1993, and I thought it right to maintain something of the flavour of the lecture hall in the final text. The prose is therefore a little more pungent, the generalisations a little less qualified and the structure a little more overt than is customary. In addition, all eight chapters were designed to stand by themselves as well as having a stacking mechanism in place for the construction of a greater whole. They were nevertheless not designed as a comprehensive treatment of religion and identity in the British Isles, but rather as a series of investigations of particular religious and political cultures at the height of their power and influence. I have chosen the British archipelago as a whole, not because it is the current fashion so to do, but because the process of comparison and contrast adds immeasurably to the range of conceptual frameworks available to the historian of religious traditions. With so much new British history really an extended version of old English history, I make no apology for devoting more than half the text to the Celtic fringes and for concentrating more on the heart and soul of religious cultures than on their ecclesiastical superstructures, though inevitably, the latter sometimes set the parameters for the former. In any comparative treatment of religion in four countries over two centuries the temptation is to stress similarities at the expense of differences, but temptation, at times, needs to be resisted. I have tried to make comparisons whenever appropriate, but the limits were unfortunately set by the current state of knowledge and my own historical competence.

I wish to record my thanks to those who attended the lectures in Birmingham and sustained such remarkably lively discussions afterwards. I am particularly grateful to a stimulating group of specialists who talked about these issues more intelligently and for longer than I can easily reflect in the text. These included Bob Bushaway, Clive Field, Mike Snape, Sean MacDougall, Geoffrey Robson, John Bourne and a number of research students. My special thanks are due to the Cadbury trustees and to Frances Young and the staff of the Theology and History departments in the University of Birmingham for their quite remarkable hospitality. I am grateful also to the tolerance of my colleagues in Queen's and to the generosity of the Nuffield Foundation without which the final text would never have reached even its present state of coherence. My greatest debt of all is to Hugh McLeod whose formidable knowledge of the religious history of industrial Britain was worn with sufficient lightness and good humour as not to embarrass his guest.

## CHAPTER I

# The Church of England: a great English consensus?

It has been unusually difficult for historians to offer satisfactory organising principles for the study of religion in British society in the long eighteenth century (c. 1689–1832).[1] One reason for that is that many of the dominant historiographical traditions of the eighteenth-century Church had their origins in the period of constitutional revolution between 1828 and 1835 when the terms under which the Established Churches in Britain operated were forever altered. The ideologues of the early Oxford Movement and enthusiastic evangelicals had much in common in decrying both the theory and practice of Whig erastianism which in their view had spiritually impoverished the Church by subjecting it to political manipulation through lay-controlled patronage. Similarly, both Nonconformists and anticlerical radicals had a vested interest in exposing establishment defects, especially those occasioned by excessive wealth and pastoral neglect.[2] Even those as ideologically far apart as Irish Catholics and utilitarian radicals regarded the episcopal Established Churches of the eighteenth century as bulwarks of unmerited privileges enjoyed by the few against the legitimate interests of the many. Hence many treatments of religion in this period are dominated by either attacks or defences of Established Churches in which moral judgements often take the place of realistic assessments of how churches could be expected to operate in an eighteenth-century setting.

An equally important historiographical problem to be aware of is that assessments of the Church of England in particular often depend on whether a date of c.1740 is chosen as the start or the end of a period

---

[1] Important landmarks in the historiography include N. Sykes, *Church and State in England in the Eighteenth Century* (Cambridge, 1934); G. F. A. Best, *Temporal Pillars* (Cambridge, 1964); A. D. Gilbert, *Religion and Society in Industrial England* (London, 1976); J. C. D. Clark, *English Society 1688–1832* (Cambridge, 1985); and J. Walsh, C. Haydon and S. Taylor (eds.), *The Church of England c. 1689–c. 1833: From Toleration to Tractarianism* (Cambridge, 1993).

[2] J. Wade (ed.), *The Extraordinary Black Book* (London, 1832).

of study. In the latter case it seems appropriate to emphasise the ecclesiastical continuities with the Caroline past, the comparative weakness of religious dissent in England, Scotland and Wales, and the relative decline of religion as a disruptive force in British politics. Conversely, although it is accepted that the establishment principle remained central to the *Weltanschauung* of ruling elites until well into the nineteenth century, social historians of religion have detected forces operating from around the middle of the eighteenth century which were inexorably eroding Established Churches throughout the British Isles. These include rapid demographic growth, the commercialisation of agriculture, an increase in the pace of industrial and urban expansion, the rise of popular evangelicalism, the growing unacceptability, especially in Scotland, of the secular exercise of ecclesiastical patronage and the renewed vitality of older forms of both Protestant and Catholic Dissent. All these, it is held, undermined the social deference and dependency upon which Established Churches relied.[3] On a statistical level at least the impact of such changes is striking. Whereas in 1750 the Established Churches in Britain accounted for over 90 per cent of all churchgoers, the proportions had altered dramatically by the time of the census on public worship in 1851. By then Nonconformity was in the ascendancy in every census registration district in Wales; in Scotland the Established Church accounted for only one third of all churchgoers (a decline unduly magnified by the disruption of 1843), in Ireland the Established Church attracted the devotion of less than 10 per cent of the population and in England Nonconformist churchgoers of all sorts made up approximately half the total.

While accepting that the statistics of churchgoing are not very reliable guides to the social influence of Established Churches, it is clear that British society was considerably more pluralistic in 1850 than it had been a century before. It is equally clear, however, that the pace of religious change in the half century after 1790 was much more rapid than in the preceding fifty years and historians need to exercise care lest in explaining the remarkable growth in alternatives to Established Churches they exaggerate both the speed and extent of their decline. The most dramatic change in the pattern of denominational adherence, for example, occurred in Wales, yet it seems probable that Welsh Nonconformity in its home county of Monmouthshire actually lost

[3]    Gilbert, *Religion and Society*; C. G. Brown, *The Social History of Religion in Scotland since 1730* (London, 1987); and idem, *The People in the Pews: Religion and Society in Scotland since 1780* (Dundee, 1993).

ground from 1700 to 1800. The real leap forward in Welsh Nonconformity took place in the first half of the nineteenth century.[4]

A third historiographical problem confronting students of eighteenth-century religion is that until quite recently wide generalisations have been made about the state of the Church of England in particular on the basis of a restricted range of local studies of dubious typicality.[5] As it is now clear that there were often enormous variations of belief and practice between neighbouring parishes within the same diocese and equally wide regional variations within the country as a whole, national projections from local studies need to be based on much wider samples than have customarily been the case. The recent upsurge of interest in eighteenth-century religion, manifested both in published works and thesis literature, has made that task easier. The aim of this chapter, then, is to seek to offer some organising principles within which to view the religious characteristics and social functions of the English Established Church in the long eighteenth century and to highlight some of the period's most important continuities and changes.

### CHURCH AND STATE

One important aspect of recent work has been the renewed emphasis on the religious foundations of much political and social ideology in the eighteenth century. Both attacks and defences of Established Churches were based more on theological and historical frameworks of understanding than on principles of utility or natural rights. Moreover, it is becoming clear that the most intellectually influential ideas on the relationship between Church and State were not so much based on Locke and Warburton as on Hooker and Filmer. Far from being regarded as a protected subsidiary of the State, the Church of England was an integral and indispensable part of the theory and practice of governing. It was therefore 'the identity of sentiment between Church and State that most impressed contemporaries about the social and political attitudes of the Church in the last two decades of the eighteenth century'. The Church as a genuinely nation-wide institution 'upheld the natural hierarchy of mutual obligations which were

---

4  E. T. Davies, *Religion in the Industrial Revolution in South Wales* (Cardiff, 1965), p. 13.
5  The most commonly cited are D. McClatchey, *Oxfordshire Clergy 1777–1869* (Oxford, 1960), and A. Warne, *Church and Society in Eighteenth-century Devon* (Newton Abbot, 1969). For more recent additions see Viviane Barrie-Curien, 'The Clergy in the Diocese of London in the Eighteenth Century', in Walsh, Haydon and Taylor (eds.), *The Church of England*, pp. 86–109, and M. Smith, *Religion in Industrial Society: Oldham and Saddleworth 1740–1865* (Oxford, 1994).

thought to provide social cohesion, and the state protected the legal establishment as the appropriate agent of benevolence and public morality'.[6] Church and State were thus regarded as interdependent; if the one suffered damage so too did the other. In Burke's words, the English regarded their church establishment 'as the foundation of their whole constitution with which, and with every part of which, it holds an indissoluble union'.[7] It must be stressed that such views were not the preserve of a coterie of High Churchmen, the intellectual vitality of whom should not be underestimated, but were the commonly accepted maxims of both governors and the governed in the eighteenth century.[8] Of course, the foundations of such beliefs were repeatedly challenged, both theologically and politically, from the deism of the early Hanoverian period and the radicalism of the 1760s to the more serious threats posed by the French Revolution in the 1790s, but they emerged, if anything, stronger than before. Some of the more radical figures within the Church either turned Unitarian or were seen to be peripheral to the main body of Anglican opinion. Although their views have disproportionately interested historians, their achievements, at least in the short term, were negligible.

Part of the badge of loyalty to Church and State in the eighteenth century was devotion to monarchy and acceptance of the State's right to have a say in ecclesiastical appointments and preferments. Whereas the former, according to Dr Clark, survived the dynastic vicissitudes of the early Hanoverian period to underpin the notion of a patriarchal society until well into the nineteenth century, the latter has been at the sharp edge of much of the criticism of the eighteenth-century Church. It is commonly alleged that the Whig exercise of patronage immeasurably weakened the spiritual vitality of the Church by subjecting it to political control and nepotism. In this area much heat is often generated by a view of patronage quite inappropriate to eighteenth-century circumstances. A recent study of ministerial patronage during the Newcastle years from 1742 to 1762, for example, has shown that patronage was not so much a tool of party as an instrument of government.[9] As the Church was recognised to have a vital role to play

6    E. R. Norman, *Church and Society in England 1770–1970* (Oxford, 1976), p. 15.
7    For Burke's views and for a wider analysis of the intellectual underpinnings of the Church of England see Clark, *English Society*.
8    P. B. Nockles, *The Oxford Movement in Context: Anglican High Churchmanship, 1760–1857* (Cambridge, 1994).
9    S. J. C. Taylor, 'Church and State in England in the Mid-Eighteenth Century: The Newcastle Years 1742–1762', PhD dissertation, Cambridge University, 1988.

in the maintenance of social stability and state security, Newcastle's priority, insofar as power was delegated to him by the king, was to select men of pastoral and administrative ability who could be relied upon to support the Hanoverian regime and steer clear of political controversy. Moreover, it was well understood that since both patrons and protégés reaped tangible benefits from one another's success, no successful system of patronage could be based upon the long-term separation of reward from ability. Uppermost in Newcastle's mind then, when making ecclesiastical appointments, were neither theological nor parliamentary considerations, but rather the need to combine the reward of talent with the good governance of the nation. Here was a policy scarcely designed to enliven the Church's holy mission, but neither was it employed to create an army of political toadies responsive to the will of those in power.

A far more serious problem for the Established Churches in Britain than the exercise of ministerial patronage and political control was the way in which appointments to livings were made throughout the country. In England about half of all advowsons were in the hands of private patrons, and pluralism rose in direct proportion to the number of livings owned by a layman. According to the most recent estimates 36 per cent of the Anglican clergy were pluralists in 1780 and only 38 per cent of parishes had resident incumbents.[10] Although there are wide regional variations there seems little doubt that pluralism was more extensive at the end of the eighteenth century than at the beginning. Nor was this a problem caused solely by lay impropriation and clerical poverty; even when there was a transfer of livings from the laity to the clergy in Norfolk in the period 1780–1830, pluralism did not decline. Moreover, the richer English clergy were as non-resident and pluralistic as their poorer Welsh counterparts. Of course, not all parishes without a resident incumbent were pastorally neglected and not all clerical pluralists were indulging in rich pickings, but it would nevertheless be foolish to underestimate the deep-seated structural and administrative problems at the heart of the eighteenth-century Church. The reason they lasted so long is not entirely attributable to the difficulties of reforming such a cumbersome institution; the fact of the matter is that neither wealthy laymen nor bishops had any great desire to alter a system from which they benefited. Perhaps the ultimate proof of

[10]   P. Virgin, *The Church in an Age of Negligence: Ecclesiastical Structure and Problems of Church Reform 1700–1840* (Cambridge, 1989), pp. 191–6.

the centrality of the Church in the eighteenth-century State is the reluctance of those in authority to tamper with it.

The criticism that the eighteenth-century Church suffered from the iron grip of Whig patronage has often gone hand in hand with the view that the Church's wealth and resources were inappropriately directed to the tasks confronting it. There is, of course, no shortage of material to support such claims whether one looks at income distribution within the Church, the utilisation of clerical manpower or the growing disparities occasioned by rapid demographic change within a relatively static parish system. Not only did the Church inherit many of its most intractable problems from the past, but by the end of the eighteenth century it had to accommodate social and economic changes of unprecedented magnitude. The Church was therefore not an easy institution for its bishops to manage even if they had been impeccable exemplars of devotion and efficiency which, of course, some were not. Recent studies of the early Georgian episcopate have nevertheless largely exonerated the bishops from allegations of fabulous wealth and ruthless exploitation of their ecclesiastical estates.[11] Some sees were, of course, exceptionally wealthy, but the majority sustained a comfortable rather than exotic life-style. In the period after 1760 rising land values did bring about a remarkable increase in the landed income of the Church and there were more bishops with aristocratic connexions. The real weakness of the Hanoverian episcopate, however, has less to do with unacceptable wealth and erastian dependency than on more prosaic structural and administrative problems. Most prelates were appointed late in life, had limited administrative experience, were required to spend much of their time in London, presided over dioceses of irregular size and poor communications, and held their jobs until death regardless of incapacitating infirmities. Without a powerful reforming stimulus from outside, such conditions were unlikely to give rise to dynamic leadership.

Below episcopal level the social structure of the Church, as with the wider society, resembled a pyramid with a broad base. At the beginning of the eighteenth century around half of Anglican livings were worth less than £50 a year and the salaries of stipendiary curates were notoriously inadequate. Detailed studies of the diocese of London

---

[11]   C. Clay, ' "The Greed of Whig Bishops"?: Church Landlords and their Lessees 1660–1760', *Past and Present*, no. 87 (May 1980), 128–57; D. R. Hirschberg, 'Episcopal Incomes and Expenses, 1660–c. 1760', in R. O'Day and F. Heal (eds.), *Princes and Paupers in the English Church 1500–1800* (Leicester, 1981), pp. 211–30.

and elsewhere have shown that there was a decline of unacceptably poor livings in the first half of the century due largely to the effects of Queen Anne's Bounty, which in modern parlance was a successful marriage of public and private capital.[12] But the results were regionally uneven with Wales and the east of England benefiting less than the midlands and the north, and most of the gains were made before 1750 and after 1800. Money alone, however, is not an adequate measure of the life and conditions of humble Hanoverian curates. As Peter Virgin has shown, out of every hundred men ordained in late Georgian England a fifth never held a benefice, a quarter died young, emigrated or went into teaching, and over a third took more than six years to find a living. Only a well-connected minority, a fifth of the total, found a benefice within five years of ordination.[13] Moreover, as is the case with all major employers in all periods, the eighteenth-century Church found it difficult to achieve a perfect balance of supply and demand. There was probably an under-supply of clergy in the middle decades of the century and an over-supply in the early nineteenth century. The former inevitably fuelled pluralism and the latter further exposed weaknesses in the Church's career structure. Most of the stresses and strains associated with such problems had to be absorbed by those at the bottom of the pile, the stipendiary and assistant curates. Stipends in the late eighteenth century were less generous than Sykes supposed, especially in the poorer dioceses of the north and Wales, and were not substantially improved until after the Stipendiary Curates Act of 1813. For the most part these worker bees of the eighteenth-century Church lived a life of peripatetic poverty with few incentives, little supervision, an absence of like-minded company and an undisguised element of rural boredom. The vast majority dutifully performed the tasks required of them, which were mainly the conduct of services and other Anglican formularies, but only an enthusiastic minority devoted themselves to a more wide-ranging pastoral ministry. As with their much wealthier bishops, therefore, such deficiencies as there were among stipendiary curates were not so much caused by excessive moral and theological inadequacy as by deep-seated structural and economic deficiencies at the heart of the Established Church. In the eighteenth century the forces, including self-interest and complacency, operating against effective reform were stronger than those on the other side, and

---

[12] I. Green, 'The First Years of Queen Anne's Bounty', in O'Day and Heal (eds.), *Princes and Paupers.*
[13] Virgin, *The Church in an Age of Negligence*, pp. 138–42.

those who grappled with ecclesiastical reform in the early nineteenth century soon appreciated the very considerable obstacles that stood in the way.

It would be misleading, however, to give the impression that the Church of England in the second half of the eighteenth century was suffering from undue economic hardship for there is much evidence to the contrary. Many clerics, especially in central and eastern counties, benefited from the widespread tithe commutation for land associated with enclosure between 1750 and 1830. Many incumbents in areas of new enclosure became substantial farmers as their average glebe size more than doubled and a new phase of parsonage-building got under way. Thus, according to Professor Ward, 'at the very time when churches within reach of revolutionary France were losing property wholesale, the Church of England was gaining it on a considerable scale throughout the midlands and the east'.[14] Similarly, a pilot study of the occupations of younger sons in the peerage, baronetage and landed gentry carried out by F. M. L. Thompson has shown that the Church was the most common identifiable career choice in the second half of the eighteenth century.[15] The Church of England was thus a more desirable occupation for younger sons after 1740 than it had been in Walpole's England. The rise in the social status of clergy – benefiting from structural changes in the English countryside – was reflected also in the remarkable increase in the proportion of clerical magistrates during the reign of George III. The most recent estimate is that clerical membership of the rural magistracy trebled in the three quarters of a century after 1761, and there is a rough correlation between counties in which tithe commutation for land was most prevalent and those with the highest proportion of clerical magistrates.[16] There were many even within the Church itself who recognised that the pastoral and judicial responsibilities of the clergy were not entirely compatible. Before assessing the implications of such developments on the position of the Church in the English countryside it is appropriate to introduce a few cautionary remarks. In the first place there are considerable regional and chronological variations that need to be taken into account. In Derbyshire, for example, it seems that the benefits of tithe commutation for land were passed on to

---

[14]    W. R. Ward, 'The Tithe Question in England in the Early Nineteenth Century', *Journal of Ecclesiastical History*, 16 (1965), 67–8.

[15]    I am grateful to Professor Thompson for allowing me to refer to these unpublished tables.

[16]    Virgin, *The Church in an Age of Negligence*, pp. 138–42.

tenants in the form of twenty-one-year leases at fixed rents. In other counties of ancient enclosure and small glebes such as Cheshire the growing weakness of the Church of England towards the end of the eighteenth century is not primarily attributable to the rising social status of the clergy, who were in any case a far from homogeneous social group in any county at any period in the eighteenth century.[17] Only a minority of Anglican clergy were wealthy and well connected, only a minority were pluralists or magistrates and only a minority were vigorous and insensitive tithe litigants. Moreover, several local studies have shown that wise use of patronage and clerical zeal could substantially improve the fortunes of the Church in areas where the social and economic structure have been traditionally regarded as antithetical to Anglican success.[18] But, even with all the necessary qualifications, there seems little doubt that the rising social status of many incumbents, especially in areas of new enclosure, did nothing for the pastoral efficiency of the Church in a period when social and religious deference was by no means unconditional. It has been suggested, for example, that the combination of enclosures, tithe collection and clerical magistrates led to more overt anticlericalism in rural England in this period than at any time since the interregnum.[19] Similarly, Ward has stated that the real tragedy for the Church in this period was not so much that 'industrialisation concentrated people where her endowments, manpower and accommodation were thinly spread, but that things went so badly where her resources were concentrated'.[20] All was not well, therefore, in the rural heartlands of the Established Church long before manufacturing and urban growth posed new problems of control for a parish system which the Georgian Church admired far too uncritically. As has been pointed out, the real problem with parishes by the late eighteenth century is that they did not easily accommodate social change on a large scale without major restructuring. As a result, the failure of the Established Church to expand from its old parish centres cost it dear in parts of the country beginning to experience economic and demographic change.[21] In such

---

[17]   R. B. Walker, 'Religious Changes in Cheshire, 1750–1850', *Journal of Ecclesiastical History*, 17 (1986), 77–94.

[18]   Smith, *Religion in Industrial Society*.

[19]   E. J. Evans, 'Some Reasons for the Growth of English Rural Anticlericalism c. 1750–1830', *Past and Present*, no. 66 (1975), 84–109.

[20]   Ward, 'The Tithe Question', 67.

[21]   P. J. Rycroft, 'Church, Chapel and Community in Craven, 1764–1851', DPhil dissertation, University of Oxford, 1988.

circumstances Anglican neglect probably counted for more than social protest in the expansion of Nonconformity.

## THE PERFORMANCE OF THE CHURCH OF ENGLAND

Turning aside from the structural problems of the Hanoverian Church to the performance of its duties, much of the recent historical writing has been kinder to the Church of England than was once the case. F. C. Mather, for example, has shown that north and west of a line from Portland Bill to the Tees the performance of two services on a Sunday was the rule, not the exception, especially in upland areas.[22] The same is true of market towns and well-populated parishes, whereas 'single duty' was more common in the lowlands of southern and eastern England where pluralism and non-residence militated against the frequency of services. A similar pattern exists for the holding of week-day services and the celebration of communion. Although weekly communion was rare outside some of the great city churches, and although quarterly communion was probably close to the average in the country as a whole, many of the more populous parishes in town and country celebrated communion more regularly than four times a year. Attendances at communion services were nevertheless low, partly due to apathy and Puritan anti-sacramentalism, but also due to the timing of services and a genuine fear of incurring personal judgement by profaning the ordinance. In a study of Restoration Wiltshire, for example, Donald Spaeth has shown that some preferred to wait until old age to lessen the risk of spoiling their sacramental devotion with subsequent sin.[23] In addition the poor were less likely to receive communion than the more wealthy.

The three most important points to be made about the public worship of the Church of England in the eighteenth century, therefore, are that paradoxically the Church was at its most diligent in those areas, including the north and Wales, where its large parishes and dispersed settlements made it pastorally vulnerable to evangelical Nonconformity. Secondly, what emerges from the welter of statistics on all aspects of public worship in this period is the sheer diversity of Church life in eighteenth-century England and how much still de-

---

[22]   F. C. Mather, 'Georgian Churchmanship Reconsidered: Some Variations in Anglican Public Worship 1714–1830', *Journal of Ecclesiastical History*, 36 (1985), 255–83.

[23]   D. A. Spaeth, 'Common Prayer? Popular Observance of the Anglican Liturgy in Restoration Wiltshire', in Susan Wright (ed.), *Parish, Church and People* (London, 1988), pp. 125–51.

pended on the personalities of the clergy in specific localities. Thirdly, it is clearly inappropriate to measure the religious and social influence of the Established Church in terms of frequency of services, church-going figures and numbers of communicants, though there is patchy evidence to suggest that all three were in decline during the course of the eighteenth century before signs of improvement can be detected in some dioceses by around 1800. Paradoxically, a more optimistic assessment of the performance of Anglican duties has gone hand in hand with a more pessimistic assessment of the extent of popular devotion to orthodox Anglican forms and services.

Evaluating the relationship between Church and State and assessing the religious performance of the Established Church, valuable though they may be, do not penetrate far enough into the essence of both official and popular Anglicanism in the long eighteenth century. This is a task that historians are now treating more seriously. After a century of fascination with the intellectual and popular alternatives to the Church of England, the time is ripe for a more sophisticated appreciation of Anglicanism itself.

## THE ESSENCE OF OFFICIAL ANGLICANISM

Anglicanism is rooted not so much in a systematic theology as in a theological method based on scripture, reason and appeals to antiquity.[24] The essence of this is flexibility and scope for different emphases within a wide tradition. It is also an intellectual rationale for the inappropriateness of engaging in controversial discussions of speculative divinity and is therefore, in part, a reaction against the High Calvinism of the Lambeth Articles of 1595 and of the Synod of Dort. Theological moderation was accompanied by a strong emphasis on the ethical implications of Christian faith. Far from being an eighteenth-century invention as is conventionally assumed, the stress on Christian ethics was a central characteristic of the plain Anglican tradition from the Reformation. Yet more central in defining the distinctiveness of the Anglican tradition was the role played by the prayer book, the Thirty-nine Articles, the liturgy and canons of the Church, the sacrament of the eucharist and the festivals of the Christian year. Once again there

---

[24] I. Green, 'Anglicanism in Stuart and Hanoverian England', in S. Gilley and W. J. Sheils (eds.), *A History of Religion in Britain: Practice and Belief from Pre-Roman Times to the Present* (Oxford, 1994), pp. 168–87; H. R. McAdoo, *The Spirit of Anglicanism* (London, 1965); and J. Spurr, *The Restoration Church of England, 1649–1689* (London, 1991).

was scope here for different interpretations and emphases (especially over the eucharist) within a broadly consensual tradition. Indeed, the unwillingness to define traditions too closely, except when pressed hard by threats of serious deviation from them, was also a characteristic feature of Anglicanism.

The Church of England was also the beneficiary of a powerful providentialism based on the glories of the Elizabethan period, the return of episcopacy and monarchy at the Restoration and the survival of Church and State against Roman Catholic plots and James's alleged attempts to copy French-style absolutism in the 1680s. The Church of England thus took seriously the notion that it was the bearer of the nation's traditions and the upholder of a truly national faith. This helps explain the zeal with which Anglicans rebutted attempts to erode or undermine the national Church. Thus, depending on where the most pressing threats were perceived to be coming from, Anglicanism has a surprisingly luxuriant literature against Roman Catholicism (from the 1650s to the 1690s), all forms of separatism, including Quakerism and other forms of Protestant Dissent (from the 1690s to the 1720s), all forms of heterodoxy, including atheism, deism, socinianism and arianism (from the 1730s to the 1740s), all forms of uncontrollable popular enthusiasm, including Methodism (from the 1740s to the 1760s), and all forms of 'jacobinical infidelity' (from the 1790s to the 1820s).[25] As a result of outside challenges and internal conflicts, therefore, an Anglican synthesis had evolved 'that rested on a shared basis of views on doctrine, worship and Church organisation which originated in the mid-sixteenth century but had been modified in response to the many challenges it had faced over the following two and a half centuries'.[26] In particular the alleged twin excesses of 'Popish superstition' and 'Puritan exclusivity' were to be avoided through stress on an inclusive national church, reasonable doctrines and Christian ethics.

The cohesion of the Hanoverian Church was thus strengthened by a cult of moderation, between the authoritarianism of Rome and the excessive individualism of radical Protestantism. In this the Church gained added strength from its apparent consonance with classical and enlightenment ideals of balance, proportion and harmony – a polite and reasonable golden mean. Even calendrical occasions encouraged balance: January 30th commemorated the execution of Charles I

---

[25]  Walsh, Haydon and Taylor (eds.), *The Church of England*, pp. 29–51; R. Hole, *Pulpits, Politics and Public Order in England* (Cambridge, 1989).

[26]  Green, 'Anglicanism in Stuart and Hanoverian England', p. 180.

(against Puritan sectaries) and November 5th celebrated the preservation of the nation from popery and superstition. There was a similar balance between lukewarmness and enthusiasm in Anglican attacks on lax religious practice on the one hand and the alleged fanaticism of the Methodists on the other.

Underpinning this Anglican consensus was a profound belief that the Established Church supplied the religious foundation for England's 'fair and beautiful constitution', 'the finest government under heaven'. 'For the clergy', states James Bradley, 'the English government with the rule of law supported by the moral precepts of the Established Church was the perfect ideal.' England was, in essence, a Christian state guided by Christian principles. All this was accompanied by a profound veneration of English law, a 'sacred barrier' against disorder and licentiousness. Even the truth of the gospel itself is described as a law in the clerical propaganda of the American revolutionary period. The social foundation for law was in turn to be found in the moral precepts of the Church. The Bishop of Rochester stated in 1780 that 'no society could subsist without government, nor government without order, nor order without laws; so neither could laws themselves avail without the aid of some powerful internal principle to enforce their operation'.[27] Such a principle was supplied by the teaching of the Established Church which promoted obedience, submission, orderliness, respect for authority, patience in suffering, civility, restraint and loyalty. Such national virtues, nurtured by the Church, were frequently contrasted with bawdy Wilkesite radicals, disloyal colonists and unreliable Dissenters. There is, of course, more than a hint of irony in the fact that such luxuriant propagandist pontifications on behalf of the Established Church conveniently ignored the part played by some churchmen both in undermining James II in 1688 and in engaging in Jacobite treason thereafter.[28] Anglican respect for the law and the constitution was nothing, if not selective.

The idea of a consensual Anglicanism underpinning a national way of life has to take into account several contrary arguments. The first is that the Church was itself cripplingly divided into theological and political parties. But episcopal biographies consistently show that their subjects had the capacity to be conscientious churchmen first and politicians second. Moreover, political High and Low Churchmanship

[27] J. E. Bradley, 'The Anglican Pulpit, the Social Order, and the Resurgence of Toryism during the American Revolution', *Albion*, 21 (1989), 361–88.

[28] G. V. Bennett, *The Tory Crisis in Church and State 1688–1730* (Oxford 1975).

did not always equate to its theological equivalents. Terms were generally used as stereotypes and represented the extremes of opinion rather than the views held by most of the bishops and the clergy. The most recent contributions on this subject tend to emphasise

the non-partisan nature of much churchmanship and the dominance of a 'Mainstream' Anglicanism, whose minor cross-currents did little to inhibit a high degree of clerical conformity, co-operation and consensus ... it is unwise to treat the history of the Church of England merely in terms of a perpetual struggle between opposing forces. That there was partisanship in the eighteenth-century Church is clear, but this is not to say that there were 'Church parties' in the High Victorian sense, well-organised, possessed of a keen sense of group identity and more or less permanently mobilised for combat.[29]

A second argument against a consensual Anglicanism is the view that the eighteenth-century Church had more than its fair share of bitter controversies: the Sacheverell affair, the Bangorian controversy, the fight against the deists, the subscription controversy and the Feathers' Tavern petition, the inner debates over coercion during the American Revolution, and so on. But threats from without could make internal cohesion even stronger and the pressure from advanced liberals paradoxically strengthened orthodoxy and gave a boost to the High Church tradition which is only now getting the attention it has for so long deserved.[30] Unlike the Church of Scotland, there were no major secessions from the eighteenth-century Church of England with the possible exception of the Methodist Plan of Pacification in 1795.[31] What is perhaps of more importance for the future fortunes of the Church, however, is that by the end of the eighteenth century the popular basis for a consensual Anglicanism was under threat from a formidable range of pressures. In response the Church of England increasingly turned its back on the national consensus it had worked so hard to create, and became more wedded to establishment values on the one hand and isolation from some of the major currents in European religion on the other. A more competitive and pluralistic religious environment was in the process of being created.[32]

---

[29]   Walsh, Haydon and Taylor (eds.), *The Church of England*, p.30. See also J. Gregory, 'The Eighteenth-Century Reformation: the Pastoral task of the Anglican Clergy after 1689', in Walsh, Haydon and Taylor (eds.), *The Church of England*, pp. 67–85.

[30]   Nockles, *The Oxford Movement in Context*; Clark, *English Society*.

[31]   D. Hempton, *Methodism and Politics in British Society 1750–1850* (London, 1984), pp. 55–84.

[32]   W. R. Ward, 'The Eighteenth-Century Church: a European View', in Walsh, Haydon and Taylor (eds.), *The Church of England*, pp. 285–98.

## THE ESSENCE OF POPULAR ANGLICANISM

While statistics alone may not be a very useful guide to the popular religious beliefs and practices of the eighteenth-century laity, finding alternative organising principles that do justice to the complexity of the subject is not easy. There is, moreover, a thinner vein of historiography to draw upon than there is for both the seventeenth and nineteenth centuries, while the ideological differences among historians are just as sharp. Edward Thompson, for example, was of the opinion that the Church was both instigator and victim of the increasing gap between patrician and plebeian cultures in the eighteenth century and consequently lost control of the ritualistic and leisure activities of the poor.[33] The sheer erastianism of the Church prevented it from exercising an effective paternalist influence over the mass of the people and left the door open for groups such as the Methodists to offer a more compelling alternative. Conversely, Jonathan Clark has suggested that the ideological centrality of Anglicanism in the Hanoverian State penetrated more deeply into the population as a whole than many suppose. Not only was the divine right of kings embedded in popular consciousness by religious celebrations of royal anniversaries and the persistence of belief in the healing powers of monarchs, but the Church was intimately involved in the life of the community through its uncontested monopoly over the rites of passage, its provision of welfare and education, its widespread distribution of popular forms of religious literature and its thorough identification with the political, legal and social institutions of the State both at the centre and in the localities.[34] Thus, the Church was not simply the religious arm of the State, but rather offered a framework of loyalty and allegiance within which other activities had their meaning. The ideological foundations of this debate render it impossible of resolution within the categories employed by Thompson and Clark, but fortunately there are other potentially more rewarding routes into the study of popular Anglicanism.

It is clear, for example, that the eighteenth-century Church enjoyed a high level of conformity, a low level of attendance, an even lower participation in communion and yet was widely, almost universally, used for baptism, confirmation, marriage and burials. It is equally clear

[33] E. P. Thompson, 'Patrician Society, Plebeian Culture', *Journal of Social History*, 7 (1974), 382–405; 'Anthropology and the Discipline of Historical Context', *Midland History*, 1 (1972), 41–55; and *Customs in Common* (London, 1991), pp. 49–55.

[34] Clark, *English Society*, pp. 161–73.

that religion, however that is to be defined, played an important part in the celebratory rhythms of the State and of the local customs associated with the agricultural calendar. In the Rogation week perambulations of the parish, for example, Bob Bushaway suggests that the Church helped underpin for the labouring poor 'the geographical basis of the community as a ceremonial unit' and 'reaffirmed an older economic and social structure'.[35] Moreover, to say that much popular celebration was impious and bawdy is not to deny the symbolic importance of the Church nor the central role occupied by many clergymen in village festivities. Similarly, to conclude that Christian ceremonies were relatively less important as religious occasions than as social events is to introduce an unhelpful distinction between the sacred and the secular into the function of religion in eighteenth-century communities. There is no denying the fact, however, that the strictly religious content of rituals and ceremonies declined towards the end of the eighteenth century, particularly in the towns.

Another fruitful line of enquiry into the religious beliefs and practices of the lower orders is to investigate the various forms of cheap literature in common circulation. The results of such enquiries are predictably ambiguous. There is no doubt that the Church, through the distribution of catechisms, tracts and manuals, and devotional and prayer aids, made a more serious attempt to communicate with the poor than was once supposed.[36] There is also a continuation of religious chapbook literature with a strong emphasis on prophecies, judgements, signs and wonders. But much chapbook literature was concerned more with popular entertainment than with piety. There is, therefore, a romantic, irreverent and disrespectful tone to much of this genre which Hannah More's Cheap Repository Tracts set out to counteract. Ironically, her best selling tracts were also her most sensational. What the various surveys of popular literature in the early modern period have shown is that, not surprisingly, there was a wide range of material to suit a wide range of tastes.[37] The reading materials of the poor, no less than their rituals and festivals, show a breadth of meaning and experience which crude divisions into two broad categories, whether based on social class

---

[35]  B. Bushaway, *By Rite: Custom, Ceremony and Community in England 1700–1800* (1982), p. 87.

[36]  I. M. Green, *The Christian's ABC: Catechisms and Catechizing in England c.1540–1740* (forthcoming, 1996). I am grateful to Dr Green for introducing me to this material.

[37]  D. M. Valenze, 'Prophecy and Popular Literature in Eighteenth-Century England', *Journal of Ecclesiastical History*, 29 (1987), 75–92; and S. Pedersen, 'Hannah More meets Simple Simon: Tracts, Chapbooks, and Popular Culture in Late Eighteenth-Century England', *Journal of British Studies*, 25 (1986), pp. 84–113.

or level of religious commitment, can never hope to encapsulate. Most communities in the eighteenth century, as with the seventeenth, contained a minority of the truly pious, some completely indifferent, and a great many more who professed what has been called an 'unspectacular orthodoxy', which was flexible enough to accommodate life-cycle changes and eclectic enough to serve a variety of religious and social functions. Such popular devotion as there was to Anglicanism in the eighteenth century was, therefore, a delicate mixture of social utility, rural entertainment and moral consensus in which the parish church and all its associated values was closely enmeshed, albeit within certain defined limits set by the community. It is possible also to demonstrate the influence of Anglicanism on popular music-making, health and healing, law and public morality and even on the common usage of language itself. None of this is to deny the importance of what historians have inadequately described as 'pagan' and 'superstitious' elements in popular religion nor to minimise the profound gap which often existed between clerical expectations and popular practices, but no treatment of religion in eighteenth-century communities can afford to underestimate the centrality of church and religion in the social life of the parish.

In many respects Anglicanism supplied a form of religion well adapted both to the demands and the lack of demands of the eighteenth-century populace. For the devout, it offered religious societies, communion, regular services and an easily transferable *domestic* piety, and for the less earnest it provided the all-important rites of passage and a range of festivals and celebrations. For many more the Church of England was at the centre of their loyalties, however vaguely they were understood or expressed. Here was a loyalty based not so much on theological conviction as on cultural and communal identification. The parish church offered continuity with the past (not least in its graveyard), a village focal point in the present and a heritage to be passed on to future generations. It was both a building to be cared for and a holy place to venerate; it was a place to ring bells and practise music; it was a place where the whole village could 'meet together with their best faces, and in their cleanliest habits'; it was a place where some detected the ancient soul of England itself and expressed their affection in the most Freudian of terms.[38] In some ways the parish

38   Walsh, Haydon and Taylor (eds.), *The Church of England*, pp. 25–8; J. Albers, ' "Papist Traitors" and "Presbyterian Rogues": Religious Identities in Eighteenth-Century Lancashire', in Walsh, Haydon and Taylor (eds.), *The Church of England*, pp. 317–33.

church was more important than the clergy. One was permanent and the other temporary. One was at the heart of the village, the other might be peripheral, geographically, socially or theologically. It was perfectly possible, therefore, to combine anticlericalism with devotion to the Church. Indeed corporate opposition to clerical shortcomings is itself one of the most cohesive and durable features of the Anglican tradition. Popular Anglicanism, as with its more elite versions, was shot through with paradoxes, ambiguities and inconsistencies.

Another route into the nature of popular Anglicanism is to try and decode the communal belligerence inflicted on Methodists, Dissenters and other religious deviants. Anti-Methodist rioting in particular was not purely an instrument of social control, but had genuinely popular motivation and support.[39] It was feared that Methodism was either an ingenious new form of popery or a recrudescence of an older Puritan tradition in opposition to a convivial village culture. Many regarded its sabbatarianism, temperance, criticisms of village sports and methodical disciplines as antithetical to community harmony. Pretending to be better than other people and driving a wedge between the 'saved' and the 'lost' were criticisms of Methodism that survived in village communities until at least the end of the nineteenth century.[40] Similarly, there were frequent allegations of Methodism splitting families, as women and children were thought to be more susceptible to emotional religion than were adult men. Early Methodism was also viewed as a religious cloak for sexual orgies (love feasts, holy kisses and spiritual trances) and as a religious pretext for appropriating money for undeclared and scurrilous purposes.[41] In addition, rumours abounded of Methodism inducing madness, encouraging witchcraft and bringing illness and misfortune.[42] Methodism was thus perceived as new, disruptive and divisive, whether in families, villages, parishes or the State. Most anti-Methodist rioters, therefore, saw themselves as acting in defence of traditional values and community solidarity. In general, however, the weapons they employed were those of ritual humiliation rather than crude violence. There was moderation, it seems, even in persecution.

[39]  J. Walsh, 'Methodism and the Mob in the Eighteenth Century', *Studies in Church History*, 8 (1972), 213–27; D. Hempton, 'Methodism and the Law, 1740–1820', *Bulletin of the John Rylands University Library of Manchester*, 30 no. 3 (1988), 93–107.

[40]  F. Thompson, *Lark Rise to Candleford* (London, 1973), pp. 209–29.

[41]  Lambeth Palace Library Mss, Secker Papers, 8, fos. 8–11, 22, 92–6.

[42]  Ibid., 8, fos. 8–10, 66, 73–4.

### THE CONSENSUS UNDER STRAIN

Although the Church of England in the long term had more to fear from the rise of popular evangelicalism within its own ranks than from alternative denominations, there were other challenges to the stability and dominance of the Established Church by the end of the eighteenth century. By 1790, for example, it seems probable that there were slightly more Roman Catholics in Britain than members of Methodist societies, though comparisons are invidious because of widely different tests of membership and levels of commitment. Estimates of the total Catholic population in Hanoverian Britain are notoriously hard to make, but according to Professor Bossy numbers began to rise from about 1720 after a century of equilibrium and began to accelerate even faster from about 1770.[43] The areas with the highest density of Catholics were Monmouthshire, Lancashire, Durham and a narrow band across the Highlands and islands of northern Scotland, but there were also appreciable numbers in many English counties as far apart as Northumberland and Hampshire. The most important change in the internal structure of the Catholic community in the modern period was caused by the impact of mass immigration from Ireland, but this did not gather pace until the end of the century. Before that there is evidence from several local studies to suggest that the English Catholic community was already changing rapidly because of its dispropor-tionate concentration in those parts of the country most affected by economic and social changes. Thus, by the end of the century probably a higher proportion of Catholics were engaged in non-agricultural occupations than the population as a whole and the consequent weakening of landlord control within Catholicism enabled the clergy to extend their influence. Certainly Bossy's estimate of a threefold increase in Catholic numbers in the four Lancashire towns of Manchester, Liverpool, Preston and Wigan in the period 1783–1800 is striking. A chronic shortage of funds and sometimes of manpower prevented the Catholic Church from fully realising the potential of its growing urban congregations.

The growth in the number of Methodists and Roman Catholics in the second half of the eighteenth century is paralleled by the growth of Old Dissent from its base level in the 1730s. It has been estimated, for example, that the number of Independents and Particular Baptists

---

[43]  J. Bossy, *The English Catholic Community 1570–1850* (London, 1975).

more than doubled in the period 1750–1800 and this growth was sustained well into the nineteenth century. Although much of this growth has been explained by the influence of evangelicalism, particularly Calvinistic Methodism, Old Dissent had its own traditions of itinerancy and evangelism upon which to draw, and the evangelical revival by no means obliterated denominational distinctions in the late eighteenth century. Evangelicalism influenced, but did not entirely transform, the theology, religious practices and politics of the Old Dissenting tradition.[44] Much of the historical interest in that tradition in the second half of the century has been focused on its political characteristics. The idea that religious dissent in this period was important in the evolution of British radicalism is not new, but it was re-stated with characteristic boldness by Jonathan Clark in his book *English Society 1688–1832*. He states that the intellectual structure of the arguments against the established social and political order – anachronistically called radicalism by historians – was ultimately based on theological, not social and economic, principles. Thus, whether one looks at Wilkes or Paine, or Price and Priestley, or even those Anglicans who drifted into Unitarianism after the failure in 1772 of the Feathers' Tavern petition against subscription to the Thirty-nine Articles, the common denominator is that religious heterodoxy was the intellectual foundation of their critique of Church and State.[45]

Although his work is a timely corrective to some trends in the historiography of late eighteenth-century radicalism, Clark's analysis, of necessity, does not penetrate very far into the Dissenting community itself. Here the picture is rather more complex and still far from complete. Many Dissenters were of course not much interested in politics, and if they were the chances are that their energies were more concentrated on local struggles for power in the boroughs than in campaigns for parliamentary reform or repeal of the Test and Corporation Acts.[46] Moreover, those so-called Rational Dissenters who formed cohesive chapel elites in the major commercial centres of the country were neither representative of Dissent as a whole nor rigidly excluded from the political structures of the towns they helped

---

[44]   D. W. Lovegrove, *Established Church, Sectarian People: Itinerancy and the Transformation of English Dissent, 1780–1830* (Cambridge, 1988).

[45]   Clark, *English Society*, ch. 5.

[46]   J. E. Bradley, 'Whigs and Nonconformists: "Slumbering Radicalism" in English Politics, 1739–1789', *Eighteenth Century Studies*, 9, no. 1 (1975), 1–27; and idem, *Religion, Revolution and English Radicalism: Nonconformity in Eighteenth-Century Politics and Society* (Cambridge, 1990).

to build.[47] It was possible for them, as with many Methodists, to be upset on occasions by the niggardly limits of religious toleration under the Toleration Act without necessarily capitulating to an all-out attack on Church and State. Many no doubt became more emboldened in the late 1780s when it seemed that political events in England and France were going their way, but a combination of Pitt's policies and Church-and-King mobs soon dampened their ardour. Rational Dissenters suffered the same kind of fate in the 1790s as did the Low Church liberals within the Established Church, as the forces of reaction made ground in all the major British religious traditions.[48] Only in the Celtic fringes, and especially in Ireland, was religious deviance a serious threat to the stability of the eighteenth-century State. To take this view is not to deny the importance of civic rivalry in the provincial towns of eighteenth-century England, where there was a surge of both Anglican and Dissenting church-building in the second half of the century which helped attract a more ambitious and talented clergy. In a number of such towns religious divisions inevitably shaded off into political and administrative divisions making it virtually impossible for the parish to function as a 'credible single focus for communal religious solidarity'.[49] This, of course, had long-term implications for the future development of social and political structures in English towns and cities.

Of more significance than the traditional threat from Roman Catholicism and religious dissent were the complex social, economic, political and intellectual changes of the period dominated by the French Revolution. Here the benchmarks are not difficult to set. They include Tom Paine's powerful critique of religious establishments in the *Rights of Man* in which he provocatively stated that religious toleration and religious intolerance were both despotisms. 'The one assumes to itself the right of withholding Liberty of Conscience, and the other of granting it. The one is the pope armed with fire and faggot, and the other is the pope selling or granting indulgences. The former is church and state, and the latter is church and traffic.'[50] Far more serious for the Church than even Paine's thunderbolts was 'a subsistence crisis of European proportions, so severe that the Speenhamland magistrates adopted the extraordinary

47  J. Seed, 'Gentlemen Dissenters: The Social and Political Meanings of Rational Dissent in the 1770s and 1780s', *Historical Journal*, 28 (1985), 299–325.
48  N. U. Murray, 'The Influence of the French Revolution on the Church of England and its Rivals, 1789–1802, DPhil dissertation, University of Oxford, 1975.
49  Wright, *Parish, Church and People*, pp. 152–202.
50  T. Paine, *Rights of Man* (Harmondsworth, 1969).

expedient of subsidising the wages of labourers actually in work'.[51] The
growth of urban radicalism, rural poverty and fear of the increasingly
exorbitant costs of poor relief challenged the old order hard at its most
vulnerable points. The influence of the clergy declined spectacularly,
one symptom of which was their inability to raise Church-and-King
mobs after 1795. 'As a working establishment', writes Ward, 'the
Church of England collapsed even quicker than that of France.'[52]

State power, weaker in England than in many other European
states, was no solution to the Church's difficulties. As the rising tide of
undenominational itinerant preaching and Sunday schools threatened
to alter the religious geography of the nation, the State first refused to
stop itinerant preaching and then launched a belated and misguided
assault on it in the shape of Lord Sidmouth's Bill in 1811. Ironically,
and revealingly, the failure of Sidmouth's Bill paved the way for an
*extension* of religious toleration as a bribe to buy the political loyalty of
enthusiastic Dissenters. In its hour of need the Church found the State
more committed to maintaining order than to propping up a national
religious establishment.[53]

The return of peace in 1815 thus saw the Church of England in a
more vulnerable position than at any time since the Restoration in
1660. Its misfortune was that 'historical factors over which it had little
or no control were increasingly disturbing the stability of the social and
administrative structure in which the clergy played so prominent a
part'.[54] Stretched by rapid demographic change, challenged by militant radicals, undermined by evangelical Dissent, picked over by
utilitarian radicals and losing control over the Celtic fringes of the
British State, the Established Church seemed to be riding a storm tide
from which there was no safe anchorage. Its inglorious and politically
inept performance during the Reform Bill crisis seemed to spell
disaster. No longer a confessional state after the constitutional revolution of 1828–32, it was in the balance, or so some of its most ardent
supporters believed, whether England would retain an Established
Church or not.[55]

[51]   W. R. Ward, 'Revival and Class Conflict in Early Nineteenth-Century Britain', in idem, *Faith and Faction* (London, 1993), pp. 285–98.

[52]   Ibid., p. 287.

[53]   D. Hempton, 'Thomas Allan and Methodist Politics 1790–1840', *History*, 67 no. 219 (1982), 13–31.

[54]   N. Gash, *Pillars of Government and Other Essays on State and Society c. 1770–c. 1880* (London, 1986), p. 18.

[55]   O. Chadwick, *The Victorian Church*, part 1 (London, 1966), pp. 7–47.

Space does not permit a detailed investigation of how the Church survived and even prospered in the Victorian era. The role of the ecclesiastical commission, the enthusiasm of evangelical and Oxford Movement clergy, the old penchant for timely and limited concession and the determination of England's propertied elite to hold on to some kind of established church all played their part. But so too, as the recent writings of a distinguished group of Oxford graduate students make clear, did the Church itself. 'If only historians would drag their gaze away from the hypnotic fascinations of Westminster and Oxford', states Arthur Burns, 'they would find a vigorous movement of diocesan revival in the Church of England stemming from the beginning of the nineteenth century.'[56] With its roots in the old High Church tradition, and encouraged by many evangelicals, the Church of England, by turning back to its historic institutions and by appealing to its past history as both a national church and a centre of community life, had begun to put its own house in order long before the shock of the constitutional revolution. If anything, the early Victorian squabbles between evangelicals and supporters of the Oxford Movement did as much to undermine the structural renewal of the Established Church as to reinvigorate its holy mission. The message from this and other comparably optimistic studies, is that the Church of England, as an historic establishment, naturally encountered severe difficulties in the half century after the French Revolution, but it was also able to build on its traditional strengths to emerge in the mid-Victorian period in a far stronger position than many anticipated. The Church of England, as a great English consensus, had taken a frightful battering, but it had within it quite unexpected powers of recovery.

On a more fundamental level, however, the decade of the 1790s was a watershed in the fortunes of the Church of England.[57] It was in this decade that the case for an Anglican monopoly of state power and popular allegiance was fatally undermined. Although in the nineteenth century the Church of England survived as an establishment and improved its efficiency as a church, it was no longer the uncontested church of the English. Deprived of the power of the old theory of obligation, and subjected to new principles of utility, the Church increasingly had to rely instead on its control of

---

[56] R. A. Burns, 'The Diocesan Revival in the Church of England c. 1825–1865', DPhil dissertation, University of Oxford, 1990, p. 319.

[57] W. R. Ward, *Religion and Society in England* (London, 1972), p. 1.

social policy. But, however vigorously Established Churchmen defended their interests, they were no match for the corrosive forces of religious pluralism, class conflict and state welfarism. The establishment principle miraculously survived, but its social foundations were swept away.

## CHAPTER 2

# *The Methodist revolution?*

The recent completion of the four-volume *History of the Methodist Church in Great Britain* (1988), a project commissioned by the Methodist Conference some forty years ago, seems an appropriate point to attempt a re-evaluation of the impact of Methodism in English society between the death of John Wesley and the outbreak of World War One.[1] Its massive bibliography, extending to some fifty pages for this period alone, and including many of the most influential historians of modern Britain, is both a tribute to the strange power Methodism has exercised over generations of research students and a revealing guide to the main turning-points of Methodist historiography.

Most obviously, there has been a marked decline in the number of words devoted to Methodist theology, spirituality and biography, and a corresponding increase in studies of the personal, social and political impact of Methodism on English localities. Such a trend was accelerated by the attention brought to the subject by the socialist historians Christopher Hill, Eric Hobsbawm and Edward Thompson,[2] whose pioneering, if sometimes crude, work stimulated a remarkably rich literature culminating in the recent publication of the History Workshop volume *Disciplines of Faith.*[3] The high quality of many of its contributions, and the fact that it was dedicated to John Walsh, who of all the eminent historians of Methodism was the most prepared to take religious motivation seriously, shows that reductionist interpretations of popular religion are almost dead and that the previously wide gulf between ecclesiastical historians and

[1] R. Davies, A. R. George and G. Rupp (eds.), *A History of the Methodist Church in Great Britain* (London, 1965–88).

[2] E. J. Hobsbawm, 'Methodism and the Threat of Revolution in Britain', *History Today*, 7 (1957), 115–24; E. P. Thompson, *The Making of the English Working Class* (London, 1963).

[3] J. Obelkevich, L. Roper and R. Samuel (eds.), *Disciplines of Faith: Studies in Religion, Politics and Patriarchy* (London, 1987).

social historians of religion is now less impassable. More recently, much of the creative work on Methodist history has concentrated on the religious experiences of ordinary people, including women and children, and the way in which those experiences were shaped by social change, family structure, gender and emotion. Despite the occasional misplaced attempt to find the holy grail of Methodism's national essence by those with an ideological axe to grind, much of this work, of necessity, has been grounded in intensive local studies that have drawn attention to the sheer variety and complexity of nineteenth-century Methodism.[4] But if the telephoto lens has brought clearer definition to the Methodism of the English regions, the wide angle has shown that regional particularity must be viewed against the backdrop of an international religious revival from the Urals in the East to the American frontier in the West.[5]

### GROWTH AND DECLINE

Most of the contested areas of Methodist historiography ultimately go back to rival explanations of its growth and decline; much else depends on positions taken on that fundamental issue. The facts themselves are not much in dispute, thanks to the convenience of class membership figures as a reasonable guide to Methodist strength, if not Methodist influence. The various Methodist connexions grew faster than the population as a whole before 1840, held their own until the middle of the 1880s, and then declined relative to the total adult population until 1906 before declining in absolute terms thereafter.[6] Both the rapidity and the chronological and geographical unevenness of Methodist growth were clearly linked to wider changes in the English economy and society, but attempts to relate spurts of Methodist growth to economic depression on the one hand and the growth of political

[4]    Many unfortunately remain unpublished, but can be traced through the bibliography in *History of the Methodist Church*, vol. IV. Among published works, the following are the most useful: R. Moore, *Pit-Men, Preachers, and Politics* (London, 1974); J. Obelkevich, *Religion and Rural Society* (Oxford, 1975); J. Rule, 'Methodism, Popular Beliefs and Village Culture in Cornwall, 1800–50', in R. D. Storch (ed.), *Popular Culture and Custom in Nineteenth-Century England* (London, 1982), pp. 48–70; and S. Yeo, *Religion and Voluntary Organisations in Crisis* (London, 1976).

[5]    W. R. Ward, *The Protestant Evangelical Awakening* (Cambridge, 1992); M. Noll, D. Bebbington and G. Rawlyk (eds.), *Evangelicalism: Comparative Studies of Popular Protestantism in North America, the British Isles and Beyond, 1700–1990* (Oxford, 1994).

[6]    R. Currie, A. Gilbert and L. Horsley, *Churches and Churchgoers: Patterns of Church Growth in the British Isles since 1700* (Oxford, 1970); A. D. Gilbert, *Religion and Society in Industrial England* (London, 1976).

radicalism on the other have not proved very fruitful.[7] There are examples of Methodist growth in periods of economic depression, including Yorkshire in the 1790s and Lancashire during the great cotton depression of the 1860s, but more generally the data is ambiguous and there is no clear pattern of relationship between religious revivals and economic changes.[8] What does seem to be the case is that whereas short sharp bursts of economic hardship or epidemics of contagious diseases could temporarily stimulate religious enthusiasm, long-term economic decline was a disaster for religious connexions dependent upon voluntary subscriptions. Similarly, the relationship between the growth of Methodism and political radicalism is more complicated than either Thompson's oscillation theory or Hobsbawm's concurrent expansion ideas would permit.[9] It is hard to resist the conclusion that religious attraction or repulsion is neither a straightforwardly economic nor political transaction.

A more constructive approach to understanding the expansion of Methodism, without in any way diminishing its distinctive theology, organisation and evangelical zeal, is to see it as part of much wider structural changes in English society in the generation overshadowed by the French Revolution.[10] In this period a complex of social tensions caused by population growth, subsistence crises and the commercialisation of agriculture, and further exacerbated by prolonged warfare, sharpened class conflict and undermined the old denominational order. Many Anglican parsons benefited from enclosure and tithe commutation at the expense of their influence among small freeholders and labourers.[11] Ironically, the rising social status of the clergy, and their unprecedented representation on the bench of magistrates, cemented the squire and parson alliance at the very time that establishment ideals were most under attack. In such circumstances the Church of England was in no position to resist a dramatic upsurge in undenominational itinerant preaching and cottage-based religion,

---

[7] For the most recent and sophisticated attempt see A. D. Gilbert, 'Religion and Political Stability in Early Industrial England', in P. O'Brien and R. Quinault (eds.), *The Industrial Revolution and British Society* (Cambridge, 1993), pp. 79–99.

[8] R. B. Walker, 'The Growth of Wesleyan Methodism in Victorian England and Wales', *Journal of Ecclesiastical History*, 34 (1973), 267–84.

[9] D. Hempton, *Methodism and Politics in British Society 1750–1850* (London, 1984), pp. 55–84.

[10] W. R. Ward, *Religion and Society in England, 1790–1850* (London, 1972); and idem, *Faith and Faction* (London, 1993), pp. 264–98.

[11] W. R. Ward, 'Church and Society in the First Half of the Nineteenth Century', in Davies (ed.), *History of the Methodist Church*, vol. II, pp. 11–96; and idem, 'The Tithe Question in England in the Early Nineteenth Century', *Journal of Ecclesiastical History*, 16 (1965), 67–81.

which even the various Methodist connexions struggled to keep under control.[12] Methodism thus made its fastest gains in areas least amenable to paternalistic influence including freehold parishes, industrial villages, mining communities, market towns, canal and sea ports, and other centres of migratory populations.[13] Obelkevich's classic local study of South Lindsey is a vivid illustration of how the Church of England's attempt to reinforce an older paternalistic, hierarchic and integrated society was vigorously challenged by more emotionally vibrant and populist forms of religion such as that offered by the Primitive Methodists.[14] The result was a mixture of class and cultural conflict which reflected the economic and social structure of the area and led to the growth of an agricultural trade unionism almost entirely under Methodist leadership.

If the explanation for the rapidity of Methodist growth in the period 1790–1840 is still contested territory among historians, so too is its continued growth at a slower pace in the Victorian period. Some regard the institutional development of nineteenth-century Wesleyanism, and ultimately of the other connexions also, as a relative success given what might have happened if self-opinionated zealots had gained control.[15] Thus Jabez Bunting and his supporters, far from debasing virginal Methodism, performed the unpleasant but necessary task of giving a structure and sense of coherence to Wesleyanism as a national connexion. The many problems and bitter controversies he encountered were not so much the result of heavy handed ecclesiastical management as the inevitable consequence of coping with the inner contradictions of Methodism which he inherited but did not create. The continued growth of Methodism throughout the nineteenth century was therefore a vindication of Bunting's strategy. Those who criticised him most, then as now, were guilty of holding a romanticised view of early Methodism's impact on the poor and consequently developed an unrealistic assessment of its potential among the industrial proletariat of Victorian England, who remained largely beyond the pale of any form of organised Christianity. Recent surveys of the

---

[12]   D. M. Valenze, *Prophetic Sons and Daughters: Female Preaching and Popular Religion in Industrial England* (Princeton, 1985).

[13]   A. Everitt, *The Pattern of Rural Dissent: The Nineteenth Century* (Leicester, 1972); J. D. Gay, *The Geography of Religion in England* (London, 1971).

[14]   Obelkevich, *Religion in Rural Society*, pp. 183–258; J. S. Werner, *The Primitive Methodist Connexion* (Madison, Wis., 1984).

[15]   J. Kent, *The Age of Disunity* (London, 1966); and idem, 'The Wesleyan Methodists to 1849', in Davies (ed.), *History of the Methodist Church*, vol. II, pp. 213–75.

social constituency of eighteenth-century Methodism seem to confirm that it drew most of its members from the upper echelons of the lower orders, and lower income groups within the middle ranks, rather than from the lowest and most desperate.[16] But neither can there be any denying the upward social mobility of mainstream Methodism in the Victorian period as 'piety, profit and paternalism' made a formidable contribution to the commercial life of the north of England and built a culture of stubborn respectability on the foundations of 'individualism, decency, self-improvement, homespun piety and public service.'[17]

An alternative picture of nineteenth-century Methodist development is presented by Professor Ward, who takes a less sympathetic view of the growth of Wesleyan connexional management than others have done. He suggests that the Wesleyan leadership, when confronted by rapid expansion in the years of high social tension between Wesley's death and Peterloo, tried to retain control by clamping down on religious revivalism, political radicalism, undenominational Sunday schools and other popular causes.[18] In the process Methodism became more centralised, more bureaucratic, more clerical and more respectable. In short, it took on all the characteristics of a religious counterrevolution to serve the interests of denominational control and discipline. While not suggesting that Methodism would ever have taken control of the urban proletariat in nineteenth-century England, Ward convincingly shows that by 1820 the Wesleyan connexion at least had changed in important respects and had consequently become less attractive to urban workers. Bunting was not, of course, the architect of all these developments; rather he grew up during their implementation and became committed through personal experience to the idea that Methodist growth had been too undisciplined and too polluted with other causes for its long-term health as a religious connexion.[19] Thus in the period of Bunting's hegemony between 1820 and 1850, when

[16] C. D. Field, 'The Social Structure of English Methodism: Eighteenth–Twentieth Centuries', *British Journal of Sociology*, 28 (1977), 199–25; idem, 'The Social Composition of English Methodism to 1830: A Membership Analysis', *Bulletin of the John Rylands University Library of Manchester*, 76 (1994), 153–69; and J. Q. Smith, 'Occupational Groups among the Early Methodists of the Keighley Circuit', *Church History*, 57 (1988), 187–96.

[17] G. E. Milburn, 'Piety, Profit and Paternalism: Methodists in Business in the North-East of England, c. 1760–1920', *Proceedings of the Wesley Historical Society*, 44 (1983), 45–92; D. Martin, 'Faith, Flour and Jam', *Times Literary Supplement*, 1 April 1983, 329–30.

[18] W. R. Ward, 'The Religion of the People and the Problem of Control, 1790–1830', in *Faith and Faction*, pp. 264–84.

[19] T. P. Bunting, *The Life of Jabez Bunting*, 2 vols. (London, 1859–87); W. R. Ward, *The Early Correspondence of Jabez Bunting, 1820–1829* (London, 1972); and idem, *Early Victorian Methodism: The Correspondence of Jabez Bunting, 1830–1858* (Oxford, 1976).

Methodism was convulsed by major secessions from which it never fully recovered, the divisive issues were not simply thrown up by problems of connexional government, but had their roots in a more general hardening of denominational boundaries which made sectarian conflict, with class overtones, the most characteristic feature of English politics in the early Victorian period.[20]

Apart from general interpretations of Methodist growth and decline in the nineteenth century there is a formidable literature now available on regional revivalism, from Cornwall to Ulster and from the Trent valley to the South Wales coalfield.[21] A number of consistent themes have emerged. Generally speaking, revivalism flourished either in very cohesive communities such as mining settlements or among rural migrants to industrial villages. Although there is some evidence to link revivalism to economic dislocation and political repression, there is a general acknowledgement that religious revivals had internal social and psychological dynamics regardless of external circumstances. While epidemic diseases and hazardous occupations could add a cutting edge of urgency to religious enthusiasm, the most consistent factor is a desire for revival and sense of expectancy within Methodist communities themselves. The existence of a population with at least a smattering of biblical knowledge and familiarity with basic Christian concepts of salvation and damnation was also important. In some regions, therefore, religious revivalism became a local tradition in its own right manifesting itself in recurring generational pulses. But by 1830 this kind of folk revivalism had become confined to the Celtic fringes of British society – in Cornwall, Wales, Ulster and parts of Scotland – and was often attributed in metropolitan and denominational newspapers to the ethnic excitability of the Celtic peoples. More charitably, historians have emphasised the existence of powerful religious cultures built partly on the desire for revival and the confident expectation that it would eventually come.

Victorian flirtations with the American new measures version of revivalism proved to be a less powerful, if more socially acceptable, alternative in many parts of England. Technique revivalism, whatever

[20] N. Gash, *Reaction and Reconstruction in English Politics, 1832–52* (Oxford, 1965); G. I. T. Machin, *Politics and the Churches in Great Britain, 1832 to 1868* (Oxford, 1977); and D. A. Gowland, *Methodist Secessions: The Origins of Free Methodism in Three Lancashire Towns* (Manchester, 1979).

[21] J. M. Turner, *Conflict and Reconciliation* (London, 1985), pp. 82–8; D. Luker, 'Revivalism in Theory and Practice: The Case of Cornish Methodism', *Journal of Ecclesiastical History*, 37 (1986) 603–19; and D. Hempton, 'Methodism in Irish Society, 1770–1830', *Transactions of the Royal Historical Society*, 5th ser., 36 (1986), 117–42.

its claimed successes in particular urban crusades may have been, was no remedy for the complex forces that were at work in the slowing down of Methodist expansion from the middle of the century.[22] Population movements from country to town and from city centres to suburbia posed new structural problems at a time when Methodist morale had taken a pounding from the reform controversies and secessions of the 1840s and 50s. From then on the various Methodist connexions, including the Primitives, which had always recruited rapidly at the bottom and lost members less rapidly at the top, made less and less impression on the unchurched English population. Such growth as still took place was largely due either to denominational migration or the natural increase of the Methodist community itself. Far from offering any long-term prospect of Methodist revitalisation, both were essentially negative developments, for they further emphasised Methodism's, especially the Wesleyan connexion's, creeping withdrawal into a respectable religious cocoon within which institutional concerns took precedence over more vital matters. Institutional order, then institutional unity, were paths guaranteed to lead to national integration and popular indifference.

### THE HALEVY THESIS REVISITED

Attempts to relate the rise and decline of Methodism to the wider social history of England during the period of the industrial revolution have occasioned strong disagreements among historians. To a remarkable extent the great French historian, Elie Halévy, set an agenda at the beginning of the twentieth century which, for good and for ill, has exercised a powerful intellectual spell over the subsequent writing of Methodist history.[23] According to Halévy, early industrial England, by comparison with its European neighbours, possessed an unusual and potentially volatile degree of political, economic and religious freedom. In Europe's most advanced capitalist country dynamic forces of anarchy and social revolution were moderated and re-directed by a powerful resurgence of Puritanism in the shape of the evangelical revival. Methodism was thus the antidote to Jacobinism and 'the free organisation of the sects was the foundation of social order in England'. Halévy stated that evangelicalism, for all its popular idiosyncrasies and

---

[22]  J. H. S. Kent, *Holding the Fort: Studies in Victorian Revivalism* (London, 1978), pp. 356–68.
[23]  G. W. Olsen (ed.), *Religion and Revolution in Early Industrial England: The Halévy Thesis and its Critics* (Lanham, Md., 1990).

bourgeois hypocrisy, was the chief engine in the creation of a free and ordered society based on widely accepted notions of 'voluntary obedience'. Paradoxical though it may seem, therefore, the freest country in Europe was saved from the frightening consequences of anarchic libertarianism by the fact that its Established Church 'left the sects outside her borders entire liberty of organisation, full power to form a host of little states within the state'.[24] Evangelicalism thus spawned a host of religious associations in the age of associations and worked for the reformation of morals, not primarily through legal coercion, but through the power of middle-class voluntaryism. English freedoms were thus saved by the exercise of characteristic English freedoms.

There is now general agreement that Halévy exaggerated both the fragility of England's *ancien régime* and the power of evangelicalism to save it from its internal contradictions. There are nevertheless two things worth saving from Halévy's set of hypotheses. The first is the importance of evangelical religion in forging a rough harmony of values between the pragmatic and moralistic middle class and the skilled and respectable sections of the English working class who were notorious in Europe for their solid virtue and capacity for organisation. The second is Halévy's emphasis on the relative tolerance of the Church of England and the capacity of the sects to separate from the establishment and from one another in an ordered and disciplined fashion. But the key here is not so much the libertarian sentiments of the sects, nor indeed their lofty principles, as any student of the bitter rivalries associated with such splits will testify, as the profound impact of legal frameworks in helping to articulate grievances and in limiting their consequences. This message emerges clearly not only from Methodism's separation from the Church of England, but also from the Kilhamite secession from the main Wesleyan connexion.[25] What Halévy attributed to the sole influence of evangelicalism was therefore built on earlier traditions of constitutional and legal chauvinism in English society. Popular evangelicalism did not create the free-born Englishman nor did it create the capacity for disciplined organisation, but it did offer a vibrant religious vehicle for both to operate outside the confines of the Established Church without seriously destabilising the English State. Similarly, evangelicals exploited, but did not create, the profound social crises of the 1790s, which effectively sealed the fate

---

[24]  E. Halévy, *The Birth of Methodism in England*, trans. by B. Semmel (Chicago, 1971); idem, *England in 1815*, vol. 1 of *A History of the English People in the Nineteenth Century* (London, 1961).

[25]  Hempton, *Methodism and Politics*, pp. 67–73.

of the Church of England as a genuinely national establishment. Thus the spectacular rise of evangelical Dissent was not a self-conscious attempt to undermine the old order in Church and State, but was rather the consequence of profound structural changes in English society which, taken together, facilitated the rise of a new denominational order. In that sense Methodism and a revived Nonconformity opened up the way for a more pluralistic and ultimately more liberal state in which the limits of toleration were gradually, if haphazardly, expanded. The Methodist revolution, as Halévy correctly diagnosed, if not always for the right reasons, was a particularly English kind of revolution.

There is now widespread agreement, therefore, that the remarkable growth of evangelical Nonconformity in the period 1790–1830 substantially undermined the Established Church, religious deference and traditional systems of dependency which had been at the heart of the old order in Church and State. Even Jonathan Clark, who is certainly no exponent of social and political determinism, has shown how English society had moved beyond the pale of the Anglican parochial system and that the opposition to Sidmouth's Bill against itinerant preaching in 1811 showed that there had been a profound shift of allegiance in the country as a whole.[26] Parallel pressures from a more radical Irish Catholicism, the old anti-exclusionist wing of Protestant Dissent, urban popular radicalism and new commercial interests did not make a constitutional revolution inevitable, but they did lay the foundations for alternative forms of politics in which religion was just as central as it had been in the ideological defences of the eighteenth-century constitution.

Methodism could not, of course, avoid the social and political tensions which accompanied its own growth. In the quarter century after the French Revolution its leadership, both clerical and lay, struggled hard to maintain the connexion's legal privileges while at the same time recruiting from sections of the population less interested in the chauvinistic traditions of the free-born Englishman than in the political and economic causes of their appalling conditions. Ironically, the secretive committee of privileges, which the Methodists had set up to guard their legal rights, soon became an inquisitorial instrument in the expulsion of disaffected radicals in the years leading up to Peterloo. This task was accomplished with such vigour, in the north of England

[26] J. C. D. Clark, *English Society, 1688–1832* (Cambridge, 1985).

in particular, that when the next great upsurge in urban popular radicalism occurred in the late 1830s the Wesleyans were relatively untroubled and were able to devote most of their energy to the defence of their denominational corner against Catholics, tractarians and radical Nonconformists. In this way class control and denominational discipline were mutually reinforced, and class tensions were to some extent redirected into sectarian conflict.[27]

It was in the first thirty years after Wesley's death, therefore, that Methodist growth most alarmed established interests, from bishops and parsons to landed and industrial magnates. At the same time, Methodism's capacity to develop qualities of self-discipline, personal responsibility and sobriety were appreciated by those able to set aside their prejudices against religious enthusiasm and who recognised that the Established Church was in no position to reclaim the unchurched. This paradox, which has generated much heat but little illumination among historians, was there from the start, and often depended on local circumstances for its resolution. In Belper, for example, which had grown from an insignificant village to the second largest town in Derbyshire, largely as a result of the entrepreneurial talents of the Strutt family, both Wesleyan and Primitive Methodism grew extraordinarily fast between 1790 and 1825. The Unitarian Strutts recognised the beneficial effects of Methodism among their work-force with restrained paternalistic generosity, but they also saw fit to launch a fund for a hugely expensive Anglican church, which architecturally dwarfed its Dissenting rivals and was opened in 1824 amid much pomp and circumstance by the Duke of Devonshire, the county's greatest landowner. Here was no exercise in crude employer coercion; the Strutts merely paid symbolic tribute to a set of social arrangements which they had come to believe were instrumental in maintaining order and stability, and which had consequently facilitated their own social advance. With so much at stake, a declaration of faith in a stable past offered more reassurance than a future clouded by unrestrained ranterism or political radicalism. The imposing Anglican monument the Strutts helped pay for was thus not meant to eliminate religious deviance, but to show the limits within which it must be seen to operate.[28]

27  Hempton, *Methodism and Politics*, pp. 85–115.
28  Valenze, *Prophetic Sons and Daughters*, pp. 159–83; E. Hopkins, 'Religious Dissent in Black Country Industrial Villages in the First Half of the Nineteenth Century', *Journal of Ecclesiastical History*, 34 (1983), 411–24.

After 1820 the Wesleyans were not entirely immune from problems caused by urban radicals within their midst, as the celebrated case of Joseph Rayner Stephens showed, but increasingly it was the Primitive and secession Methodists who were most closely bound up with radical causes in both town and country. Recent studies of Chartism in English localities, for example, have drawn attention to the importance of Methodist organisational models, the crusading zeal of local preachers, and perhaps most important, the ideological fusion of biblical warnings against social injustice with Chartist denunciations of the rich and the powerful.[29] All over the north of England in the 1830s as the anti-Poor Law, Ten Hours and anti-State Church movements shaded off into Chartism there was a sizeable minority of non-Wesleyan Methodists, conspicuous for their leadership ability, who combined a radical critique of clericalism and the religious hypocrisy of the rich with a more general humanitarian mission to reform social and political abuses. Some were willing to make chapels available for Chartist meetings, and some chapels even severed their Methodist connexions altogether, but there were also unresolved tensions between the two. As Chartists tried to create a mass movement of class solidarity, Methodist communities had alternative loyalties which caused them to repudiate Chartist bawdiness, tavern conviviality and sabbath breaking. Although many Chartist leaders were aware of the potential of religion to offer ideological legitimisation and crusading zeal to their movement, it soon became clear to Christian Chartists like the Revd William Hill, the editor of the *Northern Star*, that 'in almost all the churches and chapels, appertaining to whatever sect, the principles of social benevolence and justice, of civil equality and of political right, though recognised by the Bible, are denounced by the priesthood'.[30] Even the more radical Methodist sects, though closer in spirit to Chartist ideals than either Anglicanism or Wesleyanism, were sufficiently peripheral to mass Chartism to make large-scale theories about the relationship between Methodism and urban radicalism in these years seem rather forced.

The same cannot be said, however, of those mining and agricultural communities of England where Methodism, especially the Primitive connexion, became the dominant feature of both the religious and

---

[29]  J. Epstein and D. Thompson (eds.), *The Chartist Experience* (London, 1982), pp. 221–68; E. Yeo, 'Christianity in Chartist Struggle, 1838–42', *Past and Present*, no. 91 (1981), 109–39; H. U. Faulkner, *Chartism and the Churches* (New York, 1916); and R. Wearmouth, *Methodism and the Working-Class Movements of England, 1800–1850* (London, 1937), pp. 100–29.

[30]  Yeo, 'Christianity in Chartist Struggle', 139.

political landscape. Indeed, the contribution of Methodism to rural radicalism and agricultural trade unionism, so long ignored in the debates surrounding the Halévy thesis, has only recently attracted the attention it deserves. In East Anglia, for example, Primitive Methodism, emerging initially as a form of religious protest, became also the basis of a social protest against both the harsher realities of labouring life and 'the oligarchical troika of parson, squire and farmer'.[31] With a mixture of biblical idealism, millennial optimism and disciplined protest, both Wesleyan and Primitive Methodist local preachers brought their chapel-honed skills of public speaking and effective organisation to an agricultural trade unionism that developed a quasi-religious atmosphere of its own.

A similar combination of community solidarity built around religious forms and experiences is evident in the pit-village Methodism of the north-east of England, though here the lines of class and religious conflict are, if anything, less clear cut.[32] Once again the disciplines and opportunities of chapel life threw up a high proportion of Methodist political leaders who made their mark in trade unionism, the co-operative movement and other forms of local politics. But theirs was a trade unionism infused with moral energy to achieve fair play and just treatment from their largely Nonconformist employers, rather than an instrument for pursuing narrowly class interests as such. Hence the impact of Methodism on the mining communities of the north-east was partly responsible for the region's reluctance to exchange Liberal for Labour politics at the beginning of the twentieth century. This provincial Liberalism was based on the acceptance of a market economy, opposition to Anglican educational privileges, dislike of the Tory brewing interest, and an emphasis on mutual obligations between employers and employees, and was thus regarded as a more appropriate political vehicle than that offered by class conflict and the emerging Labour movement. The essential difference, therefore, between Methodism's relationship with Chartism and its contribution to agricultural and mining trade unionism is that within Chartism Methodism was only one strand among many influences, some of which were antithetical to Methodist piety or peripheral to Methodist interests, whereas in the other cases Methodist involvement in politics grew naturally out of its social setting and was widely approved as a legitimate expression of an essentially religious morality.

---

[31]  N. Scotland, *Methodism and the Revolt of the Field* (Gloucester, 1981), p. 175.
[32]  R. Colls, *The Collier's Rant* (London, 1977); and Moore, *Pit-Men, Preachers, and Politics*.

Whatever may be said about the relationship between Methodism and popular radicalism, or religion and social class, the fact is that most nineteenth-century Methodists encountered the world of politics either as voters or as participants in the great extra-parliamentary pressure crusades, from Sidmouth's Bill at the beginning of the century to the preoccupations of the Nonconformist Conscience at the end.[33] No sense can be made of such politics through social and economic categories alone, rather they show the profoundly religious basis – however narrow and sectarian – of much Nonconformist political behaviour. At the heart of Methodist commitment to extra-parliamentary pressure campaigns, despite the old Wesleyan no-politics rule, was a religious world-view which sought to defend denominational interests against governmental and secularist encroachments, to wage war on the moral evils of slavery, sexual licence and intemperance, and to oppose the 'heretical' advances of Roman Catholicism, tractarianism and Unitarianism.

In the period from the Great Reform Act to the end of the century, the Liberal Party was the main beneficiary of Methodist political loyalties, particularly those of the non-Wesleyan connexions, whose willingness to attack the vested interests of the Established Church went beyond that of most Wesleyans. The political allegiances of the latter were, of course, more complicated. In general their social, occupational and religious status led them to vote for the Liberal Party unless religious issues dictated otherwise. Then their evangelicalism, their distant loyalty to the Church of England and their deference to preachers and wealthy laymen within their own connexion influenced them against pro-Catholic, Unitarian or radical disestablishment candidates. Anti-Catholicism in particular was a major element in the Wesleyan Toryism of the 1830s and 40s and surfaced again in a remarkable way over Home Rule half a century later when a substantial minority of Wesleyans were committed Unionists.

As with voting, so with extra-parliamentary protest. Although the Wesleyans were of common purpose with the rest of Nonconformity in the great moral crusades against slavery and the Contagious Diseases Acts, the connexion as a whole did not support the Liberation Society nor did it approve of the disestablishment sentiments of the Free

---

[33] B. S. Turner and M. Hill, 'Methodism and the Pietist Definition of Politics: Historical Development and Contemporary Evidence', *A Sociological Yearbook of Religion in Britain*, 8, 159–80; D. Bebbington, 'Nonconformity and Electoral Sociology, 1867–1918', *Historical Journal*, 27 (1984), 633–56; and idem, *The Nonconformist Conscience* (London, 1982).

Church councils. When it came to specific matters like the removal of Nonconformist grievances over marriages and burials, the Wesleyans preferred to act through their own Committee of Privileges rather than join wholeheartedly with other Nonconformists. Thus, Methodist Liberalism as proclaimed by Hugh Price Hughes from the mid-1880s was of a distinctive hue in which anti-Catholicism, imperialism and denominational particularism were never far from the surface.[34] In saying this one is not denying the degree of homogeneity that existed in Nonconformist culture nor casting doubt on the fact that the distinctive Nonconformist values of sobriety, self-help, hard work and the free market fitted snugly into Victorian liberalism;[35] for Nonconformity offered 'an alternative establishment whose attitudes it articulated'.[36] But the Wesleyan connexion in particular, with its historic roots in Wesley's churchmanship and its long-standing commitment to Protestant Ireland and world mission, could never be as committed to a free market in religion as it was in economics. Protectionism may have been commercially undesirable but some form of it was deemed essential to maintain religious truth and eliminate heresy at home and overseas.

### THE LIMITS OF THE METHODIST REVOLUTION

The changes within Methodism over the course of the nineteenth century, as it hardened from its societary roots into a respectable denomination, have been illuminated by impressive studies of the Methodist ministry, lay spirituality, popular education and community values. The contrast, for example, between Deborah Valenze's analysis of the male and female itinerants who serviced an extensive cottage-based religion in the first half of the nineteenth century and K. D. Brown's statistical survey of Nonconformist ministers in the second half is particularly striking, even allowing for the fact that Valenze's preachers are an unrepresentative sample of Methodist preachers as a whole.[37] Indeed, it has been shown that a high doctrine of the pastoral office as opposed to itinerant flexibility and enthusiasm was already

[34] J. H. S. Kent, 'Hugh Price Hughes and the Nonconformist Conscience', in G. Bennett and J. Walsh (eds.), *Essays in Modern English Church History* (London, 1966); D. M. Thompson, *Nonconformity in the Nineteenth Century* (London, 1972); S. Koss, 'Wesleyanism and Empire', *Historical Journal*, 18 (1975); and idem, *Nonconformity in Modern British Politics* (London, 1975).
[35] J. R. Vincent, *The Formation of the British Liberal Party, 1857–1868* (Hassocks, 1976).
[36] C. Binfield, *So Down to Prayers: Studies in English Nonconformity, 1780–1920* (London, 1977), p. 132.
[37] Valenze, *Prophetic Sons and Daughters*; K. D. Brown, *A Social History of the Nonconformist Ministry in England and Wales, 1800–1930* (Oxford, 1988).

well established within the Wesleyan connexion within a quarter of a century of Wesley's death.[38] As the connexional leadership presented an increasingly respectable and authoritarian model of ministerial behaviour the more unruly preaching of revivalists and women opened up a more intimate and volatile relationship with lower-class life. Women made up a significant proportion of preachers within Primitive Methodism, the Bible Christian movement and other Methodist minorities at least until the 1840s when they disappear from the formal circuit plans, if not entirely from public ministry. The peak of their influence coincided with the high point of cottage religion within popular evangelicalism when 'unprofessional preaching in noninstitutional surroundings encompassed the immediate, tangible, and private aspects of life'.[39] The temporary emergence of female preaching on a scale not seen since the Civil War period was but one consequence of a much wider outburst of itinerant preaching between 1780 and 1830 when the Established Church's hold on the English population was substantially undermined. Moreover, itinerant preaching was not confined to the various Methodist connexions, but made an important contribution to the metamorphosis of English Calvinistic Dissent from an exclusive emphasis on the spiritual well-being of church members to a renewed concern for outsiders in hitherto untouched communities.[40]

A diluted itinerancy along with a high ratio of lay to regular preachers survived in the main Methodist connexions throughout the nineteenth century, but there were important changes in the recruitment, training and duties of the preachers. By 1900, for example, 58 per cent of all active Methodist preachers had been to theological college where the training they received was inadequate, both in educational terms and as a preparation for chapel ministry. Most recruits were from families poised uncomfortably between the middle and lower classes, with teachers, white-collar workers, clerks, small craftsmen and sons of the manse all figuring prominently. There were, moreover, disproportionately more preachers from rural areas and the Celtic fringes than from English towns and cities where the demographic pressures were most acute. Although supply and demand were in rough equilibrium, the Methodist ministry not only attracted fewer popular enthusiasts as the century went on – a fact not unrelated to the

[38]  Ward, *Faith and Faction*, pp. 225–48; J. C. Bowmer, *Pastor and People* (London, 1975).
[39]  Valenze, *Prophetic Sons and Daughters*, p. 24.
[40]  D. W. Lovegrove, *Established Church, Sectarian People: Itinerancy and the Transformation of English Dissent, 1780–1830* (Cambridge, 1988).

steady decline of an evangelical conversion as a catalyst for a preaching vocation – but was also a sufficiently unappealing career to attract men of talent from higher social groups. That a career as a Nonconformist preacher was scarcely a bed of roses in Victorian England is confirmed by the high percentage of withdrawals, particularly from Primitive Methodism, within four years of the commencement of ministry. The inconveniences of itinerancy, friction with the laity, financial pressures, moral frailty and inadequate training all played their part in creating an unsettled and often ineffective ministry, far removed from the conventional stereotypes of Nonconformist giants preaching to thousands from metropolitan pulpits.[41]

A similar spiritual retrenchment into denominational consolidation is also detectable within the Methodist laity in the second half of the nineteenth century. The class-meeting, for example, which had always been the chief means of promoting holiness both within individuals and the Wesleyan community, became the focus of an unprecedented number of attacks and defences.[42] As Wesley's writings make clear, the class had never been a uniformly successful institution within Methodism, but while religious experiences were fresh and vital its spiritual utility was above question. The problem in the later nineteenth century was that for many the classes had become dull, repetitious, ritualistic and irrelevant to their daily lives. As is the way with religious denominations, much organisational tinkering was advocated and much ink was spilt over the relationship, if any, between class-membership and church-membership, but the nub of the matter was that the decline of the class-meeting was a symptom of much more fundamental changes within both the nature of Methodism itself and its social setting. According to Henry Rack 'the Wesleyans of the later nineteenth century seemed to have lost a great deal of the confidence of their fathers, not only in the capacity of religious exercises to hold people in the church, but also in the capacity of Wesleyans to enter the world without succumbing to it and ceasing to be Wesleyans'.[43] Increasing numbers of respectable but unenthusiastic attenders and the

[41]   K. D. Brown, 'An Unsettled Ministry? Some Aspects of Nineteenth-Century British Nonconformity', *Church History*, 56 (1987), 204–23.

[42]   H. D. Rack, 'The Decline of the Class-Meeting and the Problem of Church-Membership in Nineteenth-Century Wesleyanism', *Proceedings of the Wesley Historical Society*, 39 (1973–4), 12–21; W. W. Dean, 'The Methodist Class Meeting: The Significance of its Decline', *Proceedings of the Wesley Historical Society*, 43 (1981–2), 41–48.

[43]   H. D. Rack, 'Wesleyanism and "the World" in the Later Nineteenth Century', *Proceedings of the Wesley Historical Society*, 42 (1979–80), 53–4.

counter-attractions of a more secular society left the class-meeting without the intensity of religious commitment which alone could guarantee its success. The decline of the class-meeting was accompanied also by a decline in the distinctive Methodist emphasis on entire sanctification. In the pursuit of holiness Methodists first became less ambitious and then inexorably more private in their spiritual disciplines. It would, of course, be a mistake to portray late nineteenth-century Methodism as spiritually moribund by comparison with its pristine eighteenth-century predecessor. Much energy was expended, for example, on Home Missions targeted at the urban poor, but even here it was soon apparent that the profound gap between the churched and the unchurched was as much a matter of social class as of religious preference, and was consequently unbridgeable by the relatively unimaginative methods employed. In truth, more effort was made to 'reach' the working classes than to accommodate them in meaningful cultural forms, with the result that the Methodist urban missions did more to retain the support of the faithful than to make substantial inroads into the heartland of infidelity.

One religious innovation which did attract considerable working-class support throughout the nineteenth century was Sunday school education, approximately one third of which was under the control of the various Methodist connexions by 1851.[44] The dramatic expansion of Sunday schools began in the late eighteenth century as a result of interdenominational co-operation and private philanthropy, but they soon fell victim to sectarian rivalry and political conflict.[45] By the mid nineteenth century they were firmly in the control of the religious denominations who understandably tried to exploit their potential for recruiting new church and chapel members. Within Methodism the conflicts over the control of Sunday schools were religious reflections of many of the tensions in early nineteenth-century society including class conflict and denominational competition. The Wesleyans, disturbed by reports of radical and heterodox penetration and by the apparent absence of tangible connexional benefits from the Sunday schools, pushed hard for clerical control and took a stand against teaching children how to write on the sabbath. The Wesleyan leadership, well marshalled by Bunting, was successful on both counts, but the victory

44   T. W. Laqueur, *Religion and Respectability: Sunday Schools and Working-Class Culture, 1780–1850* (New Haven, 1976).
45   A. P. Wadsworth, 'The First Manchester Sunday Schools', *Bulletin of the John Rylands University Library of Manchester*, 33 (1951), 299–326.

was costly in terms of connexional harmony and working-class allegiance, and more significantly, it never achieved its prime objective of turning the Sunday schools into chapel nurseries.[46] According to Laqueur's figures, Sunday schools attracted a remarkably high percentage of working-class children but delivered a remarkably low percentage of them into committed chapel membership. Parental pressure and the prize of literacy were clearly more effective inducements than church services and class-meetings. But if Sunday schools never quite fulfilled denominational expectations, they made an important contribution to mass literacy and to Victorian chapel culture through their anniversary celebrations, prize distributions and Whit outings. They also offered women, both young and old, a socially acceptable outlet for exercising a ministry of teaching without threatening the patriarchal conventions of chapel life.

### METHODISM DIVIDED

Pressures from without interacted with the various changes within nineteenth-century Methodism to produce manifold secessions and some spontaneous new creations. Although each revivalistic offshoot and formal secession had a unique context, many of the same themes reappear. At issue each time, from the formation of the Methodist New Connexion in 1797 to the withdrawal of the Christian Lay Churches from Primitive Methodism in the 1870s, were fundamental disagreements about the essence of the authentic Wesleyan tradition, which was, of course, sufficiently eclectic to support a range of interpretations. So much has now been written about Methodism's 'age of disunity' in this avowedly ecumenical generation that it seems pointless to rehearse the familiar explanations of how it became one of the most fissiparous religious movements in English history.[47] Nevertheless, a few broad lines of interpretation remain to be etched in. In the first place, the old dichotomy between those who interpreted Methodist secessions as the sad but inevitable consequence of stresses within the religious community itself, and those political and social historians who saw them as mere symptoms of external pressures affecting the whole of British and European society, has been an unfortunate barrier to proper historical understanding. The manifold local studies of Methodist secessions have shown conclusively that, superimposed on 'religious' disagreements

46    Ward, *Early Correspondence of Jabez Bunting*, pp. 148–52, 165–72, 228.
47    R. Currie, *Methodism Divided: A Study in the Sociology of Ecumenicalism* (London, 1968).

about the nature of the ministry, connexional management and spiritual priorities, there were undoubtedly class and cultural differences, conflicting political allegiances and social tensions which also affected the wider society.[48] The precise balance of forces varied, of course, from secession to secession and even from town to town, but they cannot be uncovered by either denominational or social reductionism. Thus, what is striking about Methodism in the first half of the nineteenth century is the way in which its internal cleavages and structures of power acted as lightning conductors for the endemic political and social tensions of the age. After mid century tensions declined but so too did the importance of what was at stake within the Methodist community. Secession, after all, can be as much a product of intense commitment as unity can be a matter of comfortable acquiescence.

A second point worth emphasising is that although Methodism's internal crises reached their peak during Bunting's period of personal ascendancy, his contribution to the shaping of Methodism, though substantial, should not be exaggerated. Consider, for example, this letter to the *Sunderland Daily Echo*: 'All confidence is at an end ... this division has been effected by a Conference clique ... infatuated by a love of power characteristic of the whole priestly hierarchy; they seek not the chief good but little circuits and large salaries.'[49] This letter might have been written by a string of Methodist radicals from Alexander Kilham in the 1790s to the authors of the Fly Sheets in the 1840s, but it was in fact an attack on the Primitive Methodist preachers of the north-east of England in 1877. The point is that once Methodism became established in an area over several generations and benefited from the upward mobility of its social constituency, there were inexorable structural pressures within the connexional system towards a more 'centralised and disciplined church structure, towards the growing authority of Conference over local affairs, towards a more refined and less evangelical ministry exercising its duties in smaller circuits, and towards more dignity in chapel-design and worship'. Those who swam with the tide, including Bunting, thought, mistakenly as it turned out, that it was possible to construct a Methodism which

48   Hempton, *Methodism and Politics*, pp. 67–73, 92–8, 197–202; Gowland, *Methodist Secessions*; and D. C. Dews, 'Methodism in Leeds from 1791–1861', 2 vols., MPhil dissertation, University of Bradford, 1984.

49   G. E. Milburn, 'Tensions in Primitive Methodism in the Eighteen-Seventies', *Proceedings of the Wesley Historical Society*, 40 (1976), 93–101, 135–43.

was both evangelistic and ecclesiastical, popular and cultivated, disciplined and flexible, professional and spontaneous, lively and restrained. As with all strongly held positions their ideology served their own interests, and legitimised their power within the connexion, which is why their opponents were often motivated as much by a sense of exclusion as a desire to return to primitive simplicity. Secession was the final proof that this was a genuine contest and that there was something vital at stake in the result. Moreover, some of the problems encountered by Methodist connexions in the nineteenth century were specific neither to themselves nor to the nineteenth century, but were deeply embedded within the historical traditions of English religion and society dating back at least as far as the Reformation. Anticlericalism, especially when clerical wealth, status and legal powers were in evidence, anti-centralisation, and opposition to an urbane liturgical uniformity were, and still are, consistent characteristics of English popular Protestantism which frustrated Archbishop Laud as much as Jabez Bunting. The final proof that the *embourgeoisement* of Methodism was not a specifically English disease comes from the United States, where precisely the same processes happened at a similar stage in the evolution of Methodism as a religious denomination.[50] What is striking about this comparison, however, is that American Methodism achieved wealth, respectability and social status with comparatively few secessions (on those issues at least), while English Methodism reflected the social tensions of a more class-conscious society in many of its internal conflicts. Methodist secessions on both sides of the Atlantic are therefore useful barometers of what was fundamentally at stake in the wider social and cultural environment.

## METHODIST IDENTITIES

The Victorian Nonconformist world of men, chapels and politics, so long dominant in Methodist historiography and cemented forever in the new official history, has given way in recent times to imaginative attempts to rediscover the human (including the female) face of Methodism in its many different cultural settings. Penetrating to the essence of Methodism's impact on ordinary people and their communities has brought forth fresh work utilising fresh materials and

[50]    J. Wigger, 'Taking Heaven by Storm: Methodism and the Popularization of American Christianity 1720–1820', PhD dissertation, University of Notre Dame, 1994; N. Hatch, 'The Puzzle of American Methodism', *Church History*, 63 (1994), 175–89.

reaching fresh conclusions which has done much to supersede the old models of repression and release made popular by Thompson and others. The problem with Methodism, or perhaps more optimistically its greatest strength, is the way in which its hard disciplines and tender mercies could be adapted to a wide variety of social circumstances not only in the British Isles but throughout the world.[51] This may be dispiriting for those ideologically committed to either the Halévy thesis or some convenient and crimping alternative, but it suggests that theoretical sophistication is no substitute for imaginative sympathy and cultural sensitivity in re-creating the history of popular religious movements.[52] Space permits only two brief examples of these qualities, both from the north-east of England but from different social ranks.

Robert Colls has sought to explain the strength of Primitive Methodism in the pit villages of the region by drawing attention to the 'reactive exchanges' between popular evangelicalism and mining culture in which the boundary lines between the secular and the sacred were almost obliterated.[53] Such exchanges were promoted by vernacular preaching, the appropriation of popular tunes and the emotional resonances of Methodism with its combination of passion and piety, zeal and order, faith and works, thrift and charity, Puritanism and decency, individualism and community, and verve and vulgarity. But exchange also took place

at the deepest meanings of life and death: in the zeal for a righteous death from a community whose traditional funeral rites were meticulous; in the capacity for mutuality of a class who had little else to offer each other; in the taste for a sudden salvation from a people whose lives were always a lottery and the translation from nothing to enough, illness to health, life to death was often arbitrary.

Such a faith was unselfconsciously all-embracing: it set standards for domestic economy and cleanliness; it educated the young and offered eternal bliss to the old; its festivals and choral entertainments were at the centre of village life; its values informed public debate and wage negotiations; it even altered the language and the oral traditions at the

---

[51]    For an example of the range of possible interpretations opened up by historians of Methodism in the United States, see R. Richey, K. Rowe and J. M. Schmidt (eds.), *Perspectives on American Methodism: Interpretive Essays* (Nashville, Tenn., 1993).

[52]    See, for example, H. McLeod, 'New Perspectives on Victorian Working-Class Religion: The Oral Evidence', *Oral History*, 14 (1986), 31–49; D. Hempton, 'Popular Religion and Irreligion in Victorian Fiction', *Historical Studies*, 16 (1987), 177–96; and D. Clark, *Between Pulpit and Pew: Folk Religion in a North Yorkshire Fishing Village* (Cambridge, 1982).

[53]    Colls, *Collier's Rant*.

very heart of the community. Not surprisingly this culture withstood everything the nineteenth century could throw at it, but the twentieth-century combination of economic and ecclesiastical rationalisation has inexorably undermined its social foundations.

A more familiar kind of cultural exchange between Methodism and society, going on in the same region at the same time, has been illuminated by the work of Geoffrey Milburn.[54] His formidable list of Methodist entrepreneurs bound together by intermarriage and business interests is itself a testimony to the commercial utility of evangelical Nonconformist values. Most of these Methodist entrepreneurial families had their origins among the skilled artisans, small tradesmen, farmers and white-collar workers of the north-east, with only a few from lower working-class backgrounds. With no apparent incompatibility between gold and the gospel, wealth was carefully husbanded over several generations of hard work, prudential marriages and self-discipline. The wealth earned was solidly and respectably enjoyed and not conspicuously consumed. Although some abandoned religious morality in the pursuit of gain, most gained without indecent pursuit, and were thus able to give some of what they received with clear paternalistic consciences. They were men who knew that 'religion, self-discipline, temperance and hard work had been good for them, and they sought to employ whatever means they could, in their homes, Sunday schools, chapels, businesses and communities, to persuade, exhort and even oblige others to live by the same lights'.[55] Here was a culture of 'piety, profit and paternalism' which dominated great tracts of provincial England in the Victorian period and which produced immense fortunes for Methodists like Joseph Rank (flour-milling) and Sir William Hartley (jam-making). With pardonable poetic exaggeration David Martin has stated that Victorian and Edwardian Methodism was 'not about Acts and Insurrections but about groceries. The Methodist grocer, like the Nonconformist Conscience, is, or was, a byword. Methodism is rooted and grounded not only in "faith alone" but in flour and jam.'[56] There was, however, a sufficient residue of Wesleyan teaching on stewardship to ensure that wealth and power were softened by public duty and religious philanthropy except in a few notorious cases where Nonconformist grit got the better of Christian generosity.

[54] Milburn, 'Piety, Profit and Paternalism', 45–92.
[55] Ibid., 66.
[56] Martin, 'Faith, Flour and Jam', 329.

Explorations of the diverse ways in which Methodism both created and re-made religious cultures are sure to continue and will be all the more rewarding for the international comparative dimension without which the evangelical revival is too easily portrayed as a mere epiphenomenon.[57] As national boundaries have become less of an impediment in the reconstruction of popular religion so too have gender barriers. Mention has already been made of Deborah Valenze's pioneering work on the tough minority of female itinerant preachers in early industrial England, but the less unconventional Methodist wives, mothers and daughters are as silent in the connexional histories as they are in nineteenth-century ecclesiastical records, despite the fact that they were almost certainly a numerical majority.[58] In early Methodism women made important contributions as class and prayer-group leaders, and by visiting the sick and offering hospitality to itinerants. Later in the century they became the organisational and financial backbone of the ubiquitous evangelical societies and managed chapel tea meetings, bazaars and special events.[59] But it was in the home that women had their most strategic influence as angels of frugality, temperance and fidelity in the cult of domesticity promoted by Victorian evangelicals. Women were the day to day guardians of values, instructors of children and supporters of husbands in the pursuit of family piety. Women's 'essential nature', so it was held, was especially receptive to spiritual qualities of submissiveness, gentleness and purity, while it fell to the lot of men to take the lead in resolution, energy and firmness. In the chapels men made policy and women followed, men preached and women listened, men were the trustees of buildings and women cleaned them, men ran the Sunday schools and women taught in them, men constructed their own social theology and women obeyed as unto God. With research on this whole area set to increase in the next decade it is worth striking three obvious but cautionary notes. The first is that it is too easy to represent women as sacrificial victims in the male-dominated world of nineteenth-century popular Protestantism when in fact most were willing participants in a campaign of moral reformation which offered tangible benefits to them as well as to their families. Secondly, women are no more a cohesive social group than men, therefore a shared gender does not in itself

[57] Noll, Bebbington and Rawlyk (eds.), *Evangelicalism*; G. Rawlyk and M. Noll, *Amazing Grace: Evangelicalism in Australia, Britain, Canada and the United States* (Montreal and Kingston, 1994).
[58] C. D. Field, 'Social Composition of English Methodism', 153–69.
[59] F. Prochaska, *Women and Philanthropy in Nineteenth-Century England* (Oxford, 1980).

produce a common experience. The social filters of class, age and personal circumstances are not gender specific. Thirdly, in the historical task of reconstructing the lives of women in nineteenth-century religion, modern concepts of gender differentiation and equality may present as substantial a barrier as contemporary male propaganda. The past's vulgarity is after all an essential part of the past.

The future agenda of nineteenth-century Methodist studies looks set to be dominated by the trends already mentioned, along with ever more sophisticated attempts to explore the religious meanings and experiences of ordinary people at work, at home, at leisure and in the community as well as in church or chapel. Oral and literary evidence together with recent work on music and hymnody, England's 'common religion', testify to the emotional resonances at the core of much popular religious behaviour without which religious institutions are as dry as husks.[60] But the most fruitful opportunities probably lie in the international spread of popular Protestantism in the eighteenth and nineteenth centuries and its impact on different kinds of societies from central Europe to America's expanding frontier. The intensive local studies of English Methodism in the past twenty years may only achieve their full significance as part of a much larger picture. Only then will both the typicality and the particularity of the Methodist revolution in England be properly appreciated. Ironically, that is exactly what Elie Halévy tried to unravel all those years ago. His ghost apparently lives on.

[60]   J. Obelkevich, 'Music and Religion in the Nineteenth Century', in Obelkevich, Roper and Samuel (eds.), *Disciplines of Faith*, pp. 550–65.

## CHAPTER 3

# Evangelical enthusiasm and national identity in Scotland and Wales

The same processes of rapid social change and the growth of evangelical religion that transformed the religious landscape in England in the eighteenth and nineteenth centuries made an even more dramatic impact on the religious history of Scotland and Wales. Indeed, so profound was the impact of religious change in this period that it helped shape the cultural and national identities of both countries. The aim of this chapter is to explore the complex relationship between evangelical enthusiasm and national identity by investigating the rise of Nonconformist Liberalism in Wales and the attempts to realise the historic ideal of the godly commonwealth in Scotland. In each country evangelical enthusiasm contributed both to the expression of national distinctiveness and to a shared British Protestant nationalism. This is no easy tale to tell because religion was inextricably bound up with unprecedented social and economic changes and with the consequent distribution of wealth and power in the Celtic peripheries of the British State. As Professor Robbins stated in his presidential address to the Ecclesiastical History Society 'modern British history, perhaps more than the history of any other European state, discloses a complex inter-relationship between political attitudes, ecclesiastical allegiances and cultural traditions. The Christian religion in the British Isles, in its divided condition, has in turn been deeply involved in the cultural and political divisions of modern Britain and Ireland.'[1] Nowhere was this more patently true than in Wales and Scotland in the period of the industrial revolution.

By the mid-Victorian period it seemed that there were two particularly noteworthy features of the religious landscape in Wales. The first was the strength of evangelical Nonconformity. Wales appeared to have become a federation of chapels with remarkably high levels of

---

[1]    K. Robbins, 'Religion and Identity in Modern British History', in S. Mews (ed.), *Religion and National Identity, Studies in Church History*, 18 (1982), 465–87.

religious adherence among all social ranks including the working classes. The figures speak for themselves, but unfortunately they are more reliable for buildings and sittings than they are for attenders and communicants. In 1810 there were about 829 Anglican churches in Wales compared with 430 chapels (not inclusive of the 525 Methodist institutions which were notionally still part of the Established Church). By 1832 the number of chapels, Dissenting and Methodist, was 1,420. By 1905 there were 4,526 chapels compared with 1,546 buildings connected with the establishment. In some counties this trend was even more dramatic over the course of the nineteenth century. The religious census of 1851, for all its very considerable methodological weaknesses, told a similar tale of Nonconformist success and Anglican weakness and of Welsh religiosity by comparison with neighbouring England.[2] For example, Horace Mann devised a simple statistical ratio to show that churches, even to be minimally effective, should offer sittings for 58.4 per cent of the population in each census registration district. Every single registration county in Wales surpassed that figure, some by a considerable margin. In terms of attendances the figure for Wales is 84.7 per cent of the population, of which the Established Church accounted for less than a fifth. Naturally, the Nonconformist habit of attending more than once on Sundays inflated both the national figure and its superiority over the Church of Wales. There is unfortunately no reliable way of estimating the total number of Welsh people attending church on census registration Sunday let alone the number who were either habitual attenders or habitual non-attenders. Nevertheless, the most informed estimates suggest that Nonconformist worshippers outnumbered Anglicans on a ratio of about 4:1.

E. T. Davies's local study of Welsh religion in the rapidly industrialising counties of Glamorgan and Monmouthshire is yet more suggestive.[3] The percentage of worshippers in Monmouthshire (52 per cent) was higher than the national average for England and Wales and was considerably higher than the average for English industrial regions. Moreover, within Monmouthshire the percentage of attenders was particularly high in the industrial areas. The Pontypool, Abergavenny and Merthyr Tydfil Unions all recorded figures of between 64 per cent

---

[2]   R. Currie, A. Gilbert and L. Horsley (eds.), *Churches and Churchgoers: Patterns of Church Growth in the British Isles since 1700* (Oxford, 1977); I. G. Jones and D. Williams (eds.), *The Religious Census of 1851: A Calendar of the Returns Relating to Wales* (Cardiff, 1976); and P. Jenkins, *A History of Modern Wales 1536–1990* (London, 1992), ch. 10.

[3]   E. T. Davies, *Religion in the Industrial Revolution in South Wales* (Cardiff, 1965).

and 74 per cent. The percentage of worshippers was also much higher in Welsh-speaking Nonconformist areas than in English-speaking Anglican areas and English-speaking Nonconformity was not as successful as Welsh-speaking Nonconformity. While it must be pointed out that a sizeable minority of the Welsh working classes were not chapel attenders, and still more were regular or occasional chapel attenders but not chapel members, a much higher percentage of the Welsh working classes were church attenders than their English counterparts.

A second remarkable feature of Welsh religion in the mid-Victorian period was the apparent confluence of Nonconformity, Liberalism and Welsh national identity. To be Welsh, it seemed, was to be a Nonconformist, to be a Nonconformist was to be a Liberal. How was this pattern established? What were its chief characteristics, ambiguities and limitations? Why did such a powerful tradition decline so quickly in the early twentieth century? These are the questions which we must now address. In answering the first of these questions I shall try to offer a fresh approach to some familiar material by borrowing Lawrence Stone's typology from his book on the origins of the English Civil War in which he looks at preconditions, precipitants and triggers.

## PRECONDITIONS

The roots of mid-Victorian Welsh Nonconformity go back to the sixteenth and seventeenth centuries, but it was in the eighteenth century that the most dramatic changes began to take place. In the Oxford History of Wales 1642–1780 Geraint Jenkins states that 'the emergence of Methodism, the rejuvenation of Dissent and the growth of literacy were formative forces in the making of modern Wales'.[4] One might add to this list the remarkable growth in the publication of Welsh religious literature in the eighteenth century, part of an international growth in pious publications which is only now receiving due recognition in the historiography of a century too often dominated by concepts of enlightenment and rationalism.[5]

The early growth of Methodism in Wales, as in other parts of the British Isles, was not as dramatic as denominational hagiographers

[4]   G. H. Jenkins, *The Foundations of Modern Wales 1642–1780* (Oxford, 1987), p. 342.
[5]   G. Williams, *Religion, Language and Nationality in Wales* (Cardiff, 1979), p. 135; S. O'Brien, 'Eighteenth-Century Publishing Networks in the First Years of Transatlantic Evangelicalism', in M. A. Noll, D. W. Bebbington and G. A. Rawlyk (eds.), *Evangelicalism: Comparative Studies of Popular Protestantism in North America, the British Isles, and Beyond, 1700–1990* (Oxford, 1994), pp. 38–57.

have suggested and was beset with personality clashes, theological disputes, periods of apparent decline and strong opposition.[6] The two dominant personalities, Howel Harris and Daniel Rowland, it should be remembered, were converted several years before John Wesley and were never as thoroughly under English guidance and control as their Irish counterparts. In his international history of the great awakening Ward regards the Welsh revival as part of a wider European tradition of resistance to the religious, political and cultural encroachments of the established churches. He states that

There were two great paradoxes in Wales. A sustained campaign to assimilate Wales to the English language, culture and religious establishment generated by way of reaction a religious revival which ended by being Welsh, evangelical and dissenting; though the elite which launched the revival was almost as anglicising as the official policy it sought to supplement. And it was characteristic that the successes of a movement which, in the period of this study, was led by men of powerful English ties and a strong international awareness of what was happening in the Protestant world as a whole, were deeply marked by the highly decentralised, indeed tribal, structure of Welsh society.[7]

The paradoxes thus described carried forth echoes into the nature of Welsh Nonconformist evangelicalism until well into the nineteenth century.

The ramshackle nature of the Established Church's parochial structure in the eighteenth century and its insensitive refusal to appoint a single Welsh-speaking bishop from 1724 to 1870 was an open invitation for evangelical enthusiasts to revive the grass-roots without necessarily mounting a direct challenge to establishment control.[8] Not surprisingly, Methodists and dissenting evangelicals achieved their greatest initial successes in the large, remote and poorly administered parishes of south Wales. After 1780 the Welsh-speaking Calvinistic Methodists began to make gains in north Wales which thereafter became their strongest territory. But Methodism did not sweep Wales in the eighteenth century. It achieved more among the middling sort than the poor and made little impact on the superstitious folk religion of the bulk of the population. What it did was to offer a Welsh-speaking, emotionally resonant and infinitely adaptable form of popular religion which the Established Church ultimately could not

---

[6]    E. D. Evans, *A History of Wales 1660–1815* (Cardiff, 1976), pp. 70–123.
[7]    W. R. Ward, *The Protestant Evangelical Awakening* (Cambridge, 1992), pp. 316–17.
[8]    Jenkins, *Foundations of Modern Wales*, pp. 342–85.

contain and which had the capacity to quicken the pace of Dissenting growth in the later eighteenth century.

Alongside the Methodist revival of the eighteenth century was a remarkable growth of Welsh literacy as a result of the circulating schools of Griffith Jones, a Welsh country parson who was engaged in distinctly evangelical pursuits some quarter of a century before the alleged beginnings of the evangelical revival in Britain. Described as 'the most striking enterprise in mass religious education undertaken anywhere in Great Britain or its empire in the eighteenth century' the circulating schools movement, despite being run on a shoestring, taught over a third of the Welsh population how to read.[9] Although Jones was himself a devoted Anglican his educational initiative, more than any other factor, helped preserve the Welsh language and laid the foundation for the future success of Methodism and evangelical Nonconformity by securing a popular base for the remarkable increase of Welsh-language religious publishing in the eighteenth century.

The danger with the approach adopted in this chapter, as with Stone's explanation of the causes of the English Civil War, is to look only for the antecedents of a tradition which one knows, with the benefit of hindsight, to be triumphant at a later date. But the subsequent triumph of a distinctly radical Nonconformity was by no means obvious in the late eighteenth and early nineteenth centuries. Although the inflexions of power, notably land, law, politics and Established Church, were in the hands of an anglicised elite, it is now becoming clearer that not all landlords were rapacious any more than all Welsh clergymen were cultural imperialists and ineffective pastors. Though poorly endowed and operating in a poor country, the Established Church made commendable efforts in terms of religious services, church-building and education, and, ironically, it was the Anglicans who were the most effective promoters of the Welsh cultural revival in the period 1815–47.[10] Before the nineteenth century there is not much evidence of a general ground swell of opposition to the Established Church and there is much evidence to the contrary. Nonconformity, moreover, was a far from homogeneous force. Not only were there religious rivalries between the Old Dissenting tradition and the new enthusiasts, but there was an enormous political gap between the 'Friends of Liberty' tradition of some rationalist Dissenters and the vigorous loyalism of many of the Methodist leaders. In addition, the early history of Welsh radicalism, far from being dominated by Nonconformist religious concerns, was characterised more by the ritualised traditional protests of the Rebecca rioters and the Scotch Cattle movement, and by the more politically sophisticated Chartist movement which established a strong base in the south Wales coalfield and gave rise to perhaps the most serious insurrectionary movement in nineteenth-century Britain in the shape of the Newport rising of 1839.[11]

## PRECIPITANTS

Although the Blue Books controversy of 1847 is often seen as the first great awakening of Welsh Nonconformist self-consciousness, the processes had begun much earlier with the transformation of the Welsh economy and racial structure. The most dramatic were of course the rapid industrial, demographic and social changes which by the 1840s, according to Philip Jenkins, had transformed Wales into one of the most modern societies in Europe.[12] Not only had Wales the largest iron industry in the world by that date, but it was using its rapidly growing population to exploit its mineral resources 'on a scale such as to defy imagination'. In the first half of the nineteenth century Wales was in reality a frontier society with a number of rapidly shifting boundaries between town and country, land and industry, Welsh-speaking and English-speaking, religion and irreligion and Church and Dissent.[13] As in all frontier societies the most assiduous suppliers of public buildings and community values were in the best position to assert a long-term cultural hegemony. In that context the Nonconformist achievement was quite astonishing. According to the 1851 religious census, Nonconformist chapel-building at the end of each of the first five decades of the century was running at more than one new chapel a week.[14] Financed both by employer paternalism (and self-interest) and voluntary subscriptions, Welsh Nonconformists transformed the religious topography of the nation in a more remarkable

[11]  T. Herbert and G. E. Jones (eds.), *People and Protest: Wales 1815–1880* (Cardiff, 1988).
[12]  Jenkins, *History of Modern Wales*, ch. 15.
[13]  I. G. Jones, *Communities: Essays in the Social History of Victorian Wales* (Llandysul, Dyfed, 1987).
[14]  E. T. Davies, *A New History of Wales: Religion and Society in the Nineteenth Century* (Llandybie, Dyfed, 1981), p. 26.

way than was possible in any other part of the British Isles. Although they varied in style and size from little brick-built halls to great classical cathedrals, the ubiquitous Nonconformist chapels, with their biblical names reminding the faithful of Old Testament holy places and New Testament deliverances, seemed to declare that Wales was both a holy nation and a largely Nonconformist one.

The Established Church also saw the need to engage in church-building, but outside areas of generous Anglican gentry it was dependent for funds on the goodwill of the Church Building commissioners, the Church Building Society and the resourcefulness of its local supporters. Professor I. G. Jones has shown how all three failed to meet the bill for the rebuilding of St Michael's in Aberystwyth in the period 1828–33.[15] Fatally, recourse was made to an increased church rate to finance a church-yard wall to keep out the sea. A different kind of torrent erupted when many local Nonconformists refused to pay and the five Nonconformist ministers in the town were insensitively summoned before the magistracy and had their goods distrained and subsequently auctioned. The previously harmonious and co-operative relationship between Church and Dissent was shattered as Anglicanism became 'identified with despotic and irresponsible government' and 'Nonconformity with liberal democracy'. Church rates were eventually made voluntary in 1856, but the Aberystwyth case is but a particularly acute local example of how religious energy in a more competitive landscape could easily be transformed into a cultural and political struggle. Similar processes were at work in some other Welsh conflicts in this period. The Rebecca Riots, for example, though a product of the grim poverty of the farming community of south-west Wales in the 1830s and 40s, were frequently directed against all forms of financial exactions including tolls, rates and tithes.[16] The latter foreshadowed the more ferocious tithe war of the 1880s when a fervent Liberal and Nonconformist nationalism lay behind the more immediate agitation of the issue itself. The division between Church and Nonconformity, one of the frontiers mentioned earlier, thus had the capacity to offer an easily available and well-understood category within which a wide range of new and traditional grievances could be expressed. The fact that Anglicanism was by and large the religion of

15  Jones, *Communities*, pp. 70–87.
16  D. J. V. Jones, *Rebecca's Children* (Oxford, 1989); Herbert and Jones (eds.), *People and Protest*, pp. 113–38.

the landed, legal and governing elite was an unsought blessing for Welsh Nonconformists.

Prys Morgan's pioneering essay on Welsh cultural nationalism in *The Invention of Tradition* points to 'the treason of the Blue Books' as a major turning-point in the evolution of Welsh identity in the nineteenth century. The Royal Commission into the state of Welsh education set out with some unfortunate presuppositions about the backward and turbulent nature of Welsh society. The commissioners of enquiry were three young English lawyers who took their evidence disproportionately from among the Anglicised clergy and gentry. Their report in 1847 was a scathing attack on the inadequacy of Welsh daily education and the limitations of the admittedly more successful Sunday-school education offered by the chapels. A combination of exclusively religious instruction and the use of the Welsh language had effectively cut off the Welsh population from wider, and the clear implication was better, social and cultural influences. Displaying a powerful combination of religious, linguistic and cultural arrogance, the commissioners portrayed the Welsh people as remorselessly narrow-minded religious enthusiasts whose theological vocabulary was more impressive than their habits and morals. The report was received in Wales as a slur on the nation, its language and its religion. On the other hand

The action taken as a result of the brouhaha over the Blue Books was paradoxical and contradictory. On the one hand it made the Welsh more nationalistic and Anglophobe than they had ever been before, on the other it made the Welsh concerned to answer the criticisms of the commissioners by becoming more like the English, by turning themselves into practical, hard-headed, business-like English-speaking Britons.[17]

In more religious terms it helped draw in the Calvinistic Methodists to a more powerful and united Nonconformist federation and reinforced both Welsh Nonconformist particularity and commitment to self-improvement. As Morgan has shown, the Blue Books controversy heralded the demise of the Anglican patriot tradition and enabled the Nonconformists to parade themselves as the real guarantors of Welshness. They took the task so seriously that they effectively invented another tradition of Welsh evangelical heroes slaying the dragons of

[17]    Morgan, 'The Hunt for the Welsh Past', p. 93.

popular superstition and effete churchmanship. All in all it opened up a good market for preachers' biographies and religious ephemera. Biblicism, sabbatarianism, temperance, self-improvement and hymn-singing became more influential cultural reference points than poetry, ballad-singing and romantic explorations of the Welsh distant past. Even the eisteddfodau had been brought within the reach of chapel culture.

Contemporaneously with the Blue Books controversy, the growth of ritualism within the Established Church was as influential in persuading Welsh Methodists that the establishment principle had become a cloak for popery, as it undoubtedly was for their English counterparts.[18] It was this that drew the Methodists into the wider campaigns of political Dissent and which helps to explain the great upsurge in political feeling in the watershed election at Merioneth in 1859. For those Dissenters, mostly Methodist, who retained a residual faith in the utility of established churches as instruments for Christianising the people, the growth of Anglo-Catholicism opened the door through which they entered Nonconformist Liberalism. Revealingly, this was accompanied by a shift in Nonconformist anti-Church propaganda away from concentration on clerical indifference, ecclesiastical abuses and unwarranted legal privileges to a sustained attack on the Church as an unreformed and crypto-papist institution. Welsh Calvinists were thus given a far more tasty meal on which to feed than was afforded by the unglamorous diet of mere institutional incompetence. Thus, as one Protestant consensus in Britain declined another took its place.

If ritualism offered one route into Liberal Nonconformity the demise of Chartism supplied another. Morgan Williams, the successor of John Frost as leader of Welsh Chartism, stated in 1866 that 'the working men did not have the political feelings of thirty years ago' and had instead embraced a more gradualist and pragmatic approach to political change. Nonconformist leaders of the 1860s seized the opportunity to broaden the base of support for radical Nonconformity by declaring that Chartism, unlike trade unionism, had been, after all, an English invention in the first place.[19] The reinvention of tradition was now virtually unstoppable.

By the 1860s therefore, Welsh Nonconformity, unlike its English

---

[18]   I. G. Jones, 'Parliament and People in Mid-Nineteenth-Century Wales', in Herbert and Jones (eds.), *People and Protest*, p. 43; Jenkins, *History of Modern Wales*, p. 296; and D. Hempton, *Methodism and Politics in British Society 1750–1850* (London, 1984), pp. 164–9.
[19]   Herbert and Jones (eds.), *People and Protest*, pp. 41–3.

counterpart, had a genuinely national coverage, attracted the great majority of Welsh churchgoers and had become deeply embedded in the language and culture of the nation. What it lacked, as with Irish Catholicism before the 1820s, was an effective electoral mobilisation and a clear political focus.[20] The decisive shift came in the 1860s when the Liberation Society started to mobilise Welsh voters through a vigorous registration campaign at the same time as the electorate was expanded by the Reform Act of 1867.[21] 'It was probably through the chapels and through participating in the constant work of the Liberation Society', suggests Jones in his evocative study of the south Wales colliers, 'that men learned the techniques of party organisation and of ordered public pressure on the government.'[22] The motivation was supplied by the fact that, in the words of the Liberation Society's own propaganda, Wales had become 'a nation of Nonconformists ... without a single Nonconformist representative'.[23]

Although this changed in the election of 1868 the change was not as dramatic as is conventionally assumed. Not only was there a pre-existing Liberal tradition in Wales, admittedly of a rather whiggish kind, but only three Nonconformists were elected in 1868. One was the radical Independent minister, Henry Richard, who, with working-class support, won Merthyr Tydfil for populist Liberalism against elite Liberalism. Ironically, in the light of the symbolic significance attached to this victory for Welsh Nonconformist politics, Richard bemoaned the fact that Welsh religiosity, as reflected in its periodical literature, was in effect a barrier against political mobilisation, not least because the Welsh language cut off the people from the rich literary tradition of English popular radicalism.[24] What this shows is that issues of class, privilege and power, though refracted most commonly through the prism of Welsh Nonconformist opposition to the Established Church and Anglican landowners in the period before World War One, had the capacity to take a different direction in response to a change of enemy. Socialist Wales may not therefore be as dramatic a departure from Liberal Wales as the crude arithmetic of electoral demography might suggest.

[20]   R. Williams, '*Organise! Organise! Organise!*': *A Study of Reform Agitations in Wales, 1840–1886* (Cardiff, 1991), pp. 122–36.
[21]   *Ibid.*, pp. 49–52.
[22]   Jones, *Communities*, p. 137.
[23]   Herbert and Jones (eds.), *People and Protest*, p. 52.
[24]   *Ibid.*, p. 53.

### THE MANNERS AND MORALS OF HIGH NONCONFORMITY

Although the confluence of Nonconformist religion, Liberal politics and Welsh national identity, as expressed in opposition to an older and increasingly resented Anglican pattern, was at the heart of the cultural hegemony established by the chapels in Wales in the half century before the Great War, that in itself does not do justice to the sheer religious magnetism of chapel culture itself. In reconstructing that culture one must be careful not to indulge in naive sentimentality. Self-righteous Puritanism, the ineluctable sectarianism of Dissent, carefully preserved hierarchies of class, gender and ministry, and endless theological squabbles about the nature and efficacy of grace were as much part of Nonconformist culture as its more vaunted choral unions and religious charities. For those educated in doctrine and dogma, but not much else, Nonconformist chapels opened up a pandora's box of hard-edged disputation and Calvinist conditioning which did not always end up in a sweeter appreciation of love and grace. But religion, through the instrumentality of chapels and their ubiquitous Sunday schools, offered, for good and for ill, a shared vocabulary for large numbers of people. In his book on the Welsh Sunday schools (1884) the Revd D. Evans stated that 'some time ago we passed three working men, we believe they were colliers, sitting together on a heap of stones by the roadside, and earnestly discussing the question "How to reconcile the sovereignty of God with the responsibility of man.". It struck us at the time that people of that class do not discuss such subjects anywhere out of Wales.'[25] Historians of the Durham coalfield in the same period might not agree, but the general point holds nevertheless.

At different stages in its chronological evolution Welsh Nonconformity was able to build on earlier, evangelical-inspired traditions of domestic piety, offer security and identity in a rapidly changing frontier landscape and present an opportunity for self-improvement and self-expression to those who understood their value. Nonconformity's powerful clerical dynasties, its 20,000 deacons and elders and its veritable army of lay preachers, Sunday-school teachers and literature distributors kindled the religious energies of the people in a way that the Established Church could never match. Nurtured by a factory of petty grievances against the Church and capable of massive internal

---

[25] *Ibid.*, p. 99.

revivification through the powerful impulses of folk revivalism, Welsh Nonconformity in the nineteenth century seemed to be flowing with an irresistible tide.[26] There are nevertheless four aspects to this Nonconformist surge that are frequently neglected.

The first is that this triumph of religious voluntaryism simply could not have been sustained without the wealth, however poorly distributed, generated by new industries.[27] The great era of chapel-building was as formidable an achievement for the purse as it was for piety. There is, moreover, a fragile aspect to the growth of Nonconformity arising from the difference between voluntary giving to a desirable new chapel as an expression of community solidarity and the unwelcome financial exactions of chapels as going concerns, especially when the perceived beneficiaries, the clergy, became more distant from the workplace. Clerical professionalism and upward social mobility within the ranks, both of which were facilitated by wealth creation, were double-edged swords for Welsh Nonconformity. Secondly, Welsh Nonconformity benefited from the reactive exchanges between urban and rural religion facilitated by population migrations, the maintenance of the Welsh language and the survival of notions of community. Hence the interface between rural and urban religion, which is often regarded as a fundamental cause of secularisation, probably had the reverse effect in Wales because of the relatively small size of towns and the adaptability of chapel culture to the urban landscape. Welsh Nonconformity was thus partly a beneficiary of modernisation and partly a protest against it. Similarly, Nonconformity was both rooted in emotionalism and systematically responsible for a cult of learning and self-improvement that eventually did much to undermine it. Such creative tensions, along with a vigorous element of denominational competition within a broad Nonconformist consensus, worked to the advantage of Nonconformist growth in the nineteenth century and to its disadvantage in the twentieth when tensions were resolved into contradictions.

Thirdly, Nonconformity, especially in the mining valleys, benefited from the organisational structure of the mining industry itself. Ben Rees has shown that there was a complementarity between religious

---

[26]    C. B. Turner, 'Revivalism and Welsh Society in the Nineteenth Century', in J. Obelkevich, L. Roper and R. Samuel (eds.), *Disciplines of Faith: Studies in Religion, Politics and Patriarchy* (London, 1987), pp. 311–23; and idem, 'The Nonconformist Response', in *People and Protest*, pp. 77–94.

[27]    D. G. Evans, *A History of Wales 1815–1906* (Cardiff, 1989), ch. 4.

and industrial organisations in the working practices of small teams engaged in seam mining.[28] Both mining teams and small Independent chapels had in common a strong degree of togetherness, a sense of belonging, a high degree of mutual responsibility and a humane camaraderie in the face of a potentially hostile environment. The mechanisation of the mining industry in the twentieth century helped undermine that pattern along with the community solidarity that went with it. Fourthly, although Nonconformist devotion to temperance and sabbatarianism could set up tensions between chapels and the equally ubiquitous public houses, there was a closer connexion between religion and popular entertainment in Wales than was common in most other parts of the British Isles in the nineteenth century.[29] Not only were chapels social and cultural centres, but there were particularly close links between chapels and the increasingly populist and democratic eisteddfodau. 'Every locality, every sizeable chapel in the coalfield, organised its eisteddfod as part of the annual round of its week-day activities, and there is no exaggerating the prestige and honour, both on a local and national scale, which was attached to the winning competitors.' In this way a 'chapel-orientated working class culture appropriated an essentially aristocratic and medieval literary tradition' and achieved a popular cultural congruence between religion and enjoyment which neither English nor Irish Nonconformists were able to match.[30]

Welsh Nonconformist Liberalism at its peak was neither religiously nor politically monochrome, but along with the miles of railroad track and remarkable circulation of Welsh language publications, it helped draw the nation together during a century of bewildering change. It was the good fortune of Welsh Nonconformists, and Irish Catholics for that matter, that the conflict between the Established Church and Nonconformity, and between Anglican landowners and an oppressed tenantry, offered available categories within which a whole host of other and more complex issues could be given meaning and coherence.[31] It was the misfortune of Welsh Nonconformity that the old war-cries of the pre-World War One period – disestablishment, education, land reform and temperance – were no longer the most

[28]  D. Ben Rees, *Chapels in the Valleys* (Upton, Wirral, 1975).

[29]  B. Harrison, 'Religion and Recreation in Nineteenth-Century England', *Past & Present*, no. 38 (1967), 98–125; I. Sellars, *Nineteenth-Century Nonconformity* (London, 1977), pp. 40–45.

[30]  Jones, *Communities*, p. 132.

[31]  Herbert and Jones (eds.), *People and Protest*, pp. 171–90.

important issues for the post-war industrial communities.[32] Industrial, linguistic, political and cultural changes helped undermine the strength of Welsh Nonconformity and opened up the way for the triumph of Labour, which at least in the short term was infused with Christian radical values. As the remarkable decline in churchgoing and chapel membership in twentieth-century Wales shows no sign of abating it remains to be seen whether Welsh Nonconformity is able to mount as successful a defence of its position as the Established Church in Wales, ironically, managed to do in the half century before its disestablishment.[33]

The conditions producing such a close confluence between religion and politics, and culture and national identity, in Wales simply did not operate in the same way in Scotland where there was a tiny episcopalian minority and a Presbyterian Established Church. In a country where the largest groups of Protestant churchgoers outside the Established Church were also Presbyterians (unlike the anti-episcopalianism of the English Dissenters), the great ecclesiastical issues after the Act of Union were not about the desirability or otherwise of an established church, but rather who should control that church and what kind of Presbyterianism it should represent.[34] In his study of nationalism in Scotland Christopher Harvie states that 'the various secessionist groups did not retreat into their own private theologies. Each was convinced that it was the true legatee of the Covenanters of 1639... They abused the Establishment but they never challenged the principle.'[35] Although this ignores the strength of voluntaryist sentiment in the last quarter of the nineteenth century it does help to explain how the reunion of churches in 1929 was facilitated not by disestablishment but by the creation of an attenuated establishment based on spiritual independence, self-government and a national recognition of the Church of Scotland.[36] Indeed, the principles upon

---

[32]  K. O. Morgan, *Rebirth of a Nation: Wales 1880–1980* (Oxford, 1981); idem, 'The New Liberalism and the Challenge of Labour: the Welsh Experience', *Welsh Historical Review*, 6 (1973); and D. Hopkins, 'The Rise of Labour: Llanelli, 1890–1922', in G. H. Jenkins and J. B. Smith (eds.), *Politics and Society in Wales, 1840–1922* (Cardiff, 1988), pp. 161–82.

[33]  Jenkins, *History of Modern Wales*, p. 296.

[34]  A. L. Drummond and J. Bulloch, *The Scottish Church 1688–1843: The Age of the Moderates* (Edinburgh, 1973); idem, *The Church in Victorian Scotland* (Edinburgh, 1975); C. G. Brown, *The Social History of Religion in Scotland since 1730* (London, 1987); and idem, *The People in the Pews: Religion and Society in Scotland since 1780* (Dundee, 1993).

[35]  C. Harvie, *Scotland and Nationalism: Scottish Society and Politics, 1707–1977* (London, 1977), pp. 70–1.

[36]  I. Machin, 'Voluntaryism and Reunion, 1874–1929', in N. Macdougall (ed.), *Church, Politics and Society: Scotland 1408–1929* (Edinburgh, 1983), ch. 12.

which the reunion was based seemed to awaken the ghost of Thomas
Chalmers whose early Victorian pursuit of the godly commonwealth
was grounded on similar, if rather more ambitious, principles.[37] It is
tempting to conclude from all this that while Presbyterianism in
Scotland has played a major role in defining Scottishness it has played
almost no part in fostering Scottish nationalism. Thus, the standard
histories of the rise of nationalism in Scotland devote little attention to
religion except to say that the Church of Scotland was too closely
linked to the British establishment, including the monarchy, to be a
suitable vehicle either for Home Rule or separatist convictions. There
is need for care here. The Act of Union gave the Scottish Church every
guarantee imaginable and the Church did manage to fight its way into
the Highlands. Its problem was that while being a more successful force
for national assimilation than the Church of England ever was, it ran
the risk of itself being assimilated by a system of influence; hence the
interminable disputes about patronage which inevitably raised bigger
questions about the rights of the Scots. What I wish to suggest,
therefore, is that the quarter century on either side of the great
disruption in 1843, the pivotal event in modern Scottish church history,
there were links not only between religion and Scottish national
consciousness, but also between the alleged particularity of Scottish
religion and much wider forces operating in the British Isles as a
whole.[38] In that respect, the issues raised by the disruption were
crucial, not only for the future of religion in Scotland, but for 'greater
Britain' as well.[39]

## THE GODLY COMMONWEALTH

The idea of a godly commonwealth[40] in Scotland had its origins in the
all-embracing Calvinism of the sixteenth and seventeenth centuries in
which the Church had responsibility for teaching God's laws and the

[37] S. J. Brown, *Thomas Chalmers and the Godly Commonwealth in Scotland* (Oxford, 1982).

[38] Bebbington, 'Religion and National Identity in Nineteenth Century Wales and Scotland',
*Studies in Church History*, 18 (1982) 489–503; idem, *Evangelicalism in Modern Britain: A History from
the 1730s to the 1980s* (London, 1989).

[39] J. Wolffe, *God and Greater Britain: Religion and National Life in Britain and Ireland 1843–1945*
(London, 1994).

[40] Much of what follows is based on Brown, *Thomas Chalmers*. For a different perspective on
Chalmers see B. Hilton, 'The Role of Providence in Evangelical Social Thought', in
D. Beales and G. Best (eds.), *History, Society and the Churches: Essays in Honour of Owen Chadwick*
(Cambridge, 1985), pp. 215–33; and idem, *The Age of Atonement: The Influence of Evangelicalism on
Social and Economic Thought, 1795–1865* (Oxford, 1988).

State for enforcing them. Here was a covenanted nation in which there was no separation of Church and State, secular and profane, or individual and community. Rather, all were to be brought together to create a society in social, economic and political conformity to the word of God. This high ideal foundered successively on the poverty of the Established Church, the propertied self-interest of the landed elite, the political consequences of the Act of Union with England, and the corrosive impact of the Scottish enlightenment, with its emphases on economic individualism, rationalism and religious toleration. It is no accident that the ideal of the godly commonwealth was rekindled among the fateful generation overshadowed by the French Revolution and the subsequent war against revolutionary France. The most compelling advocate of the ideal of the godly commonwealth was Thomas Chalmers, who was born in 1780, and whose spiritual and intellectual biography offers a fascinating pilgrimage through what is arguably the most important half century in the history of Western Christianity. Chalmers was brought up in rural Fife where faint echoes of the godly commonwealth ideal had survived, at least in part, as an expression of protest against Anglicisation, the landed interest and the declining social influence of Christianity. There was more than a hint of radicalism in Chalmers's early intellectual development. He disliked war, oppressive government, conspicuous consumption and economic individualism. He was an admirer of Fox and Sheridan. More concretely, he had his early ambitions thwarted by the patronage policy of Henry Dundas's supporters in East Fife, despite many years of loyal support from Chalmers's father. It is, however, in the first decade of the nineteenth century that the mainsprings of Chalmers's later career are to be found. He exhibited an intense patriotism in response to the threat of a French invasion in 1803, he wrote vigorously against the economic foundations of classical Liberalism in his first major publication in 1808 and he experienced an intense evangelical conversion, the first fruits of which became evident in 1811. Chalmers's conversion appears to have changed him from a vain, ambitious, opinionated, lazy and ineffectual parish minister into an equally vain, ambitious, opinionated, but ferociously energetic and successful, parish minister.

Apart from his vigorous parish ministry, Chalmers's early evangelical enthusiasm was channelled into establishing parish auxiliaries for the support of the British and Foreign Bible Society. In typically grand style Chalmers's declared purpose was to 'unite the entire British nation for a shared world mission ideal'. This early flirtation with an evangelical voluntary agency showed Chalmers both the potential and the limitations of religious voluntaryism as an agent for Christianising Britain and the wider world. The territorial unit of the parish seemed to offer a better way. Chalmers sought to transform his Kilmany parish into a microcosm of the godly commonwealth. Through the faithful preaching of the word, scriptural education, systematic visitation, poor relief and the harnessing of resources for community, not individual, benefit, Chalmers hoped to make Kilmany a model for every parish, not only in Scotland, but throughout the British Isles. However idealistic in theory, and however limited its success was in practice, even in Kilmany, Chalmers was not blind to the formidable obstacles blocking the way to the godly commonwealth. Chief among these, in Chalmers's eyes at least, were economic individualism and the ecclesiastical abuses of pluralities and lax clerical standards. With the benefit of hindsight, however, it is clear that Chalmers – and this was one of his besetting sins – exaggerated the success of his own parish experiment even in the predominantly rural environment of Kilmany. Moreover, the big question that had yet to be faced was how successfully the parish unit could be made work in the growing manufacturing cities of nineteenth-century Britain with all their attendant problems of mass poverty, class separation, working-class religious indifference and social welfare provision.

In his mid thirties and at the peak of his powers, Chalmers was delivered the great evangelical prize (regarded so because of its non-parochial, middle-class, evangelical congregation) of the ramshackle parish of Tron, one of the poorest and most populous parishes in the city of Glasgow. It was from a new parish created out of the western portion of Tron that Chalmers began his great parochial experiment in St John's in 1819. Although Chalmers later described St John's as the poorest parish in Glasgow, it was in fact populated chiefly by substantial labouring families with relatively modest numbers of seasonal paupers. His aim was to abolish poor relief assessments altogether in favour of self-help and communal benevolence, to endow new parish schools and to pursue a vigorous evangelical ministry with the help of dedicated lay visitors. Superficially, the experiment was an enormous short-term success: assessment-based poor relief was eliminated; four parish schools were established; and a small army of elders and Sunday-school teachers had been put to work. The real weakness of the experiment was not lack of middle-class support, nor even hostility from the civil magistrates (Chalmers's pet complaint), but the fact that it never succeeded in its main object – 'the formation of a closely-knit working-class community, united by Evangelical ideals, and centred upon the parish church'. Notwithstanding the immense energy expended upon it, the St John's experiment was based upon a highly dubious social policy and an exaggerated belief in the attractiveness of evangelical social ethics to the non-respectable working class. It nevertheless attracted considerable attention from those who fervently hoped that established churches could indeed rise to the challenge of an industrial society and from those who feared the unwelcome alternatives of social revolution or an insupportable poor rate.

Perhaps the most important result of the St John's experiment was the fact that Chalmers *believed* it had succeeded, and that if only the State would co-operate properly, the British Isles could be turned into a federation of self-regulating Christian communities. So it was that Chalmers set out on a grand design of national regeneration based on a parochial philosophy first worked out in a rural corner of the Celtic fringe. Even the warm-hearted Irish Catholics, according to Chalmers, could be brought along if they were treated fairly over Catholic Emancipation and poor relief. What Chalmers needed most, however, and what he was most unlikely to get, was State support for a massive church-building campaign.

While the Whigs vacillated and established a commission, Chalmers and the dominant evangelical party within the Scottish Church tried to meet the increasing challenge of Dissenting voluntaryists by mounting an impressive church extension campaign. Chalmers, though a committed anti-voluntaryist, used voluntaryist methods to raise money for church-building. By asking for a penny a week from the poor and by engaging in a high profile tour of the west of the country, described by one critic as a 'tour of spiritual O'Connellism', Chalmers sought to use his popularity among the Scottish people to put pressure on the Whig administration. He also tried, and failed, to persuade the urban working classes that church extension was a truly radical cause. Unable to bend the ear of government or to mobilise the world of labour, the formidable church-building campaign of the 1830s was a monument both to the power and the limitations of middle-class philanthropy. Over two hundred new churches were built in a period of seven years, but more importantly, the Church of Scotland believed it had been treated shabbily by a predominantly English administration, and many within the Church had come to see that there were formidable obstacles in the way of any church servicing the social deprivation and welfare needs of Scotland's growing urban population. Under the respective pressures of dissenting voluntaryism, Whig indifference and urban infidelity, the godly commonwealth ideal was beginning to assume some of the characteristics of a nationalist movement. With the rhetorical affluence for which he was famous, Chalmers asserted that the Church had the support of 'the great mass of the commonality in Scotland' and that the clergy were 'the tribunes of the people', the representatives of 'the unfranchised multitude'. In the middle of this endowment campaign, Chalmers was invited to Paris in 1838, ostensibly to speak to French academicians about his views on political economy and Christian social policy. But Stewart Brown states that Chalmers's trip to Paris assumed something of the flavour of a state visit by a leader of the Scottish nation and 'served to remind both his own countrymen and London that Scotland possessed a separate national identity. The Scots were not merely North Britons, and the Union of 1707 was not licence for the London government to treat their most sacred national institution with indifference and contempt.'[41] Chalmers's position as a *national* leader ought not to be pressed too far, however. In the first place his godly commonwealth ideal cut little ice with Scottish voluntaryists or with the urban working classes among whom Chalmers was never at ease. Secondly, by the late 1830s Chalmers had emerged as a vigorous champion of the defenders of established churches not only in Scotland, but throughout the British Isles. Even conservative English Wesleyans, though suspicious of the principles of ecclesiastical democracy implicit in Scottish Presbyterianism, regarded Chalmers as a key figure in the battle against the growing religious indifference of the State and the apparent apathy of the masses.[42]

The great disruption crisis in the Church of Scotland over the respective rights of lay patronage and local congregations in the appointment of ministers was thus in part a national movement directed against Westminster indifference and an anglicised landed elite.[43] It was also a powerful assertion of evangelical middle-class

---

[41] Brown, *Thomas Chalmers*, p. 273.
[42] Hempton, *Methodism and Politics*, pp. 187–90.
[43] G. Parsons, 'Church and State in Victorian Scotland: Disruption and Reunion', in Parsons (ed.), *Religion in Victorian Britain*, vol. II, *Controversies* (Manchester, 1988), pp. 107–23; G. I. T. Machin, *Politics and the Churches in Great Britain 1832–68* (Oxford, 1977); and S. J. Brown and M. Fry (eds.), *Scotland in the Age of Disruption* (Edinburgh, 1993).

values.[44] For Chalmers, the disruption was not a secession, but rather 'a tragic severing of the relationship between the true Church of Scotland and a British state which had broken its pledge to preserve the Church's integrity'. From his perspective, therefore, the Free Church was neither a gathered nor a voluntary church, but was rather a truly national church dedicated to the ideal of the godly common-wealth and vigorously opposed to unwelcome state interference. In a sense the great disruption was an ecclesiastical expression of the cultural and political ambiguities stemming from the Act of Union itself. The paradox at the heart of the disruption was pointed out by Chalmers himself at the first Free Church General Assembly in 1843: 'though we quit the Establishment, we go out on the Establishment principle; we have quit a vitiated Establishment, but would rejoice in returning to a pure one. To express it otherwise – we are the advocates for a national recognition and support of religion – and we are not voluntaries'.[45] The disruption was in reality a clash between an increasingly evangelical and aggressive national church and the growing power of a state committed to religious toleration and an enlarged social policy. In truth, the godly commonwealth ideal was incapable of realisation within the confines of a modern Liberal state, and this helps explain why Chalmers set himself against a range of the State's reforming measures from the Reform Act to the Poor Law Amendment Act. Indeed, despite their theological and cultural dissim-ilarities, there is a remarkable congruence of ideas between Scotland's most ardent advocate of the virtues of the rural parish and his counter-part in England, John Keble. Both marched against the formidable armies of utilitarianism and Liberalism. Chalmers was nevertheless anything but a defeatist, and he harnessed his quite remarkable administrative and organisational talents for a campaign to make the Free Church a great national church. As it turned out no amount of fund-raising and church-building could off-set the sectarian dynamics at work in the Free Church as it became more revivalist, more anti-Catholic and inexorably more voluntaryist, in practice if not in theory. Chalmers had increasingly relied on middle-class evangelicals to usher in the millennium of the godly commonwealth only to find that,

[44] C. G. Brown, *Social History of Religion*, pp. 149–59; A. A. MacLaren, *Religion and Social Class: The Disruption Years in Aberdeen* (London, 1974); P. Hillis, 'Presbyterianism and Social Class in Mid-Nineteenth Century Glasgow: a Study of Nine Churches', *Journal of Ecclesiastical History*, 32 (1981), 47–64; and T. C. Smout, *A Century of the Scottish People 1830–1950* (Glasgow, 1986), ch. 8.
[45] Brown, *Thomas Chalmers*, p. 337.

however energetically pursued by its devoted army of lay helpers, evangelicalism carried within it aspects of bourgeois individualism and religious sectarianism which made it an unlikely vehicle for the creation of a national faith. Ironically, this was not too dissimilar from the conclusion arrived at by Archbishop Laud in the 1630s in respect of Calvinists and Puritans, and which led to a different kind of crisis between the English and Scottish nations.

If the Free Church was an inappropriate vehicle for the realisation of the ideal of the godly commonwealth, it was by no means redundant as a medium for the expression of a Scottish identity. Despite considerable Free Church pride in the empire and widespread acceptance of the benefits of the Union, Hugh Miller was able to use the Free Church *Witness* as a forum for the statement of national grievances against the English. In this he was aided by the immense chauvinism of the English press which portrayed Scottish culture as provincial, uncultivated and remorselessly narrow-minded. In the infamous *Times* article of 1856, 'Scotland ... in Want of a Grievance', the ringing conclusion was that 'the more Scotland has striven to be a nation, the more she has sunk to be a province'.[46] By mid century the main grievance Scotland seemed to be in search of was the profound conviction that Scottish interests within the Union were being neglected as a result of ineffective and Anglicised administrative systems. The National Association for the Vindication of Scottish Rights founded in 1853 was in effect a federation of Scottish romantics, radical churchmen and administrative reformers. Professor Hanham has commented that the radical nationalism of the Free Churchman James Begg and the Scottish Dissenters 'closely resembled the radical nationalism of the Welsh nonconformists'. Common ingredients were the grievances against absentee landlords and capitalists, a determination to have a truly national education system and a prickly resistance to the imposition of English or metropolitan values. But Scotland did not have an English Established Church upon which to concentrate its grievances and its mid-nineteenth-century nationalism failed to produce either a nationalist literature or a vigorous political movement. What then of the fate of the ideal of the godly commonwealth? In the half century after the disruption neither the ecclesiastical division of the

---

[46] H. J. Hanham, 'Mid-Century Scottish Nationalism: Romantic and Radical', in R. Robson (ed.), *Ideas and Institutions of Victorian Britain* (London, 1967), pp. 174–5. See also, R. Mitchison (ed.), *The Roots of Nationalism: Studies in Northern Europe* (Edinburgh, 1980), and idem, *Life in Scotland* (London, 1978).

nation into three major strands (the Church of Scotland, the Free Church and the United Presbyterian Church), nor the prevailing social and political climate, were congenial to its further development. But religious pluralism and the sheer power of evangelical enthusiasm (an enterprising religion for an enterprising society) at least maintained, and possibly even increased, the popularity and social significance of religion in the nineteenth century.[47] Thus, the main enemies of religion in Scotland were not so much urbanisation and industrialisation, as state welfarism, the rise of the Labour movement and the growth of alternative forms of leisure. As T. C. Smout states, the 'Church of Scotland never did find a solution to the ... fundamental problems posed by the death of hell, the rise of class and the spread of other entertainment'.[48] However persuasive this may be in explaining the eventual decline of Scottish religiosity, it strikes me that some of the roots go back at least to the early nineteenth century and are highlighted in the successes and failures of Chalmers's parochial experiments in Glasgow and later in Edinburgh. Their success was owing to the power of evangelical middle-class enthusiasm when harnessed to the social aspirations of the 'respectable' working classes; their failure has to do with the complex reasons behind the alienation of the unskilled, low wage-earning and impoverished working classes from organised religion. Chalmers came to blame local civic leaders, then the State, and then the English for failing to encourage the Scottish Church in its parochial mission, but the real causes of popular indifference were both deeper and less accessible to the evangelical mind.

The respective religious experiences of Scotland and Wales in the era of the industrial revolution offer unlimited scope for comparisons and contrasts.[49] In both countries the stresses and strains of rapid economic and social change offered fresh opportunities for a vigorous and flexible evangelicalism to dominate their religious landscapes in the long nineteenth century. So profound was the impact of evangelical religion in its various forms that it helped shape not only the religious mores of the two countries but also their cultural and national

[47]   Brown, *The People in the Pews*, pp. 26–45; and idem, 'The Mechanism of Religious Growth in Urban Societies: British Cities since the Eighteenth Century', in H. McLeod (ed.), *European Religion in the Age of Great Cities 1830–1930* (London and New York, 1995), pp. 239–62.

[48]   Smout, *History of the Scottish People*, p. 205; K. M. Boyd, *Scottish Church Attitudes to Sex, Marriage and the Family 1850–1914* (Edinburgh, 1980).

[49]   K. Robbins, *Nineteenth-Century Britain: Integration and Diversity* (Oxford, 1988), pp. 63–96; J. Wolffe, *God and Greater Britain*, pp. 98–122.

identities. In both countries, evangelical enthusiasm made a strong contribution to both the expression of nationhood and the re-invention of tradition but, paradoxically, it also helped draw both countries into a wider British Protestant nationalism through a shared anti-Catholicism, imperialism and constitutional chauvinism. Out of a religious culture shaped by disciplined protest and self-improvement the Celtic fringes were able, through Liberalism, to bend the British State without breaking it and to influence it without either controlling or repudiating it. In addition, most of the Welsh and Scottish people were prepared, however grudgingly, to put up with the religious and cultural arrogance of the English, if for no other reason than economic self-interest.[50]

The differences between Scottish and Welsh religion, notwithstanding the dominance of evangelical Calvinism in both, are also striking. Welsh Nonconformity, perhaps because of the availability of the Established Church and Anglicised landowners as convenient targets, was yoked to popular radical and Liberal causes in a way that could not be matched in Scotland where the Established Church was the bearer of the nation's traditions.[51] Yet that in itself does not explain why, for example, there was no equivalent in the Scottish coalfields to the nineteenth-century religious fervour of miners in South Wales, Durham and Northumberland. The influence of social class as a solvent of religious enthusiasm seems to have worked less quickly in nineteenth-century, and perhaps more quickly in twentieth-century, Wales than in Scotland. One reason for this may be the fact that the exercise of religious leadership and spiritual discipline was more often employed as an agent of middle-class social control in Scotland than in Wales in the period of the industrial revolution. By the beginning of the twentieth century, however, the social gulf separating the clerical and lay leadership of Welsh Nonconformity from working-class chapel-goers had widened and, more importantly, was seen to matter. In that respect, industrialisation and urbanisation not only opened up fresh opportunities for churches in Wales and Scotland to help mould new communities and new identities, but also carried with them the potential for the fragmentation of social and cultural solidarities upon which a genuinely popular and inclusive religious tradition depends. There in a nutshell is the great paradox of British religious development since the eighteenth century.

[50]  M. Hechter, *Internal Colonialism: The Celtic Fringe in British National Development, 1536–1966* (London, 1975).
[51]  J. Brand, *The National Movement in Scotland* (London, 1978), pp. 128–9.

CHAPTER 4

# The making of the Irish Catholic nation

The chief irony of this subject is the fact that probably no church in the British Isles started out from a more unpromising position in the first half of the eighteenth century than the Roman Catholic Church in Ireland, yet no church was in a stronger position, both in terms of its popular allegiance and its social and political influence, by the middle of the twentieth century.[1] The aim of this chapter is to offer a series of five historical snapshots in the development of an Irish Catholic nationalism, combined with some observations on the long-term structural changes in the shape of the Catholic Church, which enabled it to become so deeply embedded in the social, political and cultural fabric of the nation. The result of these processes was the emergence of a powerful fusion of religion and identity unequalled in any other part of the British Isles with the possible exception of Protestantism in Ulster, which in turn drew strength from its implacable opposition to Catholic nationalism.[2]

## 'PROTESTANT ASCENDANCY' AND CATHOLIC PENALTIES IN THE EIGHTEENTH CENTURY

The success of William of Orange's Irish campaigns paved the way for further land transfer from Catholics to Protestants and for four decades of penal legislation against Irish Catholics.[3] After the turbulence and uncertainty of the half century from the Rebellion of 1641 to the conclusion of the Williamite campaigns in 1691 it seemed that out of a powerful mixture of revenge and self-defence, Irish Protestants, with

[1] The best one-volume history of the Roman Catholic Church in Ireland is P. Corish, *The Irish Catholic Experience: A Historical Survey* (Dublin, 1985).
[2] D. Hempton and M. Hill, *Evangelical Protestantism in Ulster Society 1740–1890* (London, 1992).
[3] For an authoritative collection of essays on the penal laws see G. O'Brien (ed.), *Catholic Ireland in the Eighteenth Century: Collected Essays of Maureen Wall* (Dublin, 1989).

72

the support of the British State, were determined to control the country through landed power, legal coercion and the Protestant Established Church.

The nature, purpose and effectiveness of the penal laws have been subjected to considerable historical revision in the past few years, particularly in the work of Bartlett and Connolly. The former has stated that from the '1730s on the penal laws were little more than an intolerable system of petty oppression to Catholics and an embarrassment to Protestants'.[4] Designed more as a control mechanism for the Catholic elite, clerical and lay, than as a rigorous instrument for the conversion of Ireland to Protestantism, the penal code's basic concern was not with religion but with property. Although there was a process of conformity among the Catholic landed elite, fewer priests conformed because the inducements were less attractive and the penalties less severe. Moreover, elements of Protestant anticlericalism, economic self-interest and sheer realism about the impossibility of converting the Catholic masses combined to ensure that the Established Church was not in a position to achieve a radical re-configuration of Irish religion even if that had been its earnest intention.

In an important book Sean Connolly, with deliberate polemical intent, has taken the process of revision one step further.[5] He rejects the notion that eighteenth-century Ireland was governed as a colony by a rapacious elite and instead suggests that Ireland was not too dissimilar from other *'ancien régime'* states in early modern Europe. Law was less arbitrary, violence less endemic, patronage less corrupt, landed power less vicious, popular disturbances less radical, culture less unenlightened and religious persecution less severe than many have supposed. The penal laws were therefore not so much a well-considered systematic code as a series of impromptu measures, loosely drafted and loosely enforced. They were neither vital to the functioning of eighteenth-century Irish society nor did they alter the shape and development of that society in any fundamental respect. Protestants were often as divided among themselves as to the required urgency and severity of penal legislation as they were from its intended victims. Finally, the penal code neither prevented the development of an influential Catholic mercantile and farming class nor the process of diocesan, parish, clerical and educational reform

---

[4]   T. Bartlett, *The Fall and Rise of the Irish Nation: The Catholic Question 1690–1830* (Dublin, 1992), pp. 17–29.

[5]   S. J. Connolly, *Religion, Law and Power: The Making of Protestant Ireland 1660–1760* (Oxford, 1992).

within the Catholic Church itself.[6] Indeed, the relative stability of eighteenth-century Ireland, however achieved, delivered better opportunities for the Catholic Church to engage in internal reform than had been afforded by the roller-coaster history of the seventeenth century. Thus Professor Corish's chapter on the eighteenth century in his wide-ranging history of the *Irish Catholic Experience* concentrates more on the difficulties of developing a counter-Reformation spirituality among a predominantly 'superstitious' peasantry than on the inconveniences of the penal code itself.[7]

Revision, like confession, is good for the historical soul, but it ought not to be pressed too far. The penal laws, however petty and unenforced, served the same function, albeit in a more draconian way, as the niggardly restrictions experienced by nineteenth-century Nonconformists in England and Wales. Paradoxically, they helped reinforce religious and political loyalties rather than contributing to their erosion. Ineffectual and haphazard the penal laws may have been, but they were still useful schoolmasters in educating their victims about the social, religious and political boundaries within which they were required to live. Moreover the Irish *'ancien régime'* was different in significant respects from its alleged English counterpart. The inconveniences of having a ruling elite adhering to a different religion from the mass of the population effectively meant that a complex set of mechanisms used in England to secure religious and political deference could not operate in the same way in Ireland. Anniversary sermons, ritualistic celebrations of past events and a range of agrarian religious festivals had more divisive connotations in Ireland than in England.[8] Theatrical religion in all its forms, far from binding the population to the Established Church of the political and landed elite, which was part of its function in England, often had the reverse effect in Ireland. The ritualised dynamics of anti-Catholicism, in particular, served entirely different functions in the two countries.[9]

[6]    D. Keogh, *The French Disease: The Catholic Church and Irish Radicalism, 1790–1800* (Dublin, 1993).

[7]    Corish, *Irish Catholic Experience*, pp. 123–50.

[8]    J. R. Hill, 'National Festivals, the State and "Protestant Ascendancy" in Ireland', *Irish Historical Studies*, 24 no. 93 (1984), 30–51; idem, 'The Disputed Lessons of Irish History 1690–1812', *Past & Present*, no. 118 (1988), 96–129; and B. Bushaway, *By Rite: Custom, Ceremony and Community in England 1700–1880* (London, 1982).

[9]    C. Haydon, *Anti-Catholicism in Eighteenth-Century England: A Political and Social Study* (Manchester, 1993); R. Eccleshall, 'Anglican Political Thought in the Century after the Revolution of 1688', in D. G. Boyce, R. Eccleshall and V. Geoghegan (eds.), *Political Thought in Ireland Since the Seventeenth Century* (London, 1993), pp. 36–72.

## PATRIOTISM AND SECTARIANISM AT THE END
## OF THE EIGHTEENTH CENTURY

'In the eighteenth century Irish patriotism had been very much a Protestant preserve. After the crucial decade of the 1790s it was well on the way to becoming a Catholic one.'[10] Corish's pithy summation of eighteenth-century religious history in Ireland points in the same direction as Bartlett's intriguingly titled book *The Fall and Rise of the Irish Nation*. It has as its main theme the way in which the emergence of an eighteenth-century Protestant nationalism became victim of French revolutionary neurosis, increased religious sectarianism, fear of an international radical conspiracy and the thorny issue of how much political power could and should be wielded by Catholics. Before these problems emerged, however, there had been a brief flowering of a kind of Irish nationhood based not on sectarian distinctions, but on a shared appreciation of Ireland's best interests in relation to Britain. As the penal code was gradually dismantled and as Britain ran into serious difficulties in North America it seemed possible that the campaign for legislative independence and free trade had the capacity to generate an inclusive, if conditional, national aspiration. Bartlett notes that 'this theme of an Irish nation negotiating as an equal with the British nation was one that was frequently found in the local addresses that arrived in Dublin Castle in the summer of 1782'.[11] But religious goodwill and the erosion of penal legislation were not the same things as trusting Catholics with real political power and the complex debates surrounding parliamentary reform soon showed that even the most advanced reformers had serious reservations about accepting Catholics as full members of the body politic. Moreover, no sooner had the debates begun than a new and more sinister form of organised sectarian violence made its appearance in County Armagh in 1784.

Agrarian outrage was, of course, not a new feature of eighteenth-century Irish society, but a distinction can be made between agrarian protest in the rest of Ireland, which was primarily concerned with resistance against externally imposed rents, tithes and enclosures, and the particular problems of south Ulster where the threat seemed to come within peasant society itself.[12] By the end of the eighteenth

---

10  Corish, *Irish Catholic Experience*, p. 150.
11  Bartlett, *The Fall and Rise of the Irish Nation*, p. 104.
12  M. Beames, *Peasants and Power: The Whiteboy Movements and their Control in Pre-Famine Ireland* (Sussex, 1983).

century, not only was Armagh one of the most populous counties in Ireland, but its population was made up of almost equal numbers of Protestants and Catholics. While this demographic equilibrium created the potential for sectarian conflict, industrial expansion helped produce 'favourable conditions for institutionalising the sectarian consciousness of the Protestant lower orders'.[13] In the first place, the rise of independent smallholders, directly employed by drapers or bleachers, caused a breakdown in traditional forms of social control, temporarily weakening the bond between Protestant gentry and Protestant weavers. Secondly, and more ominously, although Roman Catholics were latecomers to the weaving trade in the eighteenth century, the relaxation of the penal laws and the prosperity generated by the linen industry put them in a position to compete in the land market and thus challenge traditional Protestant notions of ascendancy. The acquisition of arms by Catholics through the Volunteer movement, and continuing radical demands for political concessions, further eroded social stability in Armagh.[14] This dangerous fusion of social, economic and political competition between the religious communities produced the conflicts fought out by the Protestant Peep O'Day Boys and the Catholic Defenders. While the gentry of north Armagh were at first concerned to protect the Catholic victims of Peep O'Day activities, their initial sympathy could not be maintained during the heightened tensions of the 1790s. When the Defender movement spread outside the area of its initial impact and its actions became more organised and more overtly political, Protestant landlords withdrew their support, and united with their Protestant tenantry against a threat which was thought to be linked with the contemporary bloody upheavals in France. The Orange Order and the yeomanry then became the channels through which their common Protestant – and inevitably anti-Catholic – identity was expressed.[15]

These local outbreaks of sectarian violence must also be placed in the context of increasing interdenominational tension at the national

---

[13]  D. W. Miller, *Queen's Rebels: Ulster Loyalism in Historical Perspective* (Dublin, 1978), p. 145.

[14]  D. W. Miller, 'The Armagh Troubles' in S. Clark and J. S. Donnelly (eds.), *Irish Peasants: Violence and Political Unrest 1780–1914* (Manchester, 1983), pp. 155–91; M. Elliott, *Partners in Revolution: The United Irishmen and France* (New Haven, 1982), pp. 35–50; and T. Bartlett, 'Religious Rivalries in Ireland and France in the Age of the French Revolution', *Eighteenth-Century Ireland*, 6 (1991), 57–76.

[15]  H. Senior, *Orangeism in Ireland and Britain 1795–1836* (London, 1966), p. 18; A. F. Blackstock, 'The Origin and Development of the Irish Yeomanry, 1796–c. 1807', PhD dissertation, Queen's University Belfast, 1993, ch. 7.

level. Although the later eighteenth century had seen the gradual relaxation of the penal laws, events in the 1780s and 1790s revealed the fragile limits of religious toleration. For example, while the grievances of secret societies such as the Whiteboys were economic in origin, their activities were often interpreted by the ruling class as popish conspiracies directed against the Protestant State, and were used as an argument against granting Catholic relief.[16] Similarly, although the Rightboy anti-tithe campaign of the mid 1780s focused the attention of Dublin Castle on the need for reform, conservative Protestants claimed that the Church of Ireland itself was under attack. Protestant pamphleteers whipped up public feeling in defence of the religious establishment, warned that the granting of Roman Catholic rights was irreconcilable with the maintenance of Protestant privilege, and, by drawing attention away from the issue of tithes to that of the security of Protestantism itself, ensured that in 1787 the political initiative passed from those advocating conciliation to those favouring coercion. The involvement of Church of Ireland clergy in this polemical warfare, and their prolific anti-Catholic propaganda, further underlined the importance of religion in shaping political attitudes.[17] Religious differences were thus deep-rooted, particularly in south Ulster, and involved more than a particular interpretation of Christianity:

If a person was a Catholic, it invariably meant that he was of old Gaelic stock, that his ancestors were a defeated race, that he was never to be fully trusted by the planter stock, that his intention was some day, perhaps some distant day, to become master in his own house again. And if he were a Protestant it also meant that he was a foreigner, a persecutor, a privileged person, an enemy.[18]

In the volatile 1790s, when the campaign for Roman Catholic liberties was again gathering momentum and the possibility of widespread rebellion was given credibility by events in France, those on each side of the religious divide drew deeply on religious traditions to justify their social and political stance. The language of the Defenders' catechisms

[16] M. Wall, 'The Whiteboys', in T. D. Williams (ed.), *Secret Societies in Ireland* (Dublin, 1973), pp. 13–25.
[17] J. Kelly, 'The Genesis of "Protestant Ascendancy": the Rightboy Disturbances of the 1780s and their Impact on Protestant Opinion', in G. O'Brien (ed.), *Parliament, Politics and People* (Dublin, 1989), pp. 93–127. For a different perspective see J. Liechty, 'Irish Evangelicalism, Trinity College Dublin and the Mission of the Church of Ireland at the end of the Eighteenth Century', PhD dissertation, St Patrick's College, Maynooth, 1987.
[18] P. Livingstone, *The Monaghan Story: a Documented History of the County Monaghan from the Earliest Times to 1976* (Clogher, 1980), p. 239.

is rich in biblical imagery, reflecting the mysticism and symbolism of the freemasonry on which it was modelled.[19]

The Orange Order which emerged in Armagh in September 1795 also had strong religious foundations. Meetings of the Society were opened with prayers, and members were forbidden to curse, swear or drink in the Lodge room. In this period, however, the Orange Order was probably more significant for what it represented than for what it actually did. 'While the social structure of Ulster was being drastically altered', writes David Miller, 'Orangeism sustained for Protestant workers in town and country the sense that the most important feature of the old structure – a special relationship between them and their betters – still existed.'[20]

While the conflicts between Catholics and Protestants in Armagh surged forward from the grass roots, the most sectarian and most violent of the four localised rebellions which broke out in 1798 was in Wexford and seems to have originated in the growing economic and political competition between Catholic and Protestant minor gentry and middlemen.[21] The shocking brutality of both rebels and suppressors brought forth comparisons with seventeenth-century atrocities and left a lasting scar on churches and people in post-rebellion Ireland. As the 1790s drew to their awful conclusion it seemed that religious sectarianism was, after all, a more powerful reality in Ireland than either mild reformism or radicalism based on natural rights. But the decade left another legacy of equal importance. In 1793 Catholics, subject to certain conditions, had been admitted to the electoral franchise but not to Parliament itself. Not only did the campaign for the vote mobilise Catholic political opinion in a way that could not easily be forgotten, but the concession of 1793 ensured that 'from now on there could be nothing but the Catholic Question'. The failure to deliver Emancipation as part of the set of deals facilitating the Act of Union in 1800 merely heaped frustration on top of expectation. This had a profoundly alienating effect on the Catholic middle class, so that by the beginning of the nineteenth century the Catholic question had in effect become the Irish question.[22]

19   T. Bartlett, 'Defenders and Defenderism in 1795', *Irish Historical Studies*, 24 (1985), 373–94.
20   Miller, *Queen's Rebels*, p. 56.
21   K. Whelan, 'The Catholic Community in Eighteenth-Century County Wexford', in T. P. Power and K. Whelan (eds.), *Endurance and Emergence: Catholics in Ireland in the Eighteenth Century* (Dublin, 1990), pp. 129–70.
22   Bartlett, *Fall and Rise of the Irish Nation*, p. 201.

## DANIEL O'CONNELL AND THE BIRTH OF
## CATHOLIC DEMOCRATIC NATIONALISM

Between 1800 and 1830, but more especially between 1820 and 1830, Irish politics were dominated by the struggle for Catholic Emancipation. Prior to the 1820s political activity among Irish Catholics had been largely centred upon the country houses of the landed gentry or among the wealthy merchants and lawyers of Dublin and other substantial Irish towns. O'Connell, by contrast, was conscious of the latent power of Irish Catholic numbers. Catholics were disadvantaged in almost every major respect: landed and commercial property, ecclesiastical power, legal rights and privileges, educational opportunities, and so on, but they had a massive advantage in terms of sheer numbers. Despite having the right to vote under certain well-defined terms, however, the latent power of Catholic numbers was held in check by their inability to sit in Parliament and hence their inability to use electoral power as a way of making a breakthrough into the apparatus of the British State. In essence this was what the struggle in the 1820s was all about. As Fergus O'Ferrall has it:

The early years of the 1820s set the scene for a struggle of decisive importance for Anglo-Irish relationships, for the political system in the British Isles and for the emerging character of Irish nationalism. At the heart of the struggle lay a fundamental clash over the nature of the British state, the role of religion in the state, the national identity of Irish people of different origins, the basis of property and the political privileges conferred by religion and property. Ireland became the battleground for competing ideas and forces with ultimate significance for the unity and security of the United Kingdom established in 1800. Ireland was in effect divided into two warring camps: the one, Protestant, claiming perpetual ascendancy; the other, Catholic, determined to achieve equality.[23]

One needs to be careful here not to exaggerate the homogeneity of either Catholic or Protestant Ireland in this period. Within Irish Catholicism the views and aspirations of bishops, priests, gentry families, tenant farmers, landless labourers, merchants, professionals and artisans were scarcely ever harmonised, but what they had in common was a shared set of grievances about the operation of a Protestant hegemony.[24] The more the latter was resented, and the

[23]   F. O'Ferrall, *Catholic Emancipation: Daniel O'Connell and the Birth of Irish Democracy 1820–1830* (Dublin, 1985), p. 29.
[24]   S. J. Connolly, *Priests and People in Pre-Famine Ireland 1780–1845* (Dublin, 1982); idem, *Religion and Society in Nineteenth-Century Ireland* (Dundalk, 1985).

more that that resentment could be focused on a single issue, the less important were the differences within the Catholic cause. O'Connell's achievement was to mobilise a national movement in pursuit of an agreed objective. Writing in November 1824 the Church of Ireland Bishop of Limerick, John Jebb, stated that 'there is what we of this generation have never before witnessed, a complete union of the Roman Catholic body ... In truth, an Irish Revolution has, in great measure, been effected.'[25]

What facilitated this revolution was the Catholic Association and its organisation of the Catholic rent, a penny a month subscription that formed the basis of a national political organisation.[26] The support of the Catholic Church was vital. After initial opposition the whole Irish hierarchy had swung behind the rent by the end of 1824 and meetings were held in Catholic chapels. The education issue, the beginnings of a more aggressive evangelical proselytism and a growing Church of Ireland assertiveness all combined to deliver the Catholic priesthood and their flocks into active membership of the Association which soon became the organisational umbrella for a whole host of grievances from the administration of justice to the collection of tithes, and from the abuses of landlords to the fear of the Orange Order.[27] This ability to tap into a folk history of past and present grievances gave the Catholic Association a more reliable mass following than the more abstract agitation for natural rights in the 1790s. The Liberal Protestant political and literary elite, which had championed Catholic rights under the paternalistic banner of 'Friends of the People' found it increasingly difficult to accommodate a movement based on independent political action.

As the Catholic Association harnessed its resources for the 1826 election there were major revolts by Catholic freeholders against landlord control. Many freeholders then faced a harrowing choice between loyalty to their church and loyalty to their landlord. Neither was averse to using whatever sanctions it had at its disposal to effect the right 'choice'. Although Catholic leaders had been slow to recognise the potential of the 1826 election it was clear that electoral politics offered a more substantial threat to Protestant control in Ireland than could have been envisaged at the start of the decade. A Catholic

25  Ibid., p. 56.
26  T. Wyse, *Historical Sketch of the late Catholic Association of Ireland*, 2 vols. (Dublin, 1929); J. A. Reynolds, *The Catholic Emancipation Crisis in Ireland 1823–29* (New Haven, 1954).
27  D. Bowen, *The Protestant Crusade in Ireland 1800–70* (Dublin, 1978).

democracy was emerging which the combined weight of landed property, Established Church and Westminster Parliament could not hold in check. In his letter to the Catholics of Ireland in July 1826 O'Connell stated that Irish Catholics were 'the people, emphatically the people' and that 'the Catholic people of Ireland are a nation'. *The Dublin Evening Mail* responded by stressing the danger of 'an imperium in imperio – a Roman Catholic nation subsisting independently in the bosom of a Protestant Empire'.[28]

In the midst of this political crisis the religious climate also showed signs of polarisation. Evangelical proselytism, whether through education, pious landlordism or more direct 'Second Reformation' assaults, was ironically at its most energetic at precisely the time when Catholic Ireland was least amenable to its advances.[29] As stories of converts were traded back and forth, liberal and accommodationist clergy in all the major denominations had to fight internal battles against a more militant generation. The fact that the Catholic Association was able to organise simultaneous parish meetings in two thirds of Ireland's 2,500 Catholic parishes not only persuaded the government that they were on the brink of having to deal with an alternative government based upon a popular confederacy (a veritable nightmare of British administrations throughout the period 1790–1850), but also confirmed the worst fears of political popery entertained by Irish Protestants.

The events from the Clare election to the passage of the Catholic Emancipation Act are well known. Britain's Protestant constitution had been breached by a Catholic democratic movement on the Celtic fringe of the British State.[30] For Peel, and for many others including Wilberforce, Chalmers and Bunting, it was a political, not a religious concession. If Catholic Emancipation did not solve Ireland's problems future contests would be on different grounds; 'the struggle will be, not for the abolition of civil distinctions, but for the predominance of an intolerant religion'.[31]

The Catholic Emancipation Act was a great disappointment for almost everyone. The Protestant establishment was profoundly shocked

28   O'Ferrall, *Catholic Emancipation*, pp. 144–5.
29   Bowen, *Protestant Crusade*; Hempton and Hill, *Evangelical Protestantism*; I. M. Hehir, 'New Lights and Old Enemies: the Second Reformation and the Catholics of Ireland', MA dissertation, University of Wisconsin, 1983; and R. F. Dunlop, 'Religious Conflict in Ireland during the Middle Years of the Nineteenth Century: a Theological Assessment', MLitt dissertation, Trinity College Dublin, 1994.
30   G. F. A. Best, 'The Protestant Constitution and its Supporters 1800–1829', *Transactions of the Royal Historical Society*, 5th ser. 8 (1958), pp. 105–27.
31   O'Ferrall, *Catholic Emancipation*, pp. 234–57.

by it and could never regain its old confidence. With pardonable exaggeration O'Ferrall sees the 1820s as a watershed in Irish history.

The Anglo-Irish Protestant Ascendancy found, from the 1820s, the current flowing strongly against them for the rest of the nineteenth century as the long-term implications of Emancipation became evident: the attack on the Established Church and the tithe war, disestablishment, municipal reform, the struggle over tenant right and the downfall of the landlords, the long struggle for repeal of the union, home rule and finally separation from Britain. All were based upon the restoration of Catholic power and influence.[32]

Catholic Emancipation, after the initial optimism subsided, also disappointed Irish Catholics of all social levels. Many had entertained unrealistic, almost millenarian, expectations and soon found that Catholic Emancipation had not wrought the miracles for which they had hoped. As in the rest of British society most Irish Catholics encountered government, in the main, through the exercise of law and coercion. For them impartial justice and economic improvement were the dazzling jewels held out to them by political emancipation. As with English, Welsh and Scottish Chartists a decade later, they placed hopelessly unrealistic faith in a legislative remedy for their more profound grievances.

Catholic Emancipation fundamentally altered relations between Church and State in the British Isles and helped bring to an end the long period of Tory dominance in English politics.[33] Indeed, it probably advanced the cause of Liberalism in England more than in Ireland and also acted as a boost to English popular reform movements. But how is it to be viewed in a much wider context? Some have seen it as a parallel movement to Jacksonian democracy in the United States as old established interests gave way to new expansionist forces. But although Jacksonian politics had some religious foundations, it was not yoked to a single church in the same way as O'Connell's movement in Ireland which had 'cultivated a coincidence of purpose with the Catholic Church'. Even in European terms there is a paradox at the heart of Ireland's Catholic democratic movement; in an 'era of papal conservatism and Metternichian reaction only in Ireland did the Catholic Church become committed to a great popular political struggle'.[34]

[32]　Ibid., p. 259.

[33]　G. I. T. Machin, *The Catholic Question in English Politics, 1820–30* (Oxford, 1964); N. Gash, *Reaction and Reconstruction in English Politics, 1832–52* (Oxford, 1965).

[34]　O'Ferrall, *Catholic Emancipation*, p. 284; H. McLeod, *European Religion in the Age of Great Cities* (London, 1995).

Ironically, as many continental liberals marvelled at the apparent liberalism of Catholic Ireland by comparison with other Catholic states in Europe, most English statesmen feared Irish Catholicism as an illiberal, backward and intolerant creed which created the very social misery it claimed to resist. The fact that O'Connell made few overtures to the Protestants of Ulster and that Irish democratic nationalism had a hard sectarian edge, meant that the ideological cleavage between continental liberals and English Protestant statesmen had a more earthy reality in Ireland itself. The interaction of religious and cultural loyalties with political and social aspirations had produced a set of problems with no convenient solution.

### THE MAKING OF IRISH NATIONALISM C. 1860–90

In this period a whole cluster of issues emerged which Gladstone described as 'the many branches from one trunk, and that trunk is the tree of what is called the Protestant Ascendancy'. According to Boyce 'Gladstone's declared aim was to lay the axe to the root of that tree'.[35] From the strictly religious point of view the most important issue of all was the disestablishment of the Church of Ireland. By the 1860s that church was facing an unholy alliance of English and Welsh Nonconformists, Irish Catholics, Scottish voluntaries, some fearful Anglicans, and utilitarian radicals, all lining up to disendow the Irish Church and remove state support for the Protestant religion in Ireland.[36] Irish churchmen recognised that they had little defence on either moral or utilitarian grounds. As a Presbyterian layman pointed out in 1867 'in 199 parishes there is not a single adherent of the Established Church, and 1,539 parishes, or nearly two-thirds of the whole, have not more than 100 adherents in each'.[37] The bitter pill which the Church of Ireland's defenders had to swallow is that, despite allegations to the contrary, the Church by 1869 was a more efficient, zealous and financially unexacting institution than it had been half a century earlier. Its demise as a religious establishment did not coincide with its nadir as a religious institution.

As the Church reformed its abuses to placate external criticism,

[35]   D. G. Boyce, *Nineteenth-Century Ireland: The Search for Stability* (Dublin, 1990), pp. 154–6.
[36]   G. Parsons, 'Irish Disestablishment', in idem (ed.), *Religion in Victorian Britain*, II, *Controversies* (Manchester, 1988), pp.124–46; P. M. Bell, *Disestablishment in Ireland and Wales* (London, 1969); D. H. Akenson, *The Church of Ireland: Ecclesiastical Reform and Revolution 1800–1885* (New Haven, 1971); R. B. McDowell, *The Church of Ireland, 1869–1969* (London, 1975).
[37]   A Presbyterian Layman, *Facts and Figures Regarding the Irish Church* (Belfast, 1867).

external critics began to take the higher view that no amount of reform could possibly justify the state endowment of a minority church once the majority was no longer willing to put up with it. Irish churchmen were not without arguments to justify their position, but in the political climate of the 1860s they were remarkably unconvincing. Obscurantist and antiquarian claims to be 'the Old Catholic Church of Ireland' cut no ice with an avowedly utilitarian generation and it soon became clear that there were only two possible defences. The first revolved around the implications Irish disestablishment would have for the Church of England and the second was based on the need to preserve Protestant truth against Romish error in Ireland.[38] Unfortunately, the former had two edges to it and the latter was more plausible among Irish Protestants than it was among English politicians.

Despite discussions about the possibility of concurrently endowing all the major Irish denominations, the Irish Church was duly disestablished. The principle of religious establishments, upon which the British State had relied for Christianising the people since the Reformation, had been dealt its first major blow. Secondly, Irish disestablishment was followed soon after by a Land Act which gave Irish tenant farmers rights that no British government would have dreamed of extending to English farmers. Here indeed was the rub. By the mid-Victorian period English statesmen were prepared to make concessions in Ireland which they would never contemplate closer to home. The message was loud and clear both to Irish Catholics and Irish Protestants: peculiar religious and political configurations brought forth peculiar measures.

The difficulties facing British administrations in Ireland were compounded in this period by forces operating within the Roman Catholic Church. The first was the ultramontanist leadership supplied by Cardinal Paul Cullen who had been ordained into the priesthood in the year of O'Connell's triumphant achievement of Catholic Emancipation.[39] When Cullen came to Ireland in 1849 after a lengthy sojourn in Rome he was equally suspicious of turbulent nationalism (as represented by MacHale and a section of the Irish priesthood), castle bishops and Irish Protestants. Desmond Bowen, rather exaggeratedly, portrays him as an ecclesiastical and cultural imperialist with a deep desire to produce a truly Catholic nation through parochial reform, Catholic education and the mobilisation of the church's own resources.

---

[38]  O. Chadwick, *The Victorian Church*, part 2 (London, 1970), pp. 427–39.
[39]  D. Bowen, *Paul Cardinal Cullen and the Shaping of Modern Irish Catholicism* (Dublin, 1983); for a more sympathetic view of Cullen see Corish, *Irish Catholic Experience*, pp.192–225.

Revealingly, he regarded the English Catholic leadership as represented by Wiseman and Manning as too closely implicated with the British government. Such a man was difficult to deal with by a state that was eager to make adjustments to make Ireland more governable, but was not eager to facilitate the triumph of a genuinely *Roman* Catholic culture. Such problems were compounded by the remarkable faith of nineteenth-century ecclesiastical imperialists of all kinds in the importance of a religious-based (in practice a denominationally based) national education. It was the education question, more than any other, which mobilised churches in the British Isles for political action.[40] Moreover, education, along with poor relief, posed serious problems for government as well. Increasingly during the course of the nineteenth century those responsible for devising and implementing social policy throughout the British Isles doubted both the capacity and even the desirability of church-based welfare provision.

In Ireland the disestablishment of the Church of Ireland, the growth of ultramontanism within the Catholic Church and ecclesiastical rivalry over education were given a more populist political dimension by the conjunction of two issues which did much to shape the direction of Irish Catholic nationalism: Home Rule and the land question. The agricultural crisis that began in 1878 and which led to the land war of 1878–82 gave the Irish Home Rule party a mass movement. Self-government and 'the land for the people' were thus brought together, and as long as the political leadership of the movement could control violence and suppress communistic elements, it was virtually guaranteed the support and organisational resources of the Catholic Church. As in the time of O'Connell, Irish Catholics were far from united in interest, aspiration and motivation, but the Land League

involved tenants, labourers, priests, publicans, journalists, cranks, in a kind of communal experience, in the making of a myth ... these diverse elements were collectively responsible for the creation of a sense of the 'people' versus the 'landlords', the 'people' against the state. Anyone who supported the League went down in history as patriotic; anyone who sought to discredit it could expect little political future in Ireland.[41]

What was now wanted, according to Archbishop Walsh, 'was the soil of

---

40   G. F. A. Best, 'The Religious Difficulties of National Education in England, 1800–70', *Cambridge Historical Journal*, 12 (1956), 155–73; Hempton and Hill, *Evangelical Protestantism*, pp. 52–61.

41   Boyce, *Nineteenth-Century Ireland*, pp. 172–3; P. Bew, *Land and the National Question in Ireland, 1858–82* (Dublin, 1978); and W. E. Vaughan, *Landlords and Tenants in Mid-Victorian Ireland* (Oxford, 1994).

Ireland for the Irish race rather than for a select gang of strangers and spoilers'.

The Irish Catholic hierarchy supported Home Rule, the priests supplied one in four of the personnel at the thirty-two conventions held in connection with selecting candidates for the 1885 election and Parnell recognised, as with O'Connell before him, that Church support was vital to his political cause. Thus the Irish nationalism that emerged at the end of the century was based on a powerful combination of a dispossessed people sharing a common faith and a common feeling that the Union, as it had operated in the nineteenth century, was not the best arrangement for governing a Catholic nation. The big question then, and subsequently in Irish history, was on what terms the Catholic nation planned to share the island with those who were regarded as being implicated in the seizure of land and in the imposition of an alien faith.[42] But this was a question which emerged more in retrospect than at the time, because the assumption among most of the nationalist leadership, including Parnell in his prime, was that the nation was already united and that northern Protestants would find their own accommodation once the pernicious remnants of oppressive rule were swept away. In essence, this is still the ideological foundation of constitutional nationalism and militant republicanism in Ireland.

### RELIGION AND POLITICS IN THE AGE OF REVOLUTION AND SEPARATION 1913–21

The promise or threat of Home Rule offered the same kind of driving force in Irish politics in the years 1870–1916 as Catholic Emancipation had in the years 1793–1829. Catholic Ireland was virtually a one-party nation by 1914, but this party had virtually no provincial organisation and was thus dependent, to some extent at least, on the one national institution which did have a nation-wide structure, the Roman Catholic Church. Catholic priests, in particular, combined social prestige and the mystique of education with the unique advantages of not having to seek political office for themselves or soliciting jobs for their children. In addition, Mass was the only weekly occasion when large numbers of rural Irishmen and women came together and, not surprisingly, most public meetings in the countryside were held on Sundays outside chapel doors. No fund-raising could hope to succeed without the

[42]    D. G. Boyce (ed.), *The Revolution in Ireland, 1879–1923* (London, 1988).

blessing and preferably the contribution of a priest, and no public cause could realise its popular potential without at least the silent acquiescence of the Irish priesthood.

But the relationship between church and popular nationalism was both subtle and complicated. In his perceptive case study of County Clare, David Fitzpatrick has shown that although the active support of a large minority of priests greatly facilitated the organisation of nationalism in this period, the power of the priest to initiate rather than merely co-ordinate patterns of popular behaviour was closely circumscribed.[43] Priests were facilitators, not innovators, and most understood the subtle limits beyond which it was wise not to go in either accelerating or retarding popular political causes. Nowhere was this more evident than in the Irish countryside in the wake of the 1916 rising when the politics of Home Rule swiftly gave way to the politics of separation. The church had initially responded cautiously to the turbulent politics of 1916, but both it and the Irish people became more radical by 1917.[44]

It is conventional wisdom that the church merely attached itself to the popular tide out of crude self-interest. But even self-interest can have its complexities and Fitzpatrick has unearthed an impressive array of reasons why more than half of Clare's priests attached themselves to the separatist cause in the period 1917–21. Disgust with the Irish Party, fear of socialism, fellow-feeling with the grandiose dreams of the rebels (and gratitude to them for frequently using religious terminology and concepts), all played their part. Moreover, self-interest could have economic as well as devotional dimensions. Fitzpatrick writes that 'priests in leaking churches could not afford to fight unpopular causes, and because the churches built in the wake of emancipation were far past their half lives, many of them leaked'.[45] It was more than a happy coincidence, then, that the rising excited many of the Irish clergy as much as their parishioners, and for the same reasons. Sinn Féin had thus much to gain and little to fear from its relationship with the church and the same was true in reverse. In that respect their shared dislike of conscription was an added advantage.

So far what has been offered is five brief snapshots of key periods in the

---

[43] D. Fitzpatrick, *Politics and Irish Life, 1913–21: Provincial Experience of War and Revolution* (Dublin, 1977).

[44] S. Gilley, 'The Catholic Church and Revolution', in Boyce (ed.), *Revolution in Ireland*, pp. 157–72; D. W. Miller, *Church, State and Nation in Ireland 1898–1921* (Dublin, 1973).

[45] Fitzpatrick, *Politics and Irish Life*, p. 141.

history of the relationship between Church and politics in modern Ireland, but at least of equal importance are long-term social and structural changes in the nature of Irish Catholicism which resulted in higher mass attendance figures than anywhere else in Western Europe or the United States in the nineteenth and twentieth centuries.[46]

In the early eighteenth century the Irish Catholic community, as with its English counterpart, was heavily dependent on the Catholic gentry who exercised a disproportionate influence on the evolution of the church. A combination of the penal laws, absence of tithes or state sponsorship and the almost complete lack of parochial property meant that most priests served in their native parish and were consequently deeply embedded in the life of their communities. Clerical recruitment patterns also followed well-defined patterns. Most were from farming families with an established clerical tradition of second or later sons going into the priesthood. By the end of the century this pattern of gentry paternalism and priestly dependency was undergoing some modifications. A County Wexford local study has shown how a complex of social changes led to the emergence of a less politically docile Catholic gentry, greater sectarian competition between Catholic and Protestant tenant farmers, an economic surge by urban Catholics and the emergence of a stronger Catholic professional class.[47] These changes had ramifications both for the Catholic Church and for the configuration of religion and politics in strategically important parts of eighteenth-century Ireland. By the end of the century fewer priests served in their natal parishes, lay patronage diminished in importance as episcopal control increased, chapels became bigger and more centrally located, membership of religious fraternities soared and Catholics became more active in politics. In Wexford Kevin Whelan has suggested

All these changes marked the increased professionalism of the priest in nineteenth century Ireland. It was reflected also in the adoption of distinctive clerical dress, by testamentary disposition of accumulated property to the church rather than to relatives, and by their distancing themselves from the gregarious side of community life. Once these changes were completed, a powerful mechanism was in place by which the astonishing penetration of the

---

[46]   E. Larkin, *The Historical Dimensions of Irish Catholicism* (New York, 1981); D. Miller, 'Irish Catholicism and the Great Famine', *Journal of Social History*, 9 (1975), 81–98; Corish, *Irish Catholic Experience*, pp. 166–7, 186–7.

[47]   Whelan, 'The Catholic Community', pp.129–70; L. M. Cullen, 'Catholic Social Classes under the Penal Laws', in Power and Whelan, *Endurance and Emergence*, pp.57–84.

institutional catholic church into all aspects of Wexford life in the later nineteenth century was achieved.[48]

Astonishing though this penetration may have been, not all was plain sailing for the church in the first half of the nineteenth century. A rapidly growing population, lack of resources, the persistent rural 'superstitions' of the Irish poor and inadequacies within the priesthood all combined to present a stern challenge to reforming bishops and their clergy.[49] Indeed, Connolly has suggested that in evaluating the strengths and weaknesses of the nineteenth-century church the retarding effects of penal laws and political disadvantages were not as important as the wide gap between official religious expectations and the popular religion of the Irish poor. Before the famine, popular adherence to the formal observances of the Catholic Church was low, but there was considerable attachment to the rites of passage, especially baptism and extreme unction which were almost universal. As with the Lincolnshire labourers brought to life by James Obelkevich, the inhabitants of rural Ireland subscribed to a whole range of beliefs and practices only tenuously related to orthodox Catholicism.[50] These included superstitious interpretations of historic Christian festivals, a wide range of magical practices from calendar customs to charms and omens, belief in fairies, banshees and witches, and an Irish propensity for squeezing the maximum amount of raucous entertainment from festivals and wakes which the church struggled valiantly but unsuccessfully to control. Indeed, Irish Catholicism in this period represented more of a contractual system of religious obligations than an integrated value system in which Catholic devotion penetrated all areas of life.

Moreover, as Irish society became more socially, economically and politically polarised in the first half of the nineteenth century, the gap between a more disciplined and professional clergy and the Irish rural poor probably widened. On the other side the shift to a market-orientated economy in the two decades before the famine led to a relatively high mass attendances in market towns. Some recent, and as yet unpublished, research by David Miller on the religious and economic topography of pre-famine Irish society has drawn attention to the relationship between high mass attendance and catchment areas

---

[48] Whelan, 'The Catholic Community', p.164.
[49] For different perspectives on these problems see D. Keenan, *The Catholic Church in Nineteenth-Century Ireland: A Sociological Study* (Dublin, 1983); Connolly, *Religion and Society*.
[50] J. Obelkevich, *Religion and Rural Society: South Lindsey 1825–75* (Oxford, 1976); Connolly, *Priests and People*.

with prominent central places. There is also a statistical correlation between high mass attendance and areas of more pronounced economic inequality and relatively rapid modernisation. Miller has suggested that the parts of Ireland that exhibited such characteristics – south-east Wexford for example – may well have set the pattern for the more extensive post-famine devotional revolution.

There is now widespread agreement, therefore, that the so-called 'devotional revolution' was already under way before the famine, though one still needs to be careful to match ecclesiastical achievement with rapid demographic growth, and to maintain a picture of the country as a whole and not selected areas where improvements were most rapid. The famine, which was disproportionately severe on the most economically vulnerable, nevertheless brought its own terrible remedy for some of the church's problems by opening up the way for a wealthier, more disciplined and better pastored church in which popular adherence to Catholic forms reached strikingly high levels. Professor Corish's revised estimate of mass attendance in the post 1850 period is 50–75 per cent in the four Irish cities (Belfast was particularly low), almost 100 per cent in towns, 37.5–75 per cent in English-speaking rural areas and 25–50 per cent in Irish-speaking rural areas.[51] Thus orthodox religious practice was consistently higher among urban dwellers and the better educated than among the Irish labouring poor in the west of the country. Those historians of nineteenth-century Britain who suggest too easily that urbanisation was the nemesis of organised religion would do well to ponder the Irish experience. Urban living may undermine the primitive community consensus underpinning a genuinely popular and all-embracing religious/superstitious culture, but it does not automatically usher in secularisation, however that word is to be defined.[52] Rapid social and economic change, if anything, helped the cause of the Catholic Church in Ireland. In a traditional society dragged disproportionately quickly into the modern world on the coat-tails of an expanding British economy and a fearful subsistence crisis, Catholicism in Ireland offered important symbols of culture and identity to a population determined to preserve its ties with the past.

The chief characteristics of Irish Roman Catholicism in the twentieth

---

[51]   Corish, *Irish Catholic Experience*, p. 167.
[52]   S. Bruce (ed.), *Religion and Modernization: Sociologists and Historians Debate the Secularization Thesis* (Oxford, 1992); C. G. Brown, 'The Mechanism of Religious Growth in Urban Societies: British Cities since the Eighteenth Century', in McLeod (ed.), *European Religion*, pp. 239–62.

century have their roots in two centuries and more of turbulent history. The nation of twenty-six counties formed after independence was not only overwhelmingly Catholic, but also sustained remarkably high levels of religious practice. According to many outside observers, Ireland in the first half of the twentieth century was simply the world's most devoutly Catholic country. But the sense in which Ireland was a homogeneous Catholic country was also determined by the past. As is the way in Ireland there are ambiguities unlimited. Despite a powerful tradition of deference to the clergy, for example, the clergy were unable to persuade their flocks completely to forsake Fenianism, agrarian violence and Parnell in the nineteenth century, or the Irish Republican Army in the twentieth century. Yet, as is often pointed out by bemused foreigners, Ireland has never produced an anticlerical party. Priestly influence, it seems, was more often side-stepped than resisted when emotive issues of national loyalty were at stake. Similarly, although Roman Catholicism has had a formidable cultural presence in post-independence Ireland, it is emphatically not an Established Church.[53] The church is organised and sustained on a voluntary basis and the State has no say in the appointment of bishops. Moreover, although the church has been able to make its views known on crucial matters of morality and social policy, the extent of its influence in politics is greater in the imagination of Ulster Protestants than in reality. Until relatively recently, the church's moral and ethical interventions rested on a bedrock of Catholic cultural values that were so all-pervasive they scarcely required vigorous defence. One of the church's most formidable weapons has been its control over national education at primary, secondary and tertiary levels. As John Whyte has remarked,

over most of the period since independence, the remarkable feature of educational policy in Ireland has been the reluctance of the State to touch on the entrenched positions of the Church. This is not because the Church's claims have been moderate: on the contrary, it has carved out for itself a more extensive control over education in Ireland than in any other country in the world.[54]

Control over education, as was realised by nineteenth-century churchmen of all persuasions in all parts of the British Isles, was indeed a prize worth fighting for. Ironically, the Catholic Church in Ireland

---

[53]  J. H. Whyte, *Church and State in Modern Ireland 1923–1970* (Dublin, 1971).
[54]  Ibid., p. 21. See also J. Whyte, *Interpreting Northern Ireland* (Oxford, 1991).

got better terms from the British State than were achieved by any other denomination and this hard-won momentum was carried over into independent Ireland.

As was suggested in the introduction, the chief irony of this subject is undoubtedly the fact that probably no church in the British Isles started out from a more disadvantaged position in the first half of the eighteenth century, yet no church was in a stronger position by the middle of the twentieth century. Perhaps in the divine economy of churches the last shall indeed be first. But, less piously, what this discussion has tried to show is that political and social conflicts in Ireland served to reinforce rather than to undermine religious loyalties. As recent events in central and eastern Europe have made abundantly clear, faith and ethnicity are a powerful combination, especially when laced with deep-seated grievances against those of an alien race and creed. Catholicism in Ireland thrived on adversity; it remains to be seen how it will fare against the more deadly poison of ethical revolt among its youthful urban dwellers in the late twentieth century.

## CHAPTER 5

# Ulster Protestantism: the religious foundations of rebellious Loyalism[1]

The religious geography of eighteenth-century Ireland was largely the product of land confiscations, population migrations and the colonising policies of Tudor and Stuart monarchs. In the seventeenth century nowhere else in Europe (with the possible exception of Bohemia where the entire Protestant gentry class was expropriated) experienced such a dramatic inward population movement or such an upheaval in the religious composition of its landowning elite. In 1600 more than 80 per cent of Irish land was owned by Roman Catholics, but by 1700 this proportion had fallen to around 14 per cent and was still falling. Nowhere was the impact of such changes more evident than in the ancient province of Ulster which received large numbers of Anglican and Presbyterian settlers. Religion, land ownership and ethnic identity were thus at the centre of profound divisions in Ulster society, which by the eighteenth century had a luxuriant tradition of historical conflict upon which to draw. The fact that the Church of Ireland was the Established Church of a landed minority, that Ulster Presbyterianism was virtually a state within a state, and that Roman Catholicism was the creed of a defeated race ensured that the province's religious life would have more than its fair share of turbulence.[2] To some extent this was eased in the first half of the eighteenth century by the relative stability of Hanoverian rule and by the fact that each of the major religious denominations ministered to pre-assigned communities and only occasionally attempted any kind of controversial proselytism.

Nevertheless, as the high immigration statistics show, social, economic and religious grievances were never far from the surface.

---

[1] For a fuller discussion of the issues raised by this chapter see D. Hempton and M. Hill, *Evangelical Protestantism in Ulster Society 1740–1890* (London, 1992).

[2] L. M. Cullen, *The Emergence of Modern Ireland, 1600–1920* (Dublin, 1983); R. F. Foster, *Modern Ireland 1600–1972* (London, 1988); and P. Brooke, *Ulster Presbyterianism: The Historical Perspective 1610–1970* (Dublin, 1987).

Moreover, in the second half of the eighteenth century a number of forces were at work to undermine the superficial tranquillity of Irish politics and religion. Problems of empire, trade and political control were given fresh impetus by the ideological issues at the heart of the American Revolution.[3] Rising levels of agrarian violence and political dissatisfaction posed further problems of control for the British State and for Anglo-Irish landowners. As in other parts of the British Isles, many of these tensions became more urgent in the last third of the eighteenth century as a result of the successive impacts of the American and French Revolutions.[4] Although many of the problems that came to the surface in Ireland in the 1780s and 1790s did not originate in those decades, they were brought into sharper focus by the stresses and strains of the French revolutionary period. Not surprisingly, the geographical concentration of conflict came to be centred in south Ulster. There, population migration, land transfer and industrial growth produced a competitive and potentially unstable social structure. Even the language of south Ulster in the late eighteenth century was undergoing a period of profound transformation as English spread along trading networks to the disadvantage of Irish speakers and ultimately the Irish language itself.

### THE CRUCIBLE OF THE 1790S

The Catholic Relief Act of 1793, admitting Catholics to the franchise on the same terms as Protestants, was at once a revolutionary change in the Irish political order and a mechanism for enlarging considerably 'the number of possible points for sectarian friction'.[5] The sectarian warfare of Armagh in the 1790s paralleled that of the Gard in France in its intricate connexions between rapid political, economic and social change. In both areas the peasantry clung ever more tightly to their historic religious identities as a way of safeguarding community values against the consequences of change and the perceived threat from alternative and hostile religious communities.[6] This dangerous fusion

---

3    R. B. McDowell, *Ireland in the Age of Imperialism and Revolution 1760–1801* (Oxford, 1979).
4    T. W. Moody and W. E. Vaughan (eds.), *A New History of Ireland*, vol. IV, *Eighteenth-Century Ireland 1691–1800* (Oxford, 1986).
5    T. Bartlett, *The Fall and Rise of the Irish Nation: The Catholic Question 1690–1830* (Dublin, 1992).
6    T. Bartlett, 'Religious Rivalries in France and Ireland in the Age of the French Revolution', *Eighteenth-Century Ireland*, 6 (1991), 57–96; J. C. Deming, 'Protestantism and Society in France: Revivalism and the French Reformed Church in the Department of the Gard, 1815–1848', PhD dissertation, University of Notre Dame, 1989.

of social, economic and political competition between the religious communities produced the conflicts fought out by the Protestant Orangemen and the Catholic Defenders. Religion itself had not been immune from the general competition between the two communities, but in the heightened atmosphere of the 1790s it became a more critical element. The upsurge of evangelical enthusiasm in Armagh, including the revivalistic growth of Methodism in the linen triangle of south Ulster in the late eighteenth and early nineteenth century, reveals a strong link between social disruption and religious excitement, suggesting that this new and vibrant faith met many of the needs of an anxious and vulnerable society.[7] The events of the last decades of the century, in particular, focused attention on the potential of its moral creed and its anti-Catholicism to act as compelling antidotes to civil and political unrest.

W. R. Ward has written that the generation overshadowed by the French Revolution was the most important in the modern history of western European religion, 'for the Revolution altered for ever the terms on which religious establishments, the chief device on which the nations of the West had relied for christianising the people, must work'.[8] So much is true, but the Revolution also cast its shadow over Dissenting churches in Britain and Ireland, especially in the last decade of the eighteenth century, when the relationship between political and theological radicalism came under close scrutiny. For Ulster Presbyterians, in particular, the events of the 1780s and 1790s produced new strains in their relations with the State. Many Dissenting Liberals saw in the revolutionary ardour of the times the opportunity for political and religious equality with both their episcopalian and Catholic neighbours. Although much has been written about this period of Presbyterian radicalism some points need re-emphasising.[9] In the first place the radicalism (or liberalism) which gained ground within Irish Presbyterianism in this decade was not a creation *ex nihilo*, nor was it politically monochrome. In fact the picture is altogether more complicated because there was not one radical ideology but many. One

[7]   D. Hempton, 'The Methodist Crusade in Ireland 1795–1845', *Irish Historical Studies*, 22 no. 85 (1980), 33–48; and idem, 'Methodism in Irish Society, 1770–1830', *Transactions of the Royal Historical Society*, 5th ser. 36 (1986), 117–42.

[8]   W. R. Ward, *Religion and Society in England 1790–1850* (London, 1972), p. 1.

[9]   The best treatment remains A. T. Q. Stewart, 'The Transformation of Presbyterian Radicalism in the North of Ireland, 1792–1825', MA dissertation, Queen's University Belfast, 1956. See also, Brooke, *Ulster Presbyterianism*; R. F. Holmes, *Our Irish Presbyterian Heritage* (Belfast, 1985); and idem, 'Eighteenth-Century Presbyterian Radicalism and its Eclipse', *Bulletin of the Presbyterian Historical Society of Ireland*, 3 (1973), 7–15.

strand had its origins in the Commonwealth tradition and was carried on by Dublin enlightenment coteries, such as the one dominated by Francis Hucheson in the period 1719–29, and by the Scottish universities. This antique republicanism stressed the right of resistance, electoral reform and equality before the law. Another strand could be described as a kind of high-minded Dissenting cantankerousness in its hostility to war, slavery and blood sports. Yet another strand drew its ideas and encouragement from the American and French Revolutions, Paine's *Rights of Man* and the democratic corresponding societies. As well as emphasising the diversity of radical ideology, one must be careful not to overestimate its appeal. To say that Presbyterians were to the forefront of Belfast radicalism is not the same thing as saying that Belfast radicalism was the dominant feature of Ulster Presbyterianism.

What was remarkable about the Presbyterian radicalism of the 1790s was its clubbable character, its close family and economic networks and its mercantile, professional and clerical membership. This educated elite, partly upset by the fact that it could not control the electoral politics and patronage of the town it had built, disseminated its opinions through radical newspapers, a sprinkling of Presbyterian pulpits and Belfast town meetings. This was precisely the kind of radicalism that could not sink deep roots into the Ulster countryside where Protestant and Catholic peasants were fighting a life and death struggle against smaller holdings, increasing rents and, ultimately, each other. The crude sectarianism of rural Ulster had its urban liberal counterpart in the fragmentation of radical Presbyterian opinion over Catholic relief. For if the Irish problem in the twentieth century is about what Irish Catholics plan to do with Ulster Presbyterians, the reverse was the case in the 1790s. Although there were perfectly respectable liberal reasons for not trusting Catholics with political power, while at the same time refraining from actual persecution, many Belfast Presbyterian radicals wanted to do something for the Catholics – the real issue was how much, how quickly and with what securities.[10] Long before the rebellion of the United Irishmen, therefore, Catholic Emancipation was the rock upon which the fragile unity of Presbyterian radicalism perished.

Disillusionment with revolutionary ardour was clearly in evidence from about 1793, when many Ulster liberals began to feel that the

[10] P. Brooke, 'Controversies in Ulster Presbyterianism 1790–1836', PhD dissertation, University of Cambridge, 1981; R. F. Holmes, 'Ulster Presbyterianism and Irish Nationalism', *Studies in Church History*, 18 (1982) 535–48.

French revolutionary government was deviating from the principle of liberty in both politics and religion. The French were accused of exercising a despotic power over the small nations within their control, and of setting up an irreligious regime. As the reign of Terror unfolded, it became necessary to distinguish between reforming and revolutionary actions and between the concept and the reality of political freedom for Irish Roman Catholics, particularly in the light of the sectarian outrages that were disrupting the southern border counties of Ulster. The choice was by no means clear-cut, and Presbyterian involvement in both United Irish and government forces in the manifold disturbances of 1798 reveals the lack of solidarity within the community.

The political radicalism of several of its clergy and a considerable number of the laity was a major embarrassment for the governing body of the Presbyterian Church. At its autumn meeting in 1790, anxious to clear itself from the suspicion under which it was placed, the church's religious leaders condemned the conduct of 'those few unworthy members of our Body whose conduct we can only view with grief and indignation', and reaffirmed its 'Fidelity to the Crown' and 'Attachment to the Constitution'.[11] Such protestations of loyalty from the Synod of Ulster were to some extent provoked by the fear that their much-vaunted 'special relationship' with the State was endangered. In the event, however, Ulster Presbyterians were to be offered an increased and differential *regium donum* from a government concerned to encourage a more respectable, more conservative and more loyal Dissenting leadership.[12] In this way a combination of disillusionment with French and Irish revolutionary violence, fear of a more strident Irish Catholicism, and government policy ensured that a more conservative ethos would leave its mark on nineteenth-century Ulster Presbyterianism. Throughout the eighteenth century both theological and political radicalism had coexisted with more conservative and orthodox elements in the Synod of Ulster. In the aftermath of rebellion, however, this essentially religious, middle-class community with a vested interest in social order and stability, began to reassess both its doctrinal and political position. The interrelation between the two is most plainly seen in the popular misconception, fostered by nineteenth-century Presbyterian conservatives and historians, that it was 'New-Light' ministers – that is those who opposed subscription to the

[11]   *Records of the General Synod of Ulster, 1691–1820,* 3 (Belfast, 1898), p. 208.
[12]   Brooke, 'Controversies in Ulster Presbyterianism', pp. 71–109.

Westminster Confession of Faith – who were most closely implicated in the rebellion. Unorthodox views in both religion and politics thus came to be seen as mutually reinforcing when in reality, as recent surveys have shown, no such convenient relationship can be demonstrated.[13]

The French Revolution not only altered for ever the terms on which churches throughout the western world must work, but also seemed to be the key to unlock the treasure chest of biblical prophecy.[14] Within Ulster Presbyterianism, in particular, a millenarian subculture fastened eagerly on the events of the French Revolution for signs and portents. Calvinists and Covenanters with an extravagant cosmology believed that God was hastening the downfall of popery and prelacy. Even the *Northern Star*, supposedly the journal of rational radicalism, was not above dabbling in the strange world of Antichrist, the Beast, the Millennium and Armageddon. The reason for all this millennial excitement was, of course, the revolutionary ditching of the French Catholic Church by erstwhile French Catholics. If that church had indeed reached its nemesis in the very nerve centre of the European *ancien régime* was not a new day about to dawn? In the general atmosphere of tension and unrest in Ulster in the 1790s both national and international events were infused with religious significance. By interpreting secular events as part of a divine plan, prophetical speculations offered both an explanation for contemporary turmoil and religious legitimacy for those seeking to transform the world. Local events thus acquired new significance by being placed not only in an international, but a universal setting. The full extent and impact of millennial ideology and millenarian excitement in late eighteenth-century Ulster is difficult to estimate, since it was expressed in a wide variety of academic and popular forms. Indeed, the intricate complexities of millenarian ideologies are often much misunderstood. For those with a vested interest in the world changing quickly it was perfectly possible to construct an optimistic eschatology in which temporal events were interpreted as the ushering in of a new and a better age. For those with most to lose from rapid social change, however, the reverse was generally the case, though for them divine providence was still regarded as an incomparably superior bet to the vagaries of temporal misfortunes. In addition, for those whose view of the last

[13]    D. Miller, 'Presbyterianism and "Modernization" in Ulster', *Past & Present*, no. 80 (1978), 66–90.

[14]    P. Berger, *The Social Reality of Religion* (London, 1967); J. F. C. Harrison, *The Second Coming: Popular Millenarianism: 1780–1850* (London, 1979).

times incorporated a post-millennial emphasis on a new 'gospel age' before the final curtain descended on the world, eschatological excitement could inspire a new enthusiasm for evangelism. All three strands were evident in the millenarian enthusiasms of late eighteenth-century Ulster.

Specialised theological studies on the approach of the millennium preoccupied sections of the Presbyterian community in the 1790s, with the printing and distribution of several publications lending weight to United Irish pressure for radical political reform. While expositions of the books of Daniel and Revelation often differed in precise details of interpretation, they generally agreed on the overriding significance of events in France. For Presbyterian radicals the struggle between Christ and Antichrist was identified with the struggle between liberty and despotism in a characteristic mingling of theological and political ideologies which was, and still is, a recurring feature of Ulster Protestantism. The biblical interpretation of political events, whether construed as an academic theological exercise or, more commonly, expressed in the general linking of contemporary social upheaval with the unfolding of a divine plan for mankind, invested all aspects of life with a compelling urgency. 'Be ye ready also, for the Son of Man cometh at an hour when ye think not' was a text taken up by all Presbyterian synods in the last decades of the century.[15] During years when murder and looting were commonplace, secret societies proliferated, a repressive military presence was established, and the daily newspapers were full of the dramatic occurrences in France and the progress of the war in Europe, references to the imminence of the Latter Days abounded. In the aftermath of the rebellion, when it did indeed seem that things would never be the same again, the Union debates perpetuated popular excitement and unrest. Few, however, could link political and religious principles with such ingenious simplicity as Francis Dobbs, MP for Charlemont, whose interpretations of both biblical and daily events enlivened the House of Commons in the first summer of the nineteenth century. Dobbs saw the immediate Second Coming as inevitable, given the attempt to unite Ireland with Britain, since her independence was 'written in the immutable records of Heaven'. He identified Armagh with Armageddon, and viewed the proposed union as an attempt to annihilate

---

[15]   Union Theological College Belfast, Minutes of the Associate Synod of Ireland (Burgher), 1799–1814, p. 65; NIPRO, Records of the Reformed Presbytery of Antrim, 1803–11, CR5/5A/1/2A.

God's chosen nation.[16] More seriously, the ability of Reformed Protestants in Ulster to view their temporal circumstances as part of God's special covenant relationship with his people has invested their political aspirations with the kind of ultimate sanction that does not lend itself to accommodation or consensus. According to a recent study, the cultural values of Ulster–Scots Presbyterians, as with the Afrikaners, are grounded in belief in a personal God, commitment to a particular land, unwavering hostility to perceived enemies, obedience to a divinely sanctioned legal code, adherence to a prophetical interpretation of human destiny and the employment of biblical language and thought forms to interpret the wider world. Such people are therefore 'not given to easy compromises, committed to religious or racial pluralism, or overly concerned about keeping the good opinion of the outside, profane world'.[17]

Millenarianism was not the only form of religious enthusiasm to benefit from the revolutionary excitement of the late eighteenth century. It was in this period also that the transition of evangelicalism, from a small coterie of enthusiastic Methodists and Anglicans dotted throughout Ireland to a genuinely popular movement centred on Ulster, gathered momentum and achieved revivalistic proportions in the border counties of south and south-west Ulster. As in England, the initial upsurge in undenominational itinerant preaching alarmed established Protestant interests and was seen as a threat to ecclesiastical discipline. Although there were many skirmishes on the way, it was soon apparent that evangelicalism was a sufficiently flexible religious ideology to attract both major landowners and their tenant farmers, the clergy of the Established Church and rural firebrands. As with the relationship between landowners and popular Orangeism, the elite and popular forms of evangelical enthusiasm were not always in harmony, but their shared dislike of Catholicism, irreligion and disorder laid the foundation for a greater degree of accommodation in the nineteenth century.[18]

Sectarianism, apocalypticism and evangelicalism were thus the ultimate beneficiaries of a decade which opened with enthusiasm for the rights of man and closed with disturbing evidence of the brutality of

[16]  *Memoirs of Francis Dobbs, also Genuine Reports of his Speeches in Parliament on the Subject of a Union, and his Prediction of the Second Coming of the Messiah* (Dublin, 1800).

[17]  D. H. Akenson, *God's Peoples: Covenant and Land in South Africa, Israel, and Ulster* (Montreal, 1992), p. 42; and idem, *Between Two Revolutions: Islandmagee, County Antrim, 1798–1920* (Hamden, Conn., 1979).

[18]  Hempton and Hill, *Evangelical Protestantism.*

man. Ironically, the passions and forces unleashed by revolutionary enthusiasm for natural rights gave a new urgency to religious identity. Although the failure of the United Irishmen was complete, the sectarian disturbances in Armagh and the sectarian war in Wexford left the Protestant community with an anxious understanding of its vulnerability in a predominantly Catholic nation. Far from the 'one and indivisible republic' envisaged by the would-be revolutionaries, religious identity assumed a heightened significance in the wider interplay of social and political conflict. The withdrawal of many Presbyterians from radical politics merely reinforced the view that Catholicism and disloyalty were synonymous. With the religious divide deepening as the new century dawned, the relevance of evangelical principles to local political and social circumstances was even more vigorously asserted. In these years it gained widespread acceptance and the support of the most important elements of ecclesiastical and secular society. But from a long-term perspective, evangelical religion, far from being a stabilising force in Irish society, which is how it was seen from within the tradition, was arguably the most disruptive of influences. It imbued the Ulster Protestant community with a sense of divine approval in its continued resistance to assimilation into the wider Irish culture, in which the Roman Catholic religion was regarded as its most central and most pernicious element. In the crucible of Ulster in the 1790s, historic cultural and religious divisions proved to be more powerful than abstract political ideas of natural rights and the brotherhood of humankind.

### EVANGELICAL ENTHUSIASM IN THE NINETEENTH CENTURY

In the early decades of the nineteenth century the great British evangelical societies not only established Hibernian auxiliaries, but also made Ireland one of the chief targets for their conversionist zeal.[19] In this way Ireland helped to fund its own deliverance or, more accurately, an evangelical minority contributed modest sums to organisations based in London whose more considerable assets were then used to convert the Irish and civilise their country. Such arrangements not only released far more resources for the evangelisation of Ireland than were available from within its own boundaries, but resulted in a much closer identification of interests between British and Irish Protestants

---

[19]  Ibid., pp. 47–61.

than would otherwise have been the case. Culminating in the well-known controversies of the so-called 'Second Reformation' movement, the first third of the nineteenth century saw an unprecedented attempt to convert Irish Catholics, not by the power of Established Churches or coercion by the State, but by the voluntary religious zeal of a host of evangelical societies.[20] It would be a serious misunderstanding of the evangelical mind to deny that the chief motivation for such enthusiasm was what evangelical Protestants claimed it to be, that is, an earnest desire to see 'vital religion' expand at the expense of Romish super-stition and popular indifference. But the fact that many of the societies were either founded in England or had the support of English evangelicals, and that they were patronised by Anglo-Irish landowners, ensured that there was more at stake than conversion alone. The potential for controversy was there from the start because the most common evangelical methods – preaching, teaching and the distribu-tion of literature – carried with them overtones of religious proselytism and cultural imperialism. The acrimonious disputes over the use of the Irish language, for example, both within Protestantism and between Protestants and Catholics, show that what was at stake was no less than a contest between incompatible religious and national cultures for the heart and soul of the nation. But even by 1830 it was clear that the evangelical campaign to convert the Irish peasantry could not succeed in the face of the Catholic Church's stout resistance. Ironically, there-fore, the evangelical crusade to convert Catholic Ireland contributed further to the concentration of Protestantism in Ulster. The extent to which the provincial frontier with the rest of Ireland was the chief theatre of evangelical proselytism is itself indicative of the changes that were taking place.

To state, however, that the evangelical societies failed to achieve their main objective is only part of the story. The voluntary agencies, with their preachers, teachers, distributors, collectors and visitors, bureaucratised evangelicalism and brought into being an army of subalterns beyond the immediate control of churches and their clergy. Committed to evangelical zeal and mutual improvement, this army at once destabilised the old conventional boundaries between the Protes-tant and Catholic Churches, and promoted class harmony within Ulster Protestantism. The nascent Catholic democratic nationalism of the 1820s was therefore matched by an unprecedented religious

[20]    D. Bowen, *The Protestant Crusade in Ireland 1800–1870* (Dublin, 1978).

mobilisation of the Irish Protestant laity, the ramifications of which soon became obvious in all the Irish Protestant denominations. The 1820s was as much the decade of Henry Cooke and Lord Farnham as it was of Daniel O'Connell.[21] Catholic Emancipation was thus passed in a climate of unprecedented religious competition, affecting the relations between Protestants and Catholics, tenants and landowners, and clergy and people.

Ironically, Irish Protestantism, including the Established Church, roused itself to vigorous activity at precisely the time when Irish Catholics were no longer prepared to tolerate religious proselytism or ascendancy values.[22] Moreover, it soon became clear that neither British governments nor British public opinion could be relied upon to resist Irish Catholicism with sufficient fortitude. A string of concessions, from Catholic Emancipation to the disestablishment of the Irish Church, alarmed Protestants and failed to assuage Catholic grievances. In such circumstances, religious sectarianism refused to die, and was transported by migration from rural Ulster into the city of Belfast.

### SECTARIAN CONFLICT IN BELFAST

In the late eighteenth century Belfast was a liberal market town with a predominantly Presbyterian population.[23] In 1785, for example, there were only 1,000 Roman Catholics living in Belfast, which represented around 8 per cent of the total population. This percentage doubled every twenty-five years until the mid 1830s when the proportion of Catholics stood at 32 per cent and continued to climb, possibly to around 40 per cent, in the 1840s when the ethnic tide started to turn as a result of the famine, the growth of shipbuilding, engineering and skilled trades in the 1850s, and the increased rate of Catholic emigration to other parts of Ireland and the rest of the world. The absolute numbers of Roman Catholics in Belfast nevertheless continued to grow very rapidly. There were, for example, more Roman Catholics in

---

[21]   R. F. Holmes, *Henry Cooke* (Belfast, 1981); Hempton and Hill, *Evangelical Protestantism*, pp. 47–102.

[22]   I. M. Hehir, 'New Lights and Old Enemies: the Second Reformation and the Catholics of Ireland, 1800–1835', MA dissertation, University of Wisconsin, 1983; M. Hill, 'Evangelicalism and the Churches in Ulster Society, 1770–1850', PhD dissertation, Queen's University Belfast, 1987; and A. R. Acheson, 'The Evangelicals in the Church of Ireland, 1784–1859', PhD dissertation, Queen's University Belfast, 1967.

[23]   E. Jones, *A Social Geography of Belfast* (London, 1960); J. C. Beckett and R. E. Glassock (eds.), *Belfast: The Origins and Growth of an Industrial City* (Belfast, 1967); J. C. Beckett (ed.), *Belfast: The Making of the City* (Belfast, 1983); and J. Bardon, *Belfast* (Belfast, 1982).

Belfast in 1871 than there were total inhabitants in 1831. As with other Victorian cities in the British Isles, population increase was due to migration from outside. This is particularly true of Belfast where infant mortality and fever death rates were among the highest in the British Isles. Where exactly the migrants came from is nevertheless sufficiently unclear for statistical precision, but reliable figures of household heads within street categories from the late nineteenth century show different patterns of Protestant and Catholic migration.[24] While 50 per cent of Protestant migrants came from the counties of Down and Antrim, Roman Catholics were more likely than Protestants to have been born in Belfast or to have migrated from the other counties of Ulster and from the rest of Ireland. What can be said with certainty is that whereas Catholics had migrated to Belfast in larger numbers than Protestants before and during the famine, the position was reversed from the 1860s.

Historians of ethnic conflict among migrants to American cities in the nineteenth century have drawn attention to the importance of the pre-existing structures of social, political and economic power in cities before the migrants arrived. Well-established elites were the least able to accommodate new migrant communities. Not only were such structures already well established in Belfast, but the predominantly poor and unskilled character of Catholic migrants merely confirmed Protestant notions about the baleful effects of Roman Catholicism on social and economic progress.[25] Thus, while Catholicism had been no more than an unobtrusive minority denomination, the attitude of Belfast's secure and generally prosperous Protestants had been mainly tolerant. Munificent town dwellers had expressed their liberality by contributing to the building of Belfast's first two Roman Catholic chapels in 1784 and 1815. But the course of the 1798 rebellion and subsequent political developments had led many Presbyterians to a distinctively anti-Catholic conservatism. Religious harmony in Belfast was now under threat as the traditions of sectarian strife which rural dwellers brought with them were grafted on to the tension generated by the political and religious polemics of the late 1820s and 1830s. These public demonstrations allowed the conservative and orthodox

[24]   A. C. Hepburn and B. Collins, 'Industrial Society: The Structure of Belfast, 1901', in P. Roebuck (ed.), *Plantation to Partition* (Belfast, 1981), pp. 210–28.
[25]   S. A. Royle, 'Industrialization, Urbanization and Urban Society in Post-Famine Ireland c. 1850–1921', in B. J. Graham and L. J. Proudfoot (eds.), *An Historical Geography of Ireland* (London, 1993), pp. 258–92.

elements in both politics and religion to mount a serious challenge to liberalism in all its forms. Before 1830 religious riots in the town were still rare, but in the succeeding decades clashes became more frequent.[26] Competition for jobs, the popular and controversial exhortations of evangelical clergy, the growth of a more visible Catholic presence and the activities of the Orange Order were all contributory factors.

Despite the fact that both Protestant and Catholic churches in Belfast were virtually mirror images of one another in the methods they used to christianise the unwashed multitude, the growth of the Catholic community served to confirm old Protestant stereotypes of the Roman Church.[27] Since there were far fewer Catholic churches than Protestant ones per head of population the former were generally larger and more imposing. Moreover, because of the absence of a substantial mercantile community, the Catholic Church was unable to rely on middle-class beneficence for church-building and had to depend instead on more assiduous collections to finance building costs.[28] Protestants interpreted the former as triumphalism and the latter as evidence of a ruthless church grinding down its humble adherents. In addition, the striking growth in the number of priests and religious orders fuelled the old fears of priestcraft, and the import of italianate devotional forms in the later Victorian period further persuaded evangelical puritans of the essentially foreign and superstitious nature of the Roman Church. Protestants thought they saw a growing, grasping, aggressive and intolerant church. Ironically, the correspondence of Catholic leaders in Belfast tells a rather different and more defensive tale. Preoccupied by high leakage rates, nervous of Protestant proselytism, burdened by huge debts, fearful of Orange excesses, and often divided among themselves on issues of politics, strategy and aspiration, the Belfast Catholic leadership resembled anything but the aggressive monolith of Protestant imagination.

That these religious cultures had the capacity for conflict is self-evident, but it was the multi-layered nature of such conflict which made it such a recurring feature of Belfast life in the nineteenth century. Points of conflict were legion. Open-air sermons, Orange parades, election

---

26  S. E. Baker, 'Orange and Green, Belfast 1832–1912', in H. J. Dyos and M. Wolff (eds.), *The Victorian City: Images and Realities*, vol. II (London, 1973), pp. 789–814.

27  D. Hempton and M. Hill, 'Godliness and Good Citizenship: Evangelical Protestantism and Social Control in Ulster, 1790–1850', *Saothar*, 13 (1988), 68–80.

28  A. Macauley, *Patrick Dorrian, Bishop of Down and Connor 1865–1885* (Dublin, 1987).

hustings, funeral processions, the great Protestant protest meetings in the city's botanical gardens, Catholic festivals such as the Feast Day of the Assumption, celebrations of historical events and transferred tensions from the surrounding countryside all contributed to riots at one time or another, especially in the years between 1857 and 1886.[29] All came with their processions, effigies, slogans, party tunes, banners and rituals. To a remarkable extent clubs and processions became a way of life. There were already thirty-two Orange lodges in Belfast by the 1830s and parades in a special way marked out ethnic and religious territory. Where you could 'walk' you could control. Underpinning episodic outbreaks of riotous behaviour were irreconcilable disputes over government policy and seemingly interminable local wrangles over powers and privileges. Predominantly Protestant Boards of Guardians administered workhouses for predominantly Catholic paupers amidst allegations of proselytism, a predominantly Protestant magistracy administered the law, a predominantly Protestant corporation allocated civic amenities and predominantly Protestant voters elected Protestant Members of Parliament. Even the allocation of graveyards occasioned sectarian animosity: Belfast was a city divided as much in death as it was in life. It was also the provincial focus of important changes in the foundations of Ulster politics which crystallised over the threat of Home Rule for Ireland.[30]

## HOME RULE AND THE PROTESTANT MIND

Long before Gladstone experimented with Home Rule in the mid 1880s, Ulster Protestants, despite long-standing political and denominational differences, had been thrown together by a formidable range of pressures. Disestablishment of the Irish Church, educational competition, the 'invasion of Ulster' by the Irish National League after 1883, agrarian violence, Cullen's anti-Protestant leadership of the Catholic Church, sectarianism in Belfast, and the perceived economic superiority of the Lagan valley over the rest of Ireland all coalesced to persuade Ulster Protestants that they were facing a Catholic-inspired nationalist threat to their entire way of life. Evangelical Protestantism,

[29] D. Hempton, 'Belfast: The Unique City?' in H. McLeod (ed.), *European Religion in the Age of Great Cities 1830–1930* (London, 1995), pp. 145–64.
[30] B. M. Walker, *Ulster Politics: The Formative Years, 1868–86* (Belfast, 1989); H. Patterson, *Class Conflict and Sectarianism: The Protestant Working Class and the Belfast Labour Movement 1868–1920* (Belfast, 1980).

which had helped create some of the pressures it professed to abhor, supplied many of the symbols, much of the religious legitimacy and not a few of the prejudices which were pressed into service in the debates over Home Rule at the end of the nineteenth and beginning of the twentieth centuries.

Since neither the disestablishment of the Irish Church nor various attempts at land reform had quietened Ireland, Gladstone reached the conclusion that only a well-considered and closely limited measure of self-government offered any prospect of long-term peace and stability.[31] Not surprisingly, such a bold constitutional proposal helped crystallise the differences between Irish Catholics and Protestants, and between Ulster and the rest of the country. In a remarkable way the Home Rule crisis brought into sharp focus an Irish Protestant *mentalité*, centred in Ulster, which had been forged over a quarter of a millennium of turbulent history. Moreover, the resistance to Home Rule in Ulster in the period 1885–1920 cemented a Protestant identity which subsequent events have done nothing to undermine. The inability of either the British State or Irish nationalism to coerce or accommodate this sturdy and peculiar minority has resulted in one of the most intractable problems in the modern world.

The hostile response of the Irish Protestant churches to Home Rule was no mere example of institutional posturing, for their opposition rested on a cultural bedrock of Protestant assumptions and values which were central to the emergence of a Protestant identity in Ulster.[32] A recent survey of some thirty Ulster Unionist speeches against Home Rule in 1886, for example, shows that in descending order of priority the arguments employed were as follows: the representatives of an ascendant Roman Catholicism would persecute the Protestant community; Ulster Protestants would be deprived of their imperial heritage and would thus have a reduced status in the world; Catholic nationalists had no respect for law and order and would deliver Ulster into social and economic ruin; Home Rule was a betrayal of loyalism; and Ulster would be forced to shoulder the fiscal and economic burden of Ireland under Home Rule.[33] The disproportionate number of reported speeches from Protestant ministers may partly

[31]   J. Loughlin, *Gladstone, Home Rule and the Irish Question 1882–93* (Dublin, 1986); A. O'Day, *Parnell and the First Home Rule Episode, 1884–1887* (Dublin, 1986).

[32]   A. Jackson, 'Unionist Politics and Protestant Society in Edwardian Ireland', *Historical Journal*, 33 no. 4 (1990), 839–66.

[33]   Loughlin, *Gladstone*, pp. 295–6.

account for the high profile given to religious fears in this survey, but there can be no doubt that the above issues were indeed dominant in the manifold pamphlets, speeches and meetings against Home Rule.[34] What is striking about this Ulster Protestant world-view is the number of mutually reinforcing explanations it offered for the plight in which they found themselves in 1886. It was, and still is, a remarkably cohesive ideology, embracing past, present and future as well as religion, politics and society. The only chink in its armour was its perceived inability to sustain itself against an imperialistic Catholic nationalism without the continued support of the rest of the United Kingdom. That was precisely the frailty exposed by Home Rule, and it was made harder to bear by Gladstone's and Parnell's persistent but erroneous belief that the eighteenth-century Patriot tradition was a stronger force in Irish Protestantism than Ulster loyalism. The belief persisted, against formidable evidence to the contrary, because both men wished it were so.

Ulster Protestants had an alternative view of Irish history which was relentlessly rehearsed at Orange, church and political meetings throughout the nineteenth century. The Great Protestant fleeting in Belfast against the Irish Church Bill in 1869 is a good example of its kind.[35] A huge crowd, optimistically estimated at 100,000 people, crammed into the city's botanical gardens on a bright summer's day. At the heart of the day's entertainment were the speeches, many of which were populist history lectures about the struggles and triumphs of Irish Protestants against an unchanging and disloyal Catholicism. As events and heroes were recalled to the cheers of the crowd, the virtues most admired were staunchness and unchanging principles, the evils most railed against were betrayal and accommodation. These appeals to forefathers, faith and the settlement of the land not only foreshortened the past, but helped even the most impious to believe that they were part of a tradition protected by divine providence for a quarter of a millennium. Here was a memorial and celebratory culture resonant with providential turning-points and rich in symbols. The most expert platform orators knew exactly how to manipulate their audience for the maximum applause and the crowd knew exactly how to manipulate

---

[34] For other interpretations of early Ulster Unionism see P. Buckland, *Ulster Unionism and the Origins of Northern Ireland 1886–1922* (Dublin, 1973); J. F. Harbinson, *The Ulster Unionist Party 1882–1973* (Belfast, 1973); and A. Jackson, *The Ulster Party: Irish Unionists in the House of Commons, 1884–1911* (Oxford, 1989).

[35] Anon., *The Irish Church Bill: The Great Protestant Demonstration in Belfast* (Belfast, 1869).

platform orators to tell them what they most wanted to hear. It was not only a great day out for all, but soon took its place in the tradition it was called to celebrate. As with many such meetings since the passage of Catholic Emancipation in 1829, it was a protest against British government policy, and that characteristic also became central to the tradition. But in making their protests Ulster Protestants were not so much giving expression to a contractual view of their relationship with the rest of the United Kingdom (that came later), as demonstrating their belief that the pragmatic liberalism of much government policy in Ireland in the Victorian period was based on mistaken assumptions about the real causes of Ireland's difficulties.[36] Hence the suggested remedies, culminating in Home Rule, were not only betraying Irish Protestantism, but were guaranteed to perpetuate the very problems they were designed to solve. In such circumstances the right to resist depended upon the seriousness of the threat to Protestant life, liberty and property.

The part played by evangelical religion in stiffening the resolve of Ulster Protestants against Home Rule should not be underestimated. For over a century old Reformation polarities had been given new social meanings in a province sufficiently divided on grounds of religion to sustain the crudest forms of stereotyping sanctified by theological principles. Protestants believed that having access to the 'Open Bible', being free from priestcraft and superstition and adhering to a progressive and enlightened faith were at the heart of Ulster's cultural and economic superiority over the rest of Ireland, and, equally important, of Protestant Ulster's superiority over Catholic Ulster.[37] The hotter the Protestantism, in terms of its evangelical zeal, the firmer was this belief and the sharper the antagonism against the 'whole system' of Roman Catholicism. In assessing the power of evangelical religion in Ulster Protestant ideology, Frank Wright perceptively noted that 'defence of the socialisation process of evangelical Protestantism is more of a universal concern than an actual belief in evangelicalism itself'.[38] He meant by this that Ulster Protestants, in the mass, have been more committed to the *right* to preach the reformed religion and to maintain its influence in education, culture and society than to the essence of

---

[36] The notion of a contractual relationship between Ulster loyalists and the United Kingdom is developed by D. Miller, *Queen's Rebels, Ulster Loyalism in Historical Perspective* (Dublin, 1978), pp. 65–80.

[37] *The Home Rule 'Nutshell', examined by an Irish Unionist* (Belfast and Dublin, 1912).

[38] F. Wright, 'Protestant Ideology and Politics in Ulster', *Archives Européennes de Sociologie*, 14 (1973), 213–80; idem, 'Developments in Ulster Politics, 1843–86', PhD dissertation, Queen's University Belfast, 1989.

religious belief itself. Hence the religious heroes of Ulster Protestantism have not been theologians or pietists, but rather those who have most resolutely defended the rights of Ulster Protestants to adhere to the reformed faith against the unwelcome encroachments of the Roman Church. From this perspective any concession made to Roman Catholics was by definition a weakening of historic Protestantism. The one could only make progress at the expense of the other. It was, as Professor Bruce has suggested, a zero sum game.[39]

One of the great strengths of evangelical ideology in Ulster was the way in which it could simultaneously narrow the focus to a contest between reformed religion and Catholic superstition in Ireland and widen it to an international conflict of major proportions. This was facilitated by the late Victorian expansion of the British Empire and by the post-famine migrations of Irish Catholics. Here was a clash of two world empires, one of commerce, Christianity and civilisation as exported by Great Britain and the other a sordid, embittered and disloyal Irish Catholic migration, particularly to the United States, where it created another culture in its own image. The corruptions of Tammany Hall and the ill-fated invasion of Manitoba merely confirmed the unchanging character of the Catholic Irish even when thousands of miles from home. 'The Home Rule movement', stated the Revd Gilbert Mahaffy to the YMCA, 'has been, from first to last, a movement hostile to British rule. And fostered as it has been on American soil, and supported by American dollars, it is essentially republican.'[40] Depending on circumstances, therefore, Ulster Protestants could think of themselves as either a faithful remnant of righteousness in a pagan land or as part of a great and civilising world empire. They were equally comforting and culturally reinforcing ideas. The Revd Thomas Ellis, for example, told the loyal Orangemen of Portadown in 1885 that 'we have sacrificed our duty to God and to each other too often on the altar of Popish compromise, worldly expediency and carnal selfishness'. He called upon them, as 'the faithful few among the faithless many – the loyal Sons of Judah amid the faithless men of Israel', to abandon their lax Protestantism and follow in the steps of their glorious forefathers.[41] Others, more impressed by

[39]  S. Bruce, *God Save Ulster: The Religion and Politics of Paisleyism* (Oxford, 1986).
[40]  G. Mahaffy, *The Attitude of Irish Churchmen in the Present Political Crisis*, 3rd edn (Dublin, 1886), p. 12.
[41]  T. Ellis, *God and the Nation. A Sermon Preached to the Orangemen of the District of Portadown* (Armagh, 1885).

Ulster's commercial vitality than depressed by its religious worldliness, simply wanted protection against a Roman Catholic ascendancy so that 'we shall be allowed to continue our triumphant march of Prosperity under the protection of the British flag, a United Parliament, and the Imperial Crown'. Such a framework was watertight. Ulster's success was due to the blessings of providence and the energy of its people, its failures were attributable to enemies on all sides pressing in on a loyal but vulnerable remnant. Not surprisingly such ideas frequently gave rise to racial notions of the inherent superiority of Ulster Protestants to Irish Celts.

The most important contribution of evangelicalism to Ulster Protestant ideology was its capacity to draw together old adversarial religious traditions and different social classes under the banner of a shared anti-Catholicism. As David Miller has written,

> although antipopery had been an element in evangelicalism since Wesley himself, the movement's role in creating Protestant solidarity derived from more than a new way to stigmatise the ancient enemy. The two cultures – Episcopal and Presbyterian – into which Ulster Protestants had been divided in the early eighteenth century were both fundamentally unsuited to a modern world in which religious belief and practice would not be a public duty to be enforced upon the populace, but a private choice whose very validity depended upon its being voluntary. Evangelical emphasis on the individual offered these two churches a way out of the adversarial relationship, over which one should enjoy the right to coerce the conscience, in which they had been cast in the seventeenth century.[42]

The capacity of evangelicalism to act as both a denominational and class solvent considerably expanded its power as an easily available and emotionally resonant creed of communal solidarity against a shared enemy.

The Roman Catholic Church in Ireland was thus regarded as all-pervasive in influence, monolithic in scope, imperialist in intention, persecuting in its essential nature and impoverishing in its social effects. No state in which its representatives were in control could offer any credible safeguards for the rights of religious minorities. Faced with such a possibility Ulster Protestant theology had the capacity to adapt to new circumstances. The view that all Christian citizens had a sacred duty to support lawfully constituted authorities was capable of being transformed into a sacred duty to resist religious tyranny. As with English Puritanism on the eve of the Civil Wars, the anti-Catholicism

---

[42]  D. Miller, book review in *Irish Economic and Social History*, 19 (1992), p. 122.

of Ulster Protestants was a potentially radical force, and was, of course, more capable of mass realisation than was sacrificial piety. It was propagated by a resurgent Orangeism whose rank and file of agricultural labourers and urban workers was led by Ulster landowners and baptised by the churches. Depending upon the seriousness of the crisis, Orange excesses, including pseudo-military drilling, came to be feared less than Protestant apathy. Even the licence of the Belfast Protestant mobs was defended by some religious leaders who apparently saw no incongruity between this and their earlier attacks on Fenian agrarian outrages.

Evangelicalism thus helped to build bridges between denominations, between clergy and laity, and between churches and voluntary associations. It sustained links between Irish and British organisations, from the staunchly Protestant, such as the Scottish Protestant Alliance and the Protestant Institute of Great Britain, to the politically mild such as the Evangelical Alliance and the YMCA.[43] Although most of the prolific evangelical societies devoted to Christian morality and self-improvement operated a 'no politics' principle, their very ethos contributed much to an Ulster Protestant identity. When addressing itself to the issue of Home Rule, for example, the YMCA journal stated that

The bulletin is not a political journal, but a grave national crisis such as this concerns young men, as well as others. It concerns Christian young men very specially. If carried, this bill would change the entire character of our national life. It would alter the prospects of many of us who are preparing for trades, or commercial life, or for the professions. It would have the most material influence on the religion of the nation ... but perhaps the worst feature of the proposed measure is the tremendous leverage it would give to Romanism – the curse of Ireland for generations.[44]

The formidable array of both denominational and inter-denominational improvement societies in late nineteenth-century Ulster helped create an ethos of godliness and good citizenship which was inextricably bound up with loyalty to the British way of life. Even the considerable female devotion to the temperance movement had an anti-Catholic twist in its portrayal of the drunken Bridget as its visible antithesis.[45] When the Home Rule crisis awakened the slumbering

---

[43]  J. Wolffe, *The Protestant Crusade in Great Britain, 1829–60* (Oxford, 1991).

[44]  YMCA, *Bulletin* (Belfast, 1885).

[45]  A. E. Brozyna, '"The Cursed Cup hath Cast her Down": Constructions of Female Piety in Ulster Evangelical Temperance Literature, 1863–1914', in J. Holmes and D. Urquart (eds.), *Coming into the Light: The Work, Politics and Religion of Women in Ulster 1840–1940* (Belfast, 1994), pp. 154–78.

Unionist associations in provincial Ulster, therefore, they found themselves lying on an easily politicised bed of respectable Protestant
culture. By then evangelical religion had thrown up successive generations of political preachers who unashamedly used their clerical
influence on behalf of popular Protestant causes. Their contribution
further united religion and politics in a way that boded ill for statesmen
called upon to disentangle the threads. As the Revd Thomas Ellis told
the Portadown Orangemen, he had never been able to understand
how any man 'with the Bible in his hands and who believed in the
moral government of the world by God' could separate religion from
politics. Ironically, Gladstone, who provoked much breast-beating
among Ulster Protestants, was one of a dwindling number of English
statesmen to put much store on such sentiment.

Important though the influence of evangelicalism was in forging an
Ulster Protestant identity, it would be misleading to present late
nineteenth-century Irish Protestantism in crudely monolithic terms.
Not only were there important denominational and class tensions, but
there was also a vigorous Protestant nationalist minority which
supported Home Rule.[46] Mainly religious moderates and liberal
reformers, the Protestant Home Rulers were more united in their
dislike of populist Orangeism than they were in their vision of how
Ireland under Home Rule should operate. In general terms the
Protestant Home Rulers thought of themselves as an enlightened and
tolerant minority whose opposition to landlordism and episcopalian
ascendancy helped forge a bond with some of their Catholic counterparts. Within Ulster their influence was marginal, not only because of
their small numbers, but because of the formidable pressures that could
be brought upon them by their less liberal co-religionists.[47] In this case
tradition was not only invented, but vigorously enforced.


### THE RISE OF ULSTER UNIONISM

It was in the turbulent political conditions of the 1880s that the Irish
Unionist Party was formed. Not surprisingly, perhaps, its first leader,
Colonel Edward Saunderson, was an evangelical landowner from
County Cavan, where the interface of British and Irish traditions lay

---

[46]  J. Loughlin, 'The Irish Protestant Home Rule Association and Nationalist Politics', *Irish Historical Studies*, 24 no. 95 (1985), pp. 341–60.

[47]  National Library of Ireland, Irish Protestant Home Rule Association, minutes, 13 October 1886.

exposed along the fault lines of landowners and tenants, Protestant and Catholic, paternalism and self-help, and social control and social aspiration.[48] Indeed the Saunderson interest in Cavan, from its origins in the undertakership of an Edinburgh merchant family in the early seventeenth century to its collapse with the rest of the old landed order in the early twentieth century is almost a sacramental odyssey through three centuries of Irish history. In the main the Saundersons consolidated their interest by backing the right horses in the land confiscations of the seventeenth century, played a part in the political culture of Irish whiggery in the eighteenth century and became evangelical Liberals and then evangelical Unionists in the nineteenth century. They were part of a tightly knit group of surprisingly evangelical landowners in southern Ulster, northern Leinster and northern Connacht, who acted as a great landed barrier against the rising tide of tenant influence and Catholic nationalism. It was, in essence, the last frontier of the greater British State, the Protestant Reformation and the power of landed property.

As is the way, Saunderson acquired his evangelicalism from his mother, his wife and his conversion, and although not as viciously anti-Catholic as some of his fellow Cavan landowners, his strong Protestant convictions offered an entree into both evangelical culture in Britain and popular Protestantism in Ulster. It was a perfect combination for the leadership of Irish Unionism which required the ability to influence the House of Commons and the householders of urban and rural Ulster. Saunderson was devoted to the Church of Ireland, loyal to the British monarchy, committed to the ideals of landed paternalism, and deeply hostile to the agrarian violence of the Land League and the remorseless clericalism (as he saw it) of the Irish Catholic Church. It was in the white heat of agrarian lawlessness, threats of Home Rule, and the trans-European crisis of territorial elites in the 1880s that Saunderson forsook whiggish Liberalism and embraced populist Orangeism. Although he regarded himself as a representative of Irish Unionism he became in effect the political leader of the Ulster Protestants. As Michael Davitt said of him, 'in politics he is an open, fearless fighter. He loves his God, and he loves his country – but his country is Ulster.'[49]

As his most recent biographer makes clear, Saunderson's essentially landed and paternalistic Unionism, however infused with evangelical

[48]   A. Jackson, *Colonel Edward Saunderson: Land and Loyalty in Victorian Ireland* (Oxford, 1995).
[49]   Ibid., p. 100.

enthusiasm, was not always endorsed by the industrial and professional classes of Belfast, the small farmers in the countryside or the ferociously evangelical and sectarian elements within the Belfast working class. But his staunch Protestantism, imperial jingoism and love–hate relationship with the British political elite were sufficiently attractive to his supporters for him to retain his position until the early twentieth century when his enthusiasm for proprietorial causes made him more of a liability than an asset. Saunderson nevertheless bequeathed more to the Unionist tradition in Ulster than that tradition has seen fit to recognise. This includes its earnest religious temper and its deep distrust of the nation to which it wished to be united. In the aftermath of the disastrous 1892 election campaign, for example, Saunderson told the Grand Master of the Belfast Orangemen that 'the course of events in England and Scotland should teach Ulster loyalists that, in the long run, they must trust to their own strength and unflinching determination ... if a just cause could win the support of the British voter we should now be in an overwhelming majority'.[50] Even in the high paternalistic Unionism of Saunderson, therefore, there is an implicit contractual threat to the British State that Loyalism is conditional on the defence of Protestant values.

There is something eerily symmetrical about the history of the Saunderson family in Ireland, from its seventeenth-century origins as part of the colonial policy of the British State to its collapse and subsequent investment of its remaining wealth in a portfolio of colonial stock in the twentieth century. Of equal interest for our theme, however, is the way in which evangelicalism, that most flexible and adaptable of religious ideologies, supplied the sacred framework within which the Protestant landlords of the frontier counties of Ulster resisted the apparently inexorable advance of Catholicism, nationalism and tenant rights.[51] Evangelicalism, as always, profited from the frontier and fed off its uncertainties. As the power of landlordism declined in the late nineteenth century and virtually collapsed in the early twentieth century, the frontier shifted to the industrial environs of Belfast and Derry where a vigorous Protestantism once again supplied a sacred canopy. As with the relationship between nationalist politicians and the Catholic Church, no subsequent leader of Unionism could afford to ignore the staunch Protestantism of the rank and file and hope to get away with it. In a period of extraordinarily rapid social

[50] Ibid., p. 115.
[51] Hempton and Hill, *Evangelical Protestantism*, pp. 81–102.

and political change evangelical religion was one of the central forces shaping the Ulster Protestant identity. The cumulative effects of the French Revolution, the Rebellion of the United Irishmen, the rise of popular Catholic nationalism, the growing impartiality of British governments in their relations with Irish religious denominations and the deadly toxin of religious sectarianism enhanced the influence of evangelicalism within the Ulster Protestant community. By the last quarter of the nineteenth century, evangelical religion had fundamentally shaped the outlook of that community and supplied a convenient religious explanation for its inherent sense of superiority. Economic progress, moral regeneration, a conservative social code and loyalty to the monarchy were all regarded as distinctive characteristics of Protestant Ulster. The problem was that Protestant Ulster had a Catholic majority in five of its nine counties and had a large and potentially disaffected Catholic minority in its chief city. Moreover, Ulster Protestants were increasingly regarded by both the British people and Irish nationalists as a peculiar and unpredictable tribe. The seeds of rebellious Loyalism, as our own generation has sadly discovered, were planted in disturbingly fertile soil in a narrow ground.[52]

[52]  See A. T. Q. Stewart, *The Narrow Ground: The Roots of Conflict in Ulster*, 2nd edn (London, 1989); idem, *The Ulster Crisis: Resistance to Home Rule, 1912–14* (London, 1967).

CHAPTER 6

# Religion and political culture in urban Britain

To understand the nature of Victorian civilization it is necessary to understand Victorian cities – visually, through their forms and formlessness; socially, through their structures and the chronology of their processes of change, planned and unplanned; symbolically, in literature and the arts, through their features and images; together for the light they throw on the process of urbanization; separately and comparatively in order to understand particularity and the sense of place. The world of Victorian cities was fragmented, intricate, eclectic and messy.[1]

A city's religion accents and is accented by the interaction of its topography, its economy, its culture and its politics.[2]

Such pleas for a variegated and conceptually flexible approach to the world of nineteenth-century cities are as relevant now as when they were first penned and need to be applied to religion in the city as much as to any other aspect of urban life. Indeed the sheer eclecticism of religious life in modern cities seems to defy analytical categories and broad generalisations. No sooner has one set of views established an ascendancy than they are challenged by fresh work based on different methodological frameworks and focusing often on different kinds of city. The nineteenth-century city seems to set up the kinds of problems for historians that post-modernists have identified for the entire historical enterprise. But, in the spirit of the introductory quotation from Asa Briggs, my limited ambition in this chapter is to open up a number of different ways of looking at religion and identity in nine-teenth-century British cities.

---

[1]  A. Briggs, 'The Human Aggregate', in H. J. Dyos and M. Wolff (eds.), *The Victorian City: Images and Realities*, vol. 1, (London, 1973), p. 83.
[2]  C. Binfield, '"A Crucible of Modest Though Concentrated Experiment": Religion in Sheffield c. 1840–1950', in H. McLeod (ed.), *European Religion in the Age of Great Cities* (London, 1995), p. 191.

## FACTS AND FIGURES

The year in which Charles Dickens opened his novel *Hard Times* (1854) with the words 'now what I want is Facts ... nothing but Facts', Victorians were obligingly given a feast of statistics with the publication of Horace Mann's report on the census of public worship carried out three years before. No document could more graphically highlight those characteristic Victorian preoccupations with fact-gathering, urban growth and religion. Among the myriads of facts processed by contemporaries, and by ecclesiastical historians since then, two stand out with particular clarity. The first is that more than five and a quarter million people had chosen to stay away from public worship on census Sunday and it was alleged that most non-attenders were to be found among the working classes in Britain's most populous cities. A second (and from a modern perspective more striking) fact was the sheer scale of voluntary religious activity designed to convert the heathen at home and abroad. Besides the ongoing work of churches, chapels and mission halls, over thirty million pieces of cheap religious literature were distributed by an army of domestic missionaries, and enormous sums of money were raised for church extension, clerical support and charity. Victorian Britain, it seemed, was remarkably religious and disturbingly irreligious at the same time.[3]

The facts presented in the census report, whatever may have been the methodological weaknesses and administrative frailties in the gathering of them, have served as a basis for investigating nineteenth-century urban religion for more than a century. Indeed, statistical surveys of religious practice, as distinct from investigations of attitudes, beliefs, rituals and behaviour, have still not lost their allure for sociologists and historians and it is worth pausing for a moment to summarise the results of such enquiries.[4] Generally speaking 'the larger the town, the faster its growth rate and the more industrial its

---

[3]    O. Chadwick, *The Victorian Church*, part one (London, 1966), pp. 1–6.
[4]    The most useful statistical surveys and social geographies of religion in urban and industrial Britain include: R. Currie, A. Gilbert and L. Horsley, *Churches and Churchgoers: Patterns of Church Growth in the British Isles since 1700* (Oxford, 1977); B. I. Coleman, *The Church of England in the Mid-Nineteenth Century* (London, 1980); J. D. Gay, *The Geography of Religion in England* (London, 1971); H. McLeod, 'Class, Community and Region: The Religious Geography of Nineteenth-Century England', in M. Hill (ed.), *Sociological Yearbook of Religion in Britain*, 6 (1973); idem, *Religion and Irreligion in Victorian England* (Bangor, Gwynedd, 1993), pp. 57–9; R. Gill, *Competing Convictions* (London, 1989); idem, 'Secularization and the Census Data', in S. Bruce (ed.), *Religion and Modernization: Sociologists and Historians Debate the Secularization Thesis* (Oxford, 1992), pp. 90–117; and idem, *The Myth of the Empty Church* (London, 1993).

character, the lower its level of religious practice – and particularly Anglican practice – was likely to be'.[5] Attendances were lowest of all in London, south Lancashire and west Yorkshire, and in the great provincial capitals of England's industrial expansion. Conversely, Anglican attendances held up well in southern agricultural counties and in towns with less than 25,000 inhabitants while Nonconformity scored spectacular successes in Wales, Cornwall and Lincolnshire, and in the smaller industrial communities of the west midlands, the Potteries and the north-east. Aside from the well-known national patterns a plethora of local studies have shown up considerable variations within regions, counties and even census registration districts. It has become clear that patterns of religious practice must be closely related to the diverse economic, occupational and denominational characteristics of specific regions. Local studies have shown, for example, how religious practice could vary enormously within a small cluster of industrial villages in a single county or even how the fortunes of two churches of the same denomination in the same town could fluctuate dramatically in the course of half a century.[6] The social geography of nineteenth-century religion cannot then be traced without an acute awareness of wider social and economic changes, but neither ought it to be drawn without an appreciation of those who forged new religious cultures, often in the most unlikely of places. Consequently the relationship between personal motivation and underlying economic structures in the religious life of Victorian Britain is deserving of the most sensitive treatment.

The religious census is chiefly useful as a means of comparing the relative strength of religious denominations in early Victorian England and Wales, and as such came as a disappointment to the Church of England which accounted for only half of the worshipping population. But it showed too that all denominations found it hard to sustain high levels of attendance in the larger cities, a problem which became more pronounced as the pace of urban growth remained unpredictable throughout the century. According to recent estimates the urban population increased almost tenfold between 1801 and 1911 and the percentage of the population living in cities of over 100,000 people increased from 11 per cent in 1801 to 43.6 per cent in 1901. Urban growth was most rapid in the 1820s and 1830s when a predominantly

[5]  Coleman, *The Church of England*, pp. 26–37.
[6]  G. Robson, 'Between Town and Countryside: Contrasting Patterns of Churchgoing in the Early Victorian Black Country', *Studies in Church History*, 16 (1979), 401–14.

youthful migration from the countryside reached its peak before going into decline in the second half of the nineteenth century.[7] Cities also had a significantly larger share of people in their twenties and thirties than the countryside. The real test for churches and voluntary religious organisations in the first half of the nineteenth century, therefore, was how well they could adapt to the realities of urban living and, more particularly, how much support they could attract from a predominantly youthful and mobile working class. There is need for care here, because urban and rural Britain were not as separate as is conventionally assumed. Not only was the demographic growth of Victorian cities sustained by substantial migration from the surrounding countryside (and Ireland), but most urban populations contained a circulating medium of domestic servants and casual labourers who sometimes returned to the countryside in later life. Unsurprisingly then, most towns reflected the religious characteristics of their surrounding regions, and there were more links between urban and rural churches and chapels, albeit not altogether harmonious, than was once thought.[8]

In coping with urban expansion churches not only faced financial and logistical problems in supplying enough clergy, buildings and facilities but also had to consider how older forms of religious organisation could be made to work in a new environment. The former required energy, which the Victorians did not lack, but the latter demanded a flexibility of mind and imagination which were not always equally forthcoming. Mr Rigby's opinion in Disraeli's *Coningsby* that 'want of religious faith was solely occasioned by want of churches' is meant to be comically ironical; but churches nonetheless needed suitable buildings close to the centres of population as a prerequisite for more meaningful expressions of institutional loyalty.[9] By 1820, for example, the Church of England in cities such as Birmingham, Sheffield, Leeds, Nottingham and Bradford was still relying on ancient parish boundaries and church buildings long after the first dramatic phase of urban growth had taken place. The Established Church, as a recent study of Bradford has shown, was at its most vulnerable in the fastest growing towns and cities in the fastest growing decades of the nineteenth

[7]   J. G. Williamson, *Coping with City Growth in the British Industrial Revolution* (Cambridge, 1990).
[8]   D. M. Thompson, 'Church Extension in Town and Countryside in Later Nineteenth-Century Leicestershire', *Studies in Church History*, 16 (1979), 427–40, and C. G. Brown, 'The Mechanism of Religious Growth in Urban Societies: British Cities since the Eighteenth Century', in H. McLeod (ed.), *European Religion in the Age of Great Cities* (London, 1995), pp. 239–62.
[9]   B. Disraeli, *Coningsby* (London, 1844), bk 3, ch. 2.

century, especially in those parts of the country where Nonconformity had already undermined Anglican strength in the surrounding countryside.[10] Bradford's growth rate in the 1820s and 30s was between 5 and 6 per cent per annum, which was not only double the average for British cities in the nineteenth century, but is even faster than the remarkable growth rates of third world cities in the 1960s and 70s. On the day of the religious census in 1851 less than 5 per cent of Bradford's population showed up for Anglican morning service and Nonconformist attenders outnumbered Anglicans by a ratio of three to one. Not only did Nonconformist chapel-building reach its peak in the two decades it was most needed, but the Anglican population was not availing itself of the sittings already in place. According to Theodore Koditschek, 72 per cent of Bradford's population did not attend church on census Sunday and he thinks it unlikely that more than 20 per cent of the working-class population attended any service. Koditschek's conclusions match those of other predominantly left-wing historians who have generally concentrated their work on Britain's fastest growing and most capitalistic cities.[11] These historians have not found it difficult to find evidence to support the conclusion that the vast number of early industrial workers in rapidly growing towns 'did not avoid church or chapel because there was no room for them, but because the religious culture of the mainstream denominations was alien to their experiences and needs'.[12] Moreover, non-attenders were not necessarily irreligious, they simply avoided the kind of religious institutions that were on offer to them, with the notable exception of the well-attended Sunday schools.

Ground lost by the churches in the urban demographic expansion of the early industrial revolution was not easily recovered, despite the remarkable Victorian contribution to church-building and restoration which Samuel Butler regarded as the most characteristic feature of the Victorian era.[13] Even this monumental achievement has received a recent dose of cold water in the shape of the longitudinal measurements of church accommodation and attendances in the second half of the nineteenth century carried out by Robin Gill. In a study of London,

[10] T. Koditschek, *Class Formation and Urban Industrial Society: Bradford, 1750–1850* (Cambridge, 1990), pp.252–92.
[11] See, for example, J. Foster, *Class Struggle and the Industrial Revolution: Early Industrial Capitalism in Three English Towns* (London, 1974), and the vigorous counter-attack by M. Smith, *Religion in Industrial Society: Oldham and Saddleworth 1740–1865* (Oxford, 1994).
[12] Koditschek, *Class Formation*, pp. 277–8.
[13] S. Butler, *The Way of All Flesh* (London, 1903), ch. 14.

Liverpool and eleven other major towns he concludes that both Nonconformist and Anglican church-building was too successful for its own good, especially in the last two decades of the century. Over capacity and emptier services carried their own secularising dynamic in the shape of crippling debts and the emotional turn-off of half-empty buildings. Furthermore, he suggests that the combination of free-market Nonconformist, and subsidised Anglican, church-building was disastrous for the proper regulation of supply and demand.[14] Simply having the right facilities for the right people at the right time was therefore a formidable task for nineteenth-century churchmen of all persuasions; but, as they soon came to understand, buildings alone did not create religious cultures, they merely serviced them.

## CLASS AND CULTURE

The more difficult task of forging a closer relationship with working-class communities was a much discussed topic in the nineteenth century, but few had any profound understanding of the issues at stake, much less the capacity to make the kind of changes which would have made any difference. From Mann's report on the census to conferences on working-class attitudes to religion, and from working-men's diaries and autobiographies to the comments of foreign observers, the same reasons for the non-participation of the poor in official religion appear again and again. Pew-rents, poor preaching, dull services, lack of suitable clothes, fatigue, poverty, inequality, illiteracy and the superior appeal of counter-attractions all find a place and should not be lightly dismissed. A study of pew-renting in Glasgow, for example, has shown how increased rents and higher-paid clergy went hand in hand with disapproval of an unhygienic and uncultivated working class.[15] Pew-renting was part of the *business* of church management, but it was also a device 'for creating and sustaining social exclusivity'.[16] Remarkably, the much admired Thomas Chalmers, whose parochial management schemes were so influential among nineteenth-century churchmen, presided over the church with the highest pew-rents of the ten Church

[14] Gill, 'Secularization and Census Data', pp. 90–117.
[15] C. G. Brown, 'The Costs of Pew-Renting: Church Management, Church-Going and Social Class in Nineteenth-Century Glasgow', *Journal of Ecclesiastical History*, 38 (1987), 347–61; P. Hillis, 'Presbyterianism and Social Class in Mid-Nineteenth-Century Glasgow: a Study of Nine Churches', *Journal of Ecclesiastical History*, 32 (1981), 47–64.
[16] Brown, 'The Costs of Pew-Renting', p. 361; and idem, *The Social History of Religion in Scotland since 1730* (London, 1987), pp. 101–2.

of Scotland congregations in Glasgow. Evangelical paternalism was by no means as sacrificially populist as its exponents sometimes claimed.

Next to pew-rents the most common cause of working-class complaints about church services was dull and irrelevant preaching. 'What could our young heads or hearts make of the mysteries and creeds of the pulpit', wrote Samuel Bamford, 'they were strange certainly; wonderfully incomprehensible were these matters the preachers tried to impress on us.'[17] To concentrate on specific working-class criticisms of organised religion, important though they may be, is, however, to miss the fundamental point that there was a gap, in part cultural and in part social class, between the 'respectable' religiosity of regular church-goers and those whose religion was expressed outside the confines of official denominations.[18] Separated by urban geography, cultural values, social status, wealth and, at times, feelings of resentment, the unskilled or destitute urban working classes in particular were not attracted by forms of religion that seemed to exacerbate, not diminish, such distinctions.[19] The very ethos of much Victorian and Edwardian Christianity, with its emphasis on sabbatarianism, temperance and self-help Liberalism, undoubtedly appealed to an upwardly mobile minority of the working classes but it almost certainly alienated as many as it attracted. Similarly, the weekly and annual rhythms of working-class life came to diverge more sharply from those sustained by religious institutions as churches steadily lost control over leisure. Public houses and emerging popular sports, especially football, were formidable competitors for the weekly attention of male urban labourers, whatever advantages the churches continued to enjoy through their festivals, rites of passage and influence over women and children.[20]

There were, of course, energetic and imaginative attempts to bridge this cultural chasm by all kinds of religious traditions, including Anglo-Catholicism, Christian Socialism and the Salvation Army. The Salvationists in particular (along with other undenominational missions) made striking gains in English cities in the last quarter of the nineteenth century. With citadels not unlike music halls, the Army made contact

[17] S. Bamford, *Passages in the Life of a Radical* (Oxford, 1984).

[18] J. Kent, 'The Role of Religion in the Cultural Structure of the Later Victorian City', *Transactions of the Royal Historical Society*, 5th ser., 23 (1973); idem, 'Feelings and Festivals: An Essay in Nineteenth-Century Working-Class Religion', in H. J. Dyos and M. Wolff (eds.), *The Victorian City*, vol. II (London, 1973), pp. 855–72.

[19] H. McLeod, *Class and Religion in the Late Victorian City* (London, 1974); idem, *Religion and the Working Class in Nineteenth-Century Britain* (London, 1984).

[20] B. Harrison, 'Religion and Recreation in Victorian England', *Past & Present*, no. 38 (1967), 98–125.

with working-class culture through its vernacular music, wide-ranging social concern and straightforward message. But despite its compelling mixture of energy and sentiment, entertainment and military discipline, the Salvation Army's war was not just against sin but against aspects of working-class life it defined as sin.[21] Ultimately it was as culturally dissociated from labouring life as the churches it replaced. Essentially the main difficulty facing official religion in the nineteenth century was that the 'respectability' of churches came across more as a cultural badge of middle-class values of success and sobriety than as an attractive picture of religion as a means and a way to a better life on earth as in heaven.

It would nevertheless be a mistake to conclude that urbanisation and industrialisation effectively excluded Christianity from an entire social group, for there is now overwhelming evidence to the contrary. Churches made most impact on the labouring classes when they either provided facilities of agreed social utility, or they enjoyed the kind of relationship in which religion helped express a particular culture rather than wage war against it. An example of the former is education, over which the churches, despite being in competition with one another, enjoyed a virtual monopoly until the State began to assume responsibility at the end of the century. Apart from the myriad of elementary schools in which the Church of England, with State support, enjoyed a preponderance, the most striking contribution made by the churches to the education of the people came through Sunday schools. Laqueur has estimated that by 1851 over two million pupils, representing 75 per cent of working-class children between the ages of five and ten, were enrolled in Sunday schools.[22] While not a monopoly of any one region, religious denomination or social class, Sunday schools were particularly important in northern cities where they frequently replaced church or chapel as the focus of working-class religious life. As they were cheap, and did not affect children's earning power during the week, they were well patronised by those in search of basic literacy and who either valued or tolerated the religious content of the teaching. Debate still rages about whether Sunday schools were predominantly instruments of social control, and taught by social superiors, or whether they were largely run, financed

---

21  J. Kent, *Holding the Fort* (London, 1978); G. Horridge, 'The Salvation Army in England 1855–1900', PhD dissertation, University of London, 1989.

22  T. W. Laqueur, *Religion and Respectability: Sunday Schools and Working-Class Culture, 1780–1850* (New Haven, 1976).

and taught by the workers themselves.[23] The evidence is inconclusive because examples of both are common, but what one can say with confidence is that since the Sunday school 'was the only religious institution which the nineteenth-century public in the mass had any intention of using', control was a prize worth fighting for.[24] The subsequent battles reflected many of the tensions in nineteenth-century English society including class conflict, anticlericalism, anti-centralisation and sectarianism. But Sunday schools not only occasioned disputes, they also made a distinctive contribution to working-class culture through their anniversary celebrations, street parades, Whitsun outings, book prizes and benefit societies. Moreover, these activities attracted a loyal band of activists whose lives were transformed by the weekly rhythms of preparation, prayer and planning. What Sunday schools did not do, however, was solve the recruitment problems of churches and chapels in working-class communities, for only a small minority of Sunday scholars ever graduated into committed church membership.

If holding the keys to elementary education gave the churches a limited and transitory hold on working-class children and their teachers, holding the keys to heaven and hell opened up more dramatic possibilities. Revivalism, for example, which had flourished in Methodist environs in the late eighteenth and early nineteenth centuries, especially in cohesive mining communities and among rural migrants to the manufacturing towns, offered enticingly quick rewards to the more enthusiastic Victorian Nonconformists. (Anglicans, incidentally, were never much impressed.) Apart from Cornwall, Wales, Ulster and parts of Scotland, old style community revivalism gave way to new measures in the course of the nineteenth century. Revivals moved from outdoors to indoors, were often led by the Americans Finney, Caughey and Moody, and were made more palatable to respectable church-goers. They were advertised, planned and orchestrated for maximum emotional appeal, but their long-term impact on the religion of the poor was limited. They did more to persuade church members that they were indeed urgent in reclaiming the lost than they did to persuade the lost to embrace church membership.[25] There was nevertheless a considerable sub-culture of working-class evangelists, both

[23] M. Dick, 'The Myth of the Working-Class Sunday School', *History of Education*, 9 (1980), 27–41.
[24] W. R. Ward, *Religion and Society in England 1790–1850* (London, 1972), pp. 12–16.
[25] Kent, *Holding the Fort*; R. Carwardine, *Trans-Atlantic Revivalism: Popular Evangelicalism in Britain and America, 1790–1865* (Westport, Conn., 1978).

men and women, who laboured with remarkable diligence, and not a little wit and imagination, to reclaim their fellow workers for the kingdom of heaven.

While control of education along with the apparently inexhaustible evangelism and domestic visitation of Victorian churches and voluntary agencies gave organised religion a foothold in working-class communities,[26] longer-term patterns of working-class religiosity were based on a symbiotic relationship between religious identity and other kinds of allegiance. The Roman Catholic revival in nineteenth-century Britain, for example, at first paralleled the expansion of English Nonconformity, but from 1830 the Roman Church in England acquired a new character under the influence of ultramontanism from the continent and mass immigration from Ireland. By 1860 there were some three quarters of a million Irish-born inhabitants living predominantly in the industrial towns of Lancashire, western Scotland, the north-east of England and London. Most were at least nominally Catholic, but it was a Catholicism 'rooted in an ancient Gaelic speaking tradition of native Irish spirituality and in a pre-Tridentine popular peasant culture of the home and the pilgrimage, rather than in Mass-going in a new shrine church'.[27] The ethos and atmosphere of this humble Irish culture of 'belligerent fidelity' has been vigorously brought to life by Gilley and Samuel. Separated by their nationality, religion and poverty, the Irish initially clustered together in tight slums in which survived a patriotic religiosity 'which was heartily popular because it was heartily vulgar'.[28] Primitive violence and drunkenness were rarely far from the surface in such communities, but there existed also warmth and generosity, humour and faith. There was, moreover, a gregarious familiarity between some priests and people, in marked contrast to the stiffer relationship – made so by respectability and clerical professionalism – between clergy and laity in most Protestant denominations. Equally important in cementing community solidarity were the valuable welfare and educational facilities offered by the Catholic Church and its lay organisations. Despite these advantages,

[26]  D. M. Lewis, *Lighten their Darkness: The Evangelical Mission to Working-Class London, 1828–1860* (Westport, Conn., 1986).

[27]  R. Swift and S. Gilley (eds.), *The Irish in the Victorian City* (London, 1985), p. 10.

[28]  S. Gilley, 'Vulgar Piety and the Brompton Oratory, 1850–1860', in Swift and Gilley, *The Irish*, p. 263; idem, 'Catholic Faith of the Irish Slums', in Dyos and Wolff (eds.), *The Victorian City*, vol. II, pp. 837–54; and idem, 'Irish Catholicism in Britain', in D. A. Kerr (ed.), *Comparative Studies on Governments and Non-Dominant Ethnic Groups in Europe, 1850–1940*, vol. 2, *Religion, State and Ethnic Groups* (Dartmouth, 1993), pp. 229–59.

however, and despite the emotional power of the close relationship between Celtic nationalism and Catholicism, only a minority of Irish migrants conformed to the prescribed devotions of official Catholicism. Not only did many come from parts of rural Ireland where mass-going was a minority pursuit, but the Irish settlements in England were occupationally transient and relatively starved of ecclesiastical resources until later in the century when more stable conditions prevailed. The Catholic Irish were nevertheless better church attenders than their English working-class counterparts, for as McLeod's study of late Victorian London has shown, Roman Catholicism was the only form of religion that integrated its adherents into a working-class environment instead of making them stand out from their neighbours.[29] One unpleasant by-product of Irish immigration to British cities, for which the Irish were not entirely responsible, was the outbreak of sectarian violence, especially in Liverpool where Orangeism gained a foothold early in the century. Religious conflict subsequently dominated Liverpool politics from the Great Reform Act until after the First World War, and the Labour Party did not finally capture the Liverpool City Council until 1955. Sectarian conflict may have been bad for working-class unity and Labour politics, but it kept religious issues, if not religious devotion, to the forefront of civic life in Liverpool, Glasgow and Belfast throughout the Victorian period. Ethnicity, then, was the cultural bedrock upon which many of the socially disadvantaged Irish maintained their devotion to Roman Catholicism.

What the preceding examples of popular religion have in common is an element of cultural harmony between working-class communities and the kind of religion which took root in them. This harmony had less to do with dogma or doctrine than with social utility and popular accessibility. The novels of William Hale White are the clearest literary expression of the view that religion, to be of any use to working people, had to have a tangible social function. For those who gathered in the little meeting in Drury Lane 'their trouble was not the forgiveness of sins, the fallacies of Arianism, the personality of the Holy Ghost, or the doctrine of the Eucharist. They all *wanted* something distinctly. They had great gaping needs which they longed to satisfy, intensely practical and special.'[30] Along with social utility, the cultural accessibility of religion to the poor was equally important. Leslie Stephen wrote in 'Religion as a Fine Art' that 'a religion to be of any value must retain a

---

29  McLeod, *Class and Religion*, p. 72.
30  *The Deliverance of Mark Rutherford* (London, 1893), ch. 6.

grasp upon the great mass of mankind and the mass are hopelessly vulgar and prosaic'.[31] Vulgarity was not an easy notion for religious Victorians to embrace, whatever twentieth-century critics might think of their ecclesiastical architecture and ritualistic controversies. J. C. Miller, the Anglican clergyman who tried to stem the tide of secularisation in early Victorian Birmingham, confessed that 'we have a morbid horror of being vulgar'. Instead, as students of the stained glass windows of the period will know, the Victorians preferred to portray religion as a civilising, ennobling and cultivating force in which the values and images of the Anglican public schools were conspicuous. But those within the Church of England with the closest experience of the urban poor, whether evangelical, ritualist, Christian socialist or broad church, recognised that Anglicanism would never make much of an impact on the cities while it was wedded either to a rural vision of how parish life should function or to an old-fashioned paternalistic mentality. Robert Bickersteth, the long-serving evangelical Bishop of Ripon (a see created in 1836 to cope with the manufacturing population of the West Riding of Yorkshire), made frequent appeals for working-class Anglicans to take more responsibility for church extension. Predictably, he found that working men were more eloquent in their criticism of the Church of England's shortcomings than they were desirous of reforming them. Bickersteth nevertheless did much to improve the pastoral efficiency of the Established Church in his diocese in the mid Victorian period, a contribution that was by no means uncommon in the last quarter of the nineteenth century when the number of Anglican communicants increased quite significantly.[32] Unfortunately the role of the Church of England in the industrial north from 1850 to 1900 still awaits proper historical investigation.

The Nonconformists have fared better. Matthew Arnold, stung by the 'Dissidence of Dissent and the Protestantism of the Protestant religion' (the motto of Miall's Nonconformist newspaper), and fearful of the electoral power of the 'uncultured' Nonconformist middle classes, disparagingly summed up Nonconformist culture as 'a life of jealousy of the Establishment, disputes, tea-meetings, openings of chapels, sermons'.[33] But it was also a sturdy and self-reliant culture built on the chapel foundations of pulpit oratory, fervent prayer and

[31]  L. Stephen, *Essays in Free Thinking and Plain Speaking* (London, 1873).
[32]  D. Hempton, 'Bickersteth, Bishop of Ripon: The Episcopate of a Mid-Victorian Evangelical', *Northern History*, 17 (1981), 183–202.
[33]  M. Arnold, *Culture and Anarchy* (London, 1869), pp. 26–31.

well-loved hymns, and schooled for civic service by years of petty exclusion and disciplined organisation. With their star preachers in all the great cities of provincial England, with their formidable grip on the provincial press, and with their literary societies and printed sermons, the Nonconformists loved words and loved pressing them into action for public recognition and for public service.[34] From preachers on trial to congregations 'sitting under the word', Nonconformists, who were never quite at ease with liturgy, chapel architecture or fine art, built their culture on words and built their economic power on trade and family loyalties. Long before they swept into the House of Commons in substantial numbers at the beginning of the twentieth century, this puritanical tribe had stamped its character on many of the towns and not a little of the countryside in Victorian England and Wales.[35] No literary observer captured its essence better than Arnold Bennett in *The Old Wives' Tale* (1908). Carefully nurtured family businesses, infinitely fine social and denominational distinctions, respectable lives of sturdy sobriety, visits to dark mahogany chapels, and life-long commitment to dogged, honourable values, all combined to make the Baineses and the Poveys pillars of provincial society. Even rebellious Sophia, despite running off to metropolitan Paris, managed to live a life of true Nonconformist grit in perhaps the world's least appropriate environment. What Bennett has accomplished in his novels, Binfield, the sharpest historical observer of Dissenting social mores, has accomplished through his delicately etched-in historical miniatures of provincial Nonconformist life.[36] Evangelical Dissenters, he writes, were

a society within a society, It was localized and it was atomized. It was a negation. Its accents were provincial. It was diluted and sidelined as much by its disintegrative polities as by its largely self-chosen exclusion from the norms of national culture. Yet theirs was also a society which transcended society. Its pacesetters were as often British as English and its horizons easily encompassed the Empire and great tracts beyond, for their limits were bounded only

[34] D. Fraser, 'Edward Baines', in P. Hollis (ed.), *Pressure from Without in Early Victorian England* (London, 1974), pp. 183–209.

[35] D. M. Thompson, *Nonconformity in the Nineteenth Century* (London, 1972); I. Sellers, *Nineteenth-Century Nonconformity* (London, 1977); S. Koss, *Nonconformity in Modern British Politics* (London, 1975); and D. W. Bebbington, *The Nonconformist Conscience: Chapel and Politics 1870–1914* (London, 1982).

[36] C. Binfield, *So Down to Prayers: Studies in English Nonconformity 1781–1920* (London, 1987); idem, *Pastors and People: The Biography of a Baptist Church: Queen's Road Coventry* (Gloucester, 1984); idem, '"A Crucible of Modest Though Concentrated Experiment": Religion in Sheffield c. 1840–1950', in H. McLeod (ed.), *European Religion in the Age of Great Cities 1830–1930* (London, 1995), pp. 191–215; and idem, 'Architects in Connexion: Four Methodist Generations', in J. Garnett and C. Matthew (eds.), *Revival and Religion Since 1700* (London, 1993), pp. 153–81.

by eternity. Its exclusion was increasingly more apparent than real and its polities had their own integrative force. Each had its core of professed believers. Each had its hinterland of clients and family, held together by commerce and politics and education. Affection came into it too. What to outsiders was destructive, to Dissenters was dynamic.[37]

From the urbanity of the high Congregationalists and the rationalism of the Unitarians to the volatile disciplines of the Methodists and the fractious disputations of the sectarians, English and Welsh Nonconformists had the capacity to be at once narrow-minded and expansive, intensely local and surprisingly internationalist, stubbornly inflexible and remarkably creative. Theirs was above all a culture based on committed chapel membership and voluntary zeal. Its traditions are prouder than Arnold was able to understand in his high-minded, but remarkably crude, idealisation of culture.

Although the preceding discussion of a selection of Britain's most powerful urban religious cultures tends to support the suggestion that 'a church's power to recruit arises from its proximity to, congruity with, and utility for those whom it recruits',[38] it would be a mistake to reduce urban religion to a crude social, economic and ethnic determinism in which personal motivation had no place. The plethora of studies of individual towns and cities now available for the nineteenth century make it clear that in each city there were intense pockets of religiosity carried there by zealous evangelicals, slum priests, Christian socialist missions, voluntary societies, the Salvation Army, unorthodox sects, Irish and Jewish migrants, and dutiful Anglicans. Even within the mainstream denominations the personality and talent of the clergyman or minister could make a decisive difference to the fortunes of urban congregations. But there is, nevertheless, a distinction between pockets of urban religion, sustained by unusual zeal, but unable to attract more than a committed minority, and the long-term strength of religious cultures which helped express the very heart and centre of community life. The former often depended on regular stimuli from outside, and were therefore vulnerable to allegations of paternalism and social control, whereas the latter was an indigenous and all-embracing religious species. A sense of identity and social utility were therefore

---

[37]  C. Binfield, 'Hebrews Hellenized? English Evangelical Nonconformity and Culture, 1840–1940', in S. Gilley and W. J. Sheils (eds.), *A History of Religion in Britain: Practice and Belief from Pre-Roman Times to the Present* (Oxford, 1994), pp. 322–45.
[38]  Currie, Gilbert and Horsley, *Churches and Churchgoers*, p. 90.

more important long-term factors than zeal alone in sustaining the strength of religious cultures.

### BELIEFS AND EXPERIENCES

The emphasis so far has been on explaining patterns of religious practice and the formation of religious cultures in nineteenth-century Britain, with particular reference to the urban working classes, but that in itself is not very revealing of the beliefs and experiences of ordinary people, especially non-churchgoers. New light has been shed on this dark corner of religious history in the past decade through the admittedly risky use of literary evidence, oral history and the accumulated impressions of a great army of city missioners, scripture readers and domestic visitors. Despite the teeming variety of opinions reflecting different regions, different methods of investigation, different perspectives of social class, and the more obvious differences of age, gender and occupation, there are the beginnings of a rough consensus on the prevailing religious attitudes of the great mass of the urban working classes in nineteenth-century Britain. Perhaps this is the nearest one can come to identifying a genuinely 'popular' religion, forming the social bedrock upon which all religious traditions sought to erect their particular denominational edifices. One way of approaching this landscape is through the insights offered by Victorian Britain's most popular art form, its ubiquitous novels, many of which took the form of popular serials at the time, and have become the most accessible window into Victorian civilisation ever since.[39] Dickens was the most popular of all, and Dickens had strong views about Victorian religion.

First, the perplexing mystery of the place was, who belonged to the eighteen denominations? Because whoever did, the labouring people did not. It was very strange to walk through the streets on a Sunday morning, and note how few of *them* the barbarous jangling of bells that was driving the sick and nervous mad, called away from their own close rooms, from the corners of their own streets, where they lounged listlessly, gazing at all the church and chapel going, as at a thing with which they had no manner of concern.[40]

According to John Ruskin 'Dickens' caricature, though often gross, is never mistaken. Allowing for his manner of telling them, the things he

---

[39]  For a more detailed discussion of Victorian religion and literature see D. Hempton, 'Popular Religion and Irreligion in Victorian Fiction', in T. Dunne (ed.), *The Writer as Witness: Literature as Historical Evidence* (Cork, 1987), pp. 177–96.

[40]  C. Dickens, *Hard Times* (London, 1854), ch. 5.

tells us are always true.'[41] Whatever the value of Dickens's fiction for social historians in general, however, informed critics are highly sceptical of the evidential value of his treatment of religion. His own presuppositions and biases are generally too near the surface. He admired instinctive goodness and a capacity for fancy and fun. He valued tolerance, human solidarity and good-natured charity. Above all he approved of a humanitarian form of religion which connected with the daily concerns of ordinary people. By contrast, he hated hypocrisy, dogma, enthusiasm, ritualism, nostalgic medievalism, Roman Catholicism and mysticism. He particularly disliked the revivalist/ fundamentalist wing of Dissent with its uneducated preachers, grimy chapels and rampant sectarianism. His novels are full of 'little Bethels' and Dissenting preachers with greasy complexions, bulbous eyes, lank hair, squints and physical deformities. In speech they bawl, snivel and mutilate the English language. Even the names are revealing: Melchise-dech Howler, Jabez Fireworks and Mr Glib. So clever was Dickens's language, and this is where literature is at its most pernicious from the historian's viewpoint, that his anti-Dissenting rhetoric, which was itself built on an earlier eighteenth-century dramatic tradition, has been enormously successful in convincing posterity of the hypocrisy and inadequacy of religion in Victorian England. Why then start with Dickens on religion? In the passage on Coketown religion quoted earlier, Dickens identified two issues which have subsequently occasioned much debate among social historians. Firstly, he drew attention to the apparent apathy of the labouring poor towards institutional religion, and, perhaps more importantly, he stressed the inadequacy of contemporary utilitarian and statistical diagnoses of that problem. Secondly, he pointed to the proliferation of sects in urban Britain as one aspect of a much broader lack of cohesion in British society. Victorian novels, sensitively applied, can illuminate both issues.

In *Silas Marner*, for example, George Eliot creatively inverts the conventional pattern of a relatively religious countryside contrasted with irreligious towns which seemed to have been irrefutably demonstrated by the census of religious worship in 1851. What is hinted at through Silas, however, is that the religion of the countryside was a rather pale mixture of deference, dependency, custom and community solidarity, while popular urban religion was based more on voluntary commitment to religious associations. It is only in comparatively recent

---

[41]   J. Ruskin, 'Unto this Last', ed. by P. M. Yarker (London, 1970), pp. 32–3. See also, V. Cunningham, *Everywhere Spoken Against: Dissent in the Victorian Novel* (Oxford, 1975).

times that social historians have begun to scrape away the accumulated grime of the 1851 census and its manifold interpretations to ask more fundamental questions about the processes and consequences of rural migration which lie at the heart of urban religious experience in early industrial Britain.[42] Victorian cities, one needs to be constantly reminded, grew primarily through migration from the surrounding countryside. In that respect, the opening scenes of Mrs Gaskell's *Mary Barton* fire the historical imagination as productively as the serried ranks of Blue Book statistics.

Moreover, the novels of Mrs Gaskell, Charles Kingsley and others suggest that the relative absence of formal religious observances did not necessarily mean a lack of Christian belief and practice in early Victorian cities. *Mary Barton* and *North and South*, in particular, are suffused with religious values in facing death and disaster, in establishing a rudimentary moral code, in neighbourly concern in times of economic hardship and depression, and in developing a sturdy respectability, mostly by women, in family life. How far these were the preoccupations of a Unitarian minister's wife on domestic visitation duty, and how far they accurately reflect the views of the non-dissolute Manchester poor is for the social historian to unravel. But the novels suggest that denominational adherence is not the best guide to the religion and morality of the Victorian working classes. The sheer grind of poverty and disappointment, a concern for tangible objectives rather than after-life speculations, the apparent dowdiness of religious services compared with popular recreations and public houses, and the distrust of fervent religion among male workers because it introduced unnecessary tensions in a culture seeking a convivial consensus, all played their part in limiting the appeal of organised religion. In addition, through admittedly untypical characters like John Barton and Alton Locke, the novelists portray a nascent class consciousness fuelled by dislike of bourgeois Christian morality and hypocrisy. This chimes in with Susan Budd's work on working-class biographies and with E. P. Thompson's view that religion's most serious disadvantage was that it did not offer working men practical solutions to problems of everyday life, with the notable exceptions of Sunday schools and the manifold religious welfare agencies like the St Vincent de Paul societies.[43]

42  Brown, 'Religious Growth in Urban Societies', pp. 245–54. See also, A. M. Urdank, *Religion and Society in a Cotswold Vale: Nailsworth, Gloucestershire, 1780–1865* (Berkeley, 1990).

43  S. Budd, *Varieties of Unbelief* (London, 1977); E. P. Thompson, 'Anthropology and the Discipline of Historical Context', *Midland History*, 1 no. 3 (1972), pp. 41–55.

A second characteristic of Victorian religion identified by Dickens in *Hard Times*, and one that bears particularly heavily on the theme of religion and identity, was the remarkable proliferation of religious denominations. This was not a new phenomenon, but by the time of the religious census in 1851 its urban manifestations had become more obvious. The roots of the problem went back to the period 1780–1830 when a complex set of circumstances and crises resulted in the emergence of a new class society. In England this was accompanied first of all by an explosion of non-denominational renewal and then inexorably by a drive for denominational discipline. By 1830 the old denominational order, which had been solidified by the Act of Toleration, had given way to a new one. This process was facilitated by the weakness of the English State and Established Church. The period 1828–51 was therefore accompanied by bitter sectarian conflicts which in large measure gave the character to the politics of the period. What Disraeli described in *Tancred* as 'an anarchy of creeds' had by 1890 resulted in 244 officially registered denominations, though even that was undoubtedly an under-assessment.[44] Thus, Samuel Wilberforce's comment that 'the tendency of all things round us is to break our people into separate and unsympathising classes' applied also to religion which many had hoped would act as social cement in the class divisions of mid nineteenth-century England.[45]

Early Victorian novelists were therefore writing in a period of social and religious fragmentation and this is consciously and unconsciously reflected in their fiction. Many of the 'condition of England' novels show a desire for social cohesion accompanied by dislike of class-conscious organisations and religious sectarianism. Trade unionism, Chartism and evangelical Dissent are therefore almost universally vilified, even at the expense of factual accuracy.[46] Disraeli's description of Wodgate (Willenhall) in *Sybil*, for example, is based on Blue Books, but he deliberately (and inconsistently) exaggerated the irreligion of Wodgate because the valiant Dissenting contribution did not fit his ideological scheme of a re-awakened Tory paternalism pursuing its holy mission.[47] Similarly, though less dishonestly, Dickens, for artistic

---

[44]    Cunningham, *Everywhere Spoken Against*, pp. 25–47.
[45]    Kent, 'Feelings and Festivals', pp. 855–71.
[46]    G. Carnall, 'Dickens, Mrs Gaskell, and the Preston Strike', *Victorian Studies*, 8 no. 1 (1964), pp. 31–48; P. Brantlinger, 'The Case against Trade Unions in Early Victorian Fiction', *Victorian Studies*, 13 no. 1 (1969), pp. 37–52.
[47]    S. M. Smith, 'Willenhall and Wodgate: Disraeli's Use of Blue Book Evidence', *Review of English Studies*, n. s. 13 (1962), pp. 368–84.

purposes, emphasised the divisiveness of trade unionism in *Hard Times* while writing a more favourable eye-witness account of the Preston strike for his magazine *Household Words*.[48] Dickens's aim in *Hard Times* was to highlight the inhumanity of exclusive and intolerant organisations, however worthwhile their cause, and the same idea is at the root of much fictional criticism of Dissenting religion. 'These cramping cults', wrote H. G. Wells from bitter experience, 'do indeed take an enormous toll of human love and happiness ... they make frightful breaches in human solidarity.'[49] In a period of apparent social fragmentation it is not surprising that the novelists should pinpoint the divisiveness of Dissenting religion as its most serious evil. Victorian fiction emphasises therefore the Calvinism of Dissent (though most nineteenth-century Nonconformists were not Calvinists), its detrimental effect on family cohesion, as in *Alton Locke* and *The New Machiavelli*, and its contribution to the ugliness and disorder of the urban landscape by building 'low-pitched gables up dingy streets' and riding roughshod over ancient parish boundaries. In a society nervous about its culture and stability, Dissenting religion, especially of a crudely populist variety, was castigated for being both vulgar and divisive. Such attacks from the Victorian intelligentsia were in part a self-fulfilling prophecy as the popular Dissenting press railed against the evils of fiction and gloried in their own lack of worldly wisdom. Literature is itself a vibrant historical agent.

Sensitive to the fact that the old ideal of a truly national Established Church ministering to a united people on the basis of ancient territorial units was in terminal decline, Victorian novelists attempted to recover an organic society in which religion would once again act as a cohesive force. For Disraeli this ideal was to be realised through a national church fulfilling its holy mission to the poor accompanied by England's ancient community rituals. Such medieval nostalgia was dismissed by Marx and Engels in the *Communist Manifesto* as being 'always ludicrous in its effect, through total incapacity to comprehend the march of modern history'.[50] For Kingsley the ideal was a marriage of the co-operative spirit of socialism with the moral goodness of Christianity. Inevitably this mixture contained too much Christianity for doctrinaire socialists and too much socialism for Kingsley's Anglican colleagues. It

48  Compare, for example, *Hard Times*, bk II, ch. 4 with 'On Strike' in *Household Words*, 8 (Feb., 1854), pp. 553–9.
49  H. G. Wells, *The New Machiavelli* (London, 1911), bk I, ch. 3.
50  K. Marx and F. Engels, *Manifesto of the Communist Party* (Moscow, 1969), pp. 78–80.

has survived more as a noble ideal for Christians with a social conscience, and for socialists unhappy with 'godless materialism', than it has as a practical proposition for either.

In contrast to Disraeli and Kingsley, Dickens's concern for human solidarity, tolerance, disinterested charity and fun was an attempt to celebrate an older English consensus on the social function of religion. As with Flora Thompson's treatment of religion in a village community in *Lark Rise to Candleford,* Dickens unselfconsciously draws attention to a greater degree of religio-moral homogeneity in British society than is immediately obvious from historians' concentration on the bitter sectarian conflicts of the Victorian period. Dickens's impatience with religious dogma, dislike of religious enthusiasm, contempt for notions of hell (with their implied ethical coercion), along with his emphases on human solidarity, tolerance and mutual responsibilities, helped cement his relationship with his readers. Here was a fusion of religion and national character – the English way if you like – that was based upon an avoidance of metaphysical abstractions and the pursuit of humane values. Interestingly, many of the same preoccupations are evident in the oral evidence relating to the religious experiences of those alive in the late Victorian and Edwardian periods.

Taped interviews with controlled samples of people brought up at the beginning of the twentieth century, for all the obvious limitations of such evidence, have helped etch in the religious attitudes of urban dwellers.[51] Outright scepticism and militant infidelity were rare, and the general level of religious knowledge, if anything, may have improved, not diminished, over the course of the nineteenth century, partly because of a more pervasive national integration of British society and partly because of the indefatigable efforts of city missioners of all persuasions. Non-churchgoers were therefore not generally irreligious nor even hostile to official Christianity. Describing what they were not is, of course, easier than capturing what they were, and the catch-phrases used by contemporary observers and subsequent commentators have not been entirely successful. 'Unconscious secularists', 'habitual neglecters', 'practical atheists', 'believers not belongers', and practitioners of a 'diffusive Christianity' are all insufficiently flexible to describe a complex range of beliefs and

[51]  H. McLeod, 'New Perspectives on Working-Class Religion: The Oral Evidence', *Oral History,* 14 no. 1 (1986), pp. 31–49. See also, C. G. Brown and J. D. Stephenson, ' "Sprouting Wings?" Women and Religion in Scotland c. 1890–c. 1950', in E. Breitenbach and E. Gordon (eds.), *Out of Bounds: Women in Scotland in the Nineteenth and Twentieth Centuries* (Edinburgh, 1992).

experiences that are not easily encapsulated in a single phrase or concept.[52]

The preliminary results of completed oral history projects tentatively suggest that the churchgoing minority of working people may be larger than conventional statistics indicate. In addition, even non-churchgoers sent their children to Sunday school, dressed up on Sundays, used religious affiliations to obtain jobs and welfare relief, sang hymns as a means of cementing community solidarity, respected 'practical Christian' virtues, relied heavily on Christian sexual ethics (not least as a point of departure), derived comfort from religion in times of suffering or disaster, accepted that church and chapel or Protestant and Catholic were fundamental social divisions, and used the churches' social facilities without feeling any need to attend more overtly 'religious' activities.

One important, but often neglected, aspect of popular religion amplified by oral evidence is the emotional resonance achieved by the religious music of hymns and choirs, and the happy memories of church- or chapel-organised seaside treats and social gatherings. Hymns in particular, so central to the Methodist revival in the eighteenth century, became the common currency of nineteenth-century Protestantism, reaching the peak of their influence in the 1850s and 60s when four hundred collections appeared in England alone. 'If there has been a common religion in England in the last hundred years', states Obelkevich, 'it has been based not on doctrine but on the popular hymns.'[53] Characterised by earnestness, self-absorption, sentimentality and images of military might and family bliss, hymns offered both emotional satisfaction and a shared religious language to those who found the theological abstractions of the pulpit too impenetrable. With the formation of the great choral societies, as in Huddersfield in 1836, sacred music was combined with civic pride to express Victorian Protestantism's confidence in its own culture. But ultimately the music of organs and choirs was more the vernacular of the middle and 'respectable' working classes than it was of the unwashed and the unchurched. The emotions generated by hymn-singing were, however, transportable outside church services into the home, the workplace and, on occasions, even the public house.

[52]  J. Cox, *English Churches in a Secular Society: Lambeth 1870–1930* (Oxford, 1982); G. Davie, *Religion in Britain since 1945: Believing without Belonging* (Oxford, 1994).
[53]  J. Obelkevich, 'Music and Religion in the Nineteenth Century', in J. Obelkevich, L. Roper and R. Samuel (eds.), *Disciplines of Faith: Studies in Religion, Politics and Patriarchy* (London, 1987), pp. 550–65.

Oral evidence also highlights a complex range of relationships between religious employers and their work-forces in Victorian Britain. In the great age of family businesses and voluntary initiative, employers used varying degrees of paternalism and coercion in providing religious facilities for their workers, but while deference could bring tangible rewards for obedient employees, it was never absolute nor unconditional. As the sectarian explosion of urban religion illustrates, there were generally alternative congregations available to those workers who were either sufficiently independent or disaffected to search them out. But this should not detract from the convenient harmony of factory, church and political allegiance achieved by many employers in this period, nor from their immense contribution to church-building in the High Victorian era when supply outstripped demand. Never again in British history did liberal capitalism, civic pride and religious duty combine so effectively to give urban culture such a pervasive religious character, especially in its middle-class strongholds.[54]

Above all, what the evidence from literature and taped conversations has shown is that the religious beliefs and experiences of ordinary people were not prescribed by convocation or conference, nor enforced by priests and deacons; they were not codified into a systematic theology nor recited in creeds; they were not consistent from day to day, far less over an entire life-span, nor were they the same for men and women. Generally speaking, ordinary people persistently appropriated from Christianity the view that religion was primarily about doing the best one could and doing no-one else any harm. This ethical and community-based definition of Christian living has a long history in British religion (and, of course, elsewhere) and proved to be equally resistant to Puritan preachers and nineteenth-century evangelicals. Justification by faith, irrespective of the popular attractions of conversionism and making a fresh start, was not a doctrine well understood by English labourers. Their sincere belief that a generally well-intentioned life, lived free of the worst debaucheries, would be rewarded was both more prevalent than open scepticism and more difficult for the churches to counteract. Even hell, the ultimate in doctrinal terrors, lost its grip on the urban poor who seemed more concerned with temporal inequalities than with eternal punishment. But they were not, strictly speaking, irreligious, for even at the heart of working-class London at the turn of the century, religious idioms and

[54]  S. Yeo, *Religion and Voluntary Organisations in Crisis* (London, 1976).

symbols, folk beliefs and a serious devotion to the churches' rites of passage were woven together into a meaningful religious culture. It was no less meaningful for its lack of regular institutional expression, for as one contemporary observer put it, 'Many of the poor rarely attend church, not because they are irreligious but because they have long since received and absorbed the truths by which they live; while the idea that attendance at public worship is a duty does not occur to them and does not seem credible when suggested.'[55]

What is refreshing about some of the recent work is that modern historians of popular religion have at last appropriated some of the lessons learnt by their early modern counterparts in allowing the religion of the poor to speak for itself rather than imposing pre-assigned, and often mutually exclusive, categories of analysis. Among poor Londoners at the end of the nineteenth century, therefore,

A commitment to the Christian efficacy of an orthodox ritual was often inseparable from a web of folk superstition, from the customary expectations of communal society and from an assertion of communal identity. Apparently incompatible narratives of religious belief thus formed one rationale for action in which many dimensions of belief were present. The eclectic character of popular attitudes tends to be overlooked when the actions of participants are interpreted with reference to factors external to the meanings and interpretations which the actors themselves brought to bear upon their practices.[56]

Not only in London, but in great tracts of urban Britain in the nineteenth and early twentieth centuries, there existed, beyond the realms of church attendance figures and clerical expectations, 'a network of association, attachment and identification whereby church-based symbols were incorporated as part of a distinct popular identity and heritage'.[57] Nothing could more clearly demonstrate that religious identity is more than a straightforwardly national or denominational proposition. The inhabitants of the British Isles in the long eighteenth and nineteenth centuries may have had a greater harmony of belief and practice than intricate historical discussions of class and denominational conflict might otherwise suggest.

[55] M. Loane, *The Queen's Poor* (London, 1906), quoted by S. C. Williams, 'Religious Belief and Popular Culture: A Study of the South London Borough of Southwark (c. 1880–1939)', DPhil dissertation, University of Oxford, 1993, p. 5.

[56] S. Williams, 'Urban Popular Religion and the Rites of Passage', in McLeod (ed.), *European Religion* (London, 1995), pp. 216–36.

[57] Williams, 'Religious Belief and Popular Culture', p. 289.

## CHURCH AND SOCIETY

In the churches over the course of the nineteenth century 'the change from zeal to routine, from confident aggression to worried organisational concern' betrayed an institutional introversion that boded ill for the future. They also increasingly surrendered the community ideal of the church in favour of organisations designed for a specific age and gender. This was done with the best of intentions to withstand secularisation, but probably only hastened it. Outside the churches even more dramatic changes were occurring in the early twentieth century. The growing power of the State was chipping away at the educational, charitable and institutional role of the churches at the same time as their declining control over leisure was further eroded by the emergence of national sports and a new entertainment culture. Moreover, the growth of socialism and the Labour movement finally gave political expression to the problem of class separation which had motivated, divided and ultimately weakened the churches during the course of the nineteenth century. But even here religion was far from buried. Early socialist campaigns were conducted with all the idealism, missionary enthusiasm and self-sacrifice of a gospel crusade.[58] In addition, early leaders of the Independent Labour Party in English and Welsh counties, as with Chartists in an earlier period and trade unionism throughout the century, were by no means all committed secularists. Many were from Nonconformist or Roman Catholic backgrounds. Indeed, the kind of Chartism and trade unionism that emerged in many parts of England not only relied on religious personnel and organisational structures, but was also shaped by a distinctive brand of biblical radicalism combining warnings against the rich with a desire for better social relations. Christian imperatives, based upon particular scriptural interpretations of Christ's special love for the oppressed and special hatred of oppressors, led to distinctive forms of religio-political radicalism in nineteenth-century Britain. For a significant, but often neglected, minority of those involved in the familiar radical campaigns for parliamentary reform and factory reform, the relief of poverty, trade unionism and the People's Charter, their radicalism was fired by their Christianity and their Christianity was enlivened and shaped by their radicalism. This symbiosis threw up an array of colourful characters in the industrial environs of Britain.

[58] S. Yeo, 'A New Life: The Religion of Socialism in Britain, 1883–96', *History Workshop Journal*, 4 (1977).

Although they transcended the conventional denominational boundaries, many of them seem to have cut their teeth as lay preachers in the manifold popular Protestant sects before denominational alienation accelerated their commitment to radical causes.[59] Religion, therefore, as much shaped working-class politics as suffered from its growth. Whatever ground was lost by churches in the late nineteenth and early twentieth centuries, therefore, was not primarily due to the fact they were challenged and found wanting by a vigorous Labour movement, nor even because they were threatened by the secularising dynamics of urban life diagnosed by some sociologists, but because of the inexorable diminution of the churches' sphere of public influence through suburbanisation, state welfarism, and the attractiveness and greater accessibility of leisure alternatives.[60] These changes were all facilitated by a rise in living standards which as much as anything led to the ascendancy of material over more directly spiritual values. In addition, the general attractiveness and social utility of the churches in the twentieth century were further eroded by extensions to the electoral franchise which had the effect of undermining their political usefulness. The chapel interest dominated local government elections in south Wales, for example, right down to the moment when the Attlee government turned over local government elections from a general property franchise to the general electoral register. At that point the chapel interest was ditched virtually overnight by the trade unions.

In retrospect what is remarkable about religion in urban Britain in the nineteenth century is the extent to which a predominantly evangelical pietism managed to spread its values and preoccupations far beyond the doors of the churches it controlled.[61] Its power lay not so much in its theology or dogma as in its energy and its ability to mobilise the middle-class laity – men, women and children – in an unremitting war against urban vice and irreligion. Women, in particular, were used both as collecting boxes in the countless local auxiliaries of the popular evangelical societies, and appealed to as national custodians of the evangelical virtues of temperance, charity and pious family life.[62] Evangelical energy was also at the root of many of the great 'anti'

[59] D. Hempton, *Methodism and Politics in British Society 1750–1850* (London, 1984), pp. 208–16.
[60] C. G. Brown, 'Did Urbanization Secularize Britain?', *Urban History Yearbook* (1988).
[61] D. W. Bebbington, *Evangelicalism in Modern Britain: A History from the 1730s to the 1980s* (London, 1989).
[62] F. K. Prochaska, *Women and Philanthropy in Nineteenth-Century England* (Oxford, 1980).

movements of the century, from slavery to alcohol, whose values formed the backbone of the Nonconformist Conscience and Free Church Liberalism in English cities. But evangelicalism was only the noisiest element in a revival of many religious traditions in Victorian Britain, the most notable of which was the recovery of Roman Catholic fortunes with the unlikely help of the pauper Irish. In addition, the Established Church, eclectic as ever, was administratively reformed and then spiritually enlivened by both evangelicals and High Churchmen. What gave Victorian Britain its religious temper by comparison with some other western European states was the sheer strength of its middle-class religiosity together with a much greater acceptance of religious values among the working classes than social historians, in the main, have been prepared to acknowledge. Thus, industrialisation and urbanisation, far from being the nemesis of British religion, possibly stimulated greater religiosity in the short term while eroding its popularity in the long term. In the light of these suggestions secularisation theory is not only in need of fresh analysis, but also requires a considerably revised time scale. Religious identities were not foreclosed by the growth of cities in the nineteenth century, they simply became more eclectic and more intricate.

CHAPTER 7

# *Religion and identity in the British Isles: integration and separation*

Thus far our analysis has consisted of a religious tour of the British Isles in the modern period with a number of stopping off points on the way. These have included the investigation of elite and popular Anglicanism at the peak of the Church of England's influence in the long eighteenth century; the spectacular rise of evangelical Nonconformity, particularly Methodism, in the period of the French and industrial revolutions, which increased religious pluralism, but also contributed to the relatively ordered transitions of British society in the nineteenth century; the rise of evangelical Nonconformity in Wales and its relationship to Welsh identity and Liberal politics; the attempts to realise the old sixteenth-century ideal of the godly commonwealth in Scotland and the unwillingness of the British State to fund this ideal; the rise of the Irish Catholic nation as the most conspicuously successful fusion of faith and identity anywhere in the British Isles; the role of religion in creating an Ulster Protestant world-view in opposition to a vigorous Catholic nationalism which has led to one of the most intractable problems of the modern world; and the growth of religious pluralism in urban Britain, and its consequences for national homogeneity, social class and popular belief and practice. Above all, the aim has been an attempt to bring to life the cultural power of living religious traditions and to explore the ways in which religion has interacted with other frameworks within which people in Britain and Ireland sought to express meaning and identity. What has been done so far has been relatively straightforward. What is more difficult to accomplish is to offer satisfactory organising principles for this material with sufficient flexibility to help explain over two centuries of turbulent religious history in the British Isles.

At the start of this project the intention had been to devote a chapter to factors promoting national integration on the one hand and factors promoting separation on the other as a tidy way of concluding the

143

subject; but over time it became increasingly obvious to me that many of the most important forces shaping modern religious history could be regarded as operating in both of these directions simultaneously. The precise direction they took often depended on quite specific social and political contexts, and they are therefore unamenable to the universal application of grand theories. An alternative strategy, albeit with some limitations of its own, is to highlight four of the major themes impinging directly on the relationship between faith and identity, before concluding with a range of conceptual models that offer some promising analytical possibilities. These themes have been chosen not only for their centrality to the past, but also for their importance in a lively new debate about the nature of national identity in modern Britain. They are Protestantism and anti-Catholicism, evangelicalism, imperialism and the relationship between religion and the construction of social policy.

## PROTESTANTISM AND ANTI-CATHOLICISM

British anti-Catholicism, though it had obvious points of similarity with European expressions of ideological objection to Catholic beliefs and practices, was quite unique. It was peculiarly related to popularly subscribed precepts about the ends and nature of the British state; it was chauvinistic and almost general.[1]

Edward Norman's comments on the nature of nineteenth-century English anti-Catholicism are entirely consistent with the conclusions of early modern scholars thereby showing the continuity of this feature of post-Reformation English society. It has been shown, for example, that Elizabethan and Jacobean Englishmen expressed their anxiety, apocalyptic ideology and national identity by opposing a sinister and monolithic Catholic Church.[2] Protestantism was English; it preserved freedom; it was morally pure; and it was providentially on the right side in the great cosmic battle between good and evil, between Christ and Antichrist. Roman Catholicism, on the other hand, was foreign, violent, morally corrupt, doctrinally erroneous, magical, devious, and was led by a standing army of Popes, Jesuits and priests. In the sixteenth century this powerful ideology manifested itself in a mixture

---

[1]  E. R. Norman, *Anti-Catholicism in Victorian England* (London, 1968), p. 20.
[2]  C. Z. Wiener, 'The Beleaguered Isle: a Study of Elizabethan and Early Jacobean Anti-Catholicism', *Past & Present*, no. 51 (1971), 27–62; P. Lake, 'Anti-Popery: the Structure of a Prejudice', in R. Cust and A. Hughes (eds.), *Conflict in Early Stuart England* (London, 1989), pp. 72–106.

of anxiety and creative energy and operated as a guiding star in Englishmen's view of themselves in their relations with the rest of Europe. In the seventeenth century anti-Catholicism played an important part in the destabilising of the English State in the 1640s and supplied the ideological justification for the constitutional innovations of the 1680s, from the exclusion crisis to the Glorious Revolution.[3] Thus, depending on circumstances, anti-Catholicism could serve both conservative and revolutionary ends. It is probably the most ubiquitous, most eclectic and most adaptable ideology in the post-Reformation history of the British Isles.

Until recently it was widely assumed that this powerful anti-Catholic tradition took a back seat in the more enlightened climate of the eighteenth century before re-appearing in the characteristic sectarian conflicts of the Victorian period. The Gordon Riots of 1780 are an acknowledged exception, but by concentrating on the metropolitan epicentre of the riots and by discovering elements of class hostility in them it was possible to suggest that they were not attributable to a bedrock of anti-Catholicism anything like as powerful as that which existed in the previous century.[4] More recent work on the popular world-view of eighteenth-century Englishmen, from a wide range of different sources and perspectives, has nevertheless drawn attention to a strong continuity of anti-Catholicism from the seventeenth century. Not only were there more widespread no popery disturbances in the English provinces in 1745 and 1780 than was previously thought, but anti-Catholicism remained a strong element in the traditional beliefs and moral economy of the English lower orders throughout the period.[5] It is remarkable, for example, how often early Methodism was attacked for its alleged popish beliefs and practices.[6] Thus, fear of religious novelty, chauvinistic notions of liberty, anti-French feeling and vivid ritualistic celebrations of England's Protestant past all contributed to a profound distrust of Roman Catholicism. This mental

---

[3]   J. Miller, *Popery and Politics in England, 1660–1688* (Cambridge, 1973); J. P. Kenyon, *The Popish Plot* (London, 1972).

[4]   G. Rudé, 'The Gordon Riots: a Study of the Rioters and their Victims', *Transactions of the Royal Historical Society*, 5th ser., 6 (1956).

[5]   C. Haydon, *Anti-Catholicism in Eighteenth-Century England: A Political and Social Study* (Manchester, 1993); J. Black, 'The Catholic Threat and the British Press in the 1720s and 1730s', *Journal of Religious History*, 12 (1983), 364–81.

[6]   F. Baker, 'Methodism and the '45 Rebellion', *The London Quarterly and Holborn Review* (October, 1947), 325–33; J. Walsh, 'Methodism and the Mob in the Eighteenth Century', *Studies in Church History*, 8 (1972), 213–27; and D. Hempton, 'Methodism and the Law, 1740–1820', *Bulletin of the John Rylands Library*, 70 no. 3 (1988), 93–107.

framework was rarely channelled into active hostility against Roman Catholic neighbours unless fuelled by wider dynastic or political crises. What is different about the anti-Catholicism of the later eighteenth century, however, is that among social elites, including those responsible for government, it was increasingly recognised that the English Catholic community was a relatively harmless minority worthy of a greater degree of religious toleration. This difference in perception between social superiors and the bulk of the British population, as much as anything, accounts for the events leading up to the Gordon Riots, and a similar pattern continued into the nineteenth century when the Catholic Emancipation Act was passed against the wishes of the great majority of the British people.[7]

A vigorous anti-Catholic Protestantism, suggests Linda Colley, was the most important shared element in the forging of British national identity in the eighteenth century.[8] It was built on a selective and commemorative historical tradition of providential deliverances and was disseminated through pulpits and popular print in all parts of Britain. English, Scottish, Welsh and Irish almanacs were virulently anti-Catholic and remorselessly chauvinistic. The same was true of Britain's most widely circulating works of popular piety, Foxe's *Book of Martyrs* and Bunyan's *Pilgrim's Progress*. It was no accident, then, that the first collaborative campaign between English and Scottish artisans was organised around the Gordon Riots and that the 'first genuinely nation-wide petitioning campaign that involved Welshmen and women on a massive scale was that organised against Catholic Emancipation in 1829'. Similarly, it was no accident that the issue that exposed the fragile liberalism of northern Irish Presbyterians in the 1790s was how far Roman Catholics could be trusted with the exercise of political power. Protestantism in Britain in the eighteenth century, as with Ulster in the twentieth, was more significant than mere belief and churchgoing, it was in effect a major organising principle within which other spheres of life were duly processed. Insofar as eighteenth-century Britons regarded themselves as peculiarly free and peculiarly prosperous, it was because of the blessings of Protestantism. Insofar as they could be roused to the vigorous expression of anti-French and anti-Irish sentiment, it was because of the perceived superiority of British civilisation under the guidance of a benevolent providence. Insofar as they regarded themselves free from arbitrary laws and military

7    N. Gash, *Aristocracy and People 1815–1865* (London, 1979), p. 140.
8    L. Colley, *Britons: Forging the Nation 1707–1837* (New Haven, 1992).

despotism, it was because of the liberties guaranteed by the Glorious Revolution. A shared Protestantism and anti-Catholicism did not of course dissolve the cultural and historical divisions of the British peoples, but it did offer an easily available and deeply felt principle to rally around in times of stress and strain. With a scarcely pardonable oversight of the Protestant Irish, Colley concludes that

Great Britain might be made up of three separate nations, but under God it could also be one, united nation. And as long as a sense of mission and providential destiny could be kept alive, by means of maintaining prosperity at home, by means of recurrent wars with the Catholic states of Europe, and by means of a frenetic and for a long time highly successful pursuit of empire, the Union flourished, sustained not just by convenience and profit but by belief as well. Protestantism was the foundation that made the invention of Great Britain possible.[9]

This tradition was carried into the nineteenth century and became, if anything, more vigorous as a consequence of the revival of popular Protestantism, the large-scale migration of Catholic Irish to mainland Britain and the rapidity with which Irish issues were thrust to the forefront of British political debate.[10] Although anti-Catholicism is easily dismissed as a crude expression of religious bigotry, its most recent student is well aware of the complexities that lie within such a superficially straightforward ideology. Paz suggests that anti-Catholicism in the round cannot be reduced to mere historical memory, anti-Irish sentiment, bourgeois social control, British chauvinism, evangelical enthusiasm, economic conflict or religious prurience, but that there were different varieties of anti-Catholicism that served several functions in different locations. Thus in different parts of the country anti-Catholicism could serve political, electoral and theological interests, while in others it acted as a form of raucous urban entertainment in its association with pub rioting and its deliberate challenge to a rudimentary police force. Anti-Catholicism was both meticulously organised in powerful metropolitan associations and unpredictably random in its local incidence. What is not in doubt, however, is its ubiquity and its ability to draw on many different traditions and forms of expression to maintain its vulgar vitality in many different parts of the country.

[9] Ibid., pp. 53–4.
[10] W. L. Arnstein, *Protestant versus Catholic in Mid-Victorian England* (London, 1982); J. Wolffe, *The Protestant Crusade in Great Britain, 1829–1860* (Oxford, 1991); D. G. Paz, *Anti-Catholicism in Mid-Victorian England* (Stanford, Calif., 1992).

Although British anti-Catholicism was both more than, and less than, anti-Irish sentiment, there is no doubt that the sheer scale of Irish migration, and its religious, political, racial and economic distinctiveness, brought a fresh stimulus to an old prejudice. In a curious way Irish emigration made the British Isles more culturally homogeneous by exporting the peculiar sectarian tensions of Ireland to dozens of new frontiers in British towns and cities.[11] Such frontiers were well served by a peripatetic band of anti-Catholic orators, many of whom were exported from Ireland to tell the British what poison they now had in their midst.[12] With British evangelicals working furiously for the conversion of Catholic Ireland and with the Protestant Irish engaged in a kind of no popery grand tour of Britain, anti-Catholicism both reinforced British nationalism and Irish Catholic solidarity – however far from home it happened to be.

If Irish emigration and British anti-Catholicism had the capacity to draw the British Isles closer together even in conflict, there were many other ways in which potentially destabilising tensions were to some extent etherised. For example, although British anti-Catholicism operated at every social level, its forms of expression were variegated according to social class and degree of respectability. Even in Liverpool, middle-class Conservative Party supporters were often embarrassed by violent Orange populism, however much they may have exploited it for their own political advantage. Similarly, although British evangelical Nonconformity was staunchly anti-Catholic, its hostility to the Protestant Established Churches in the British Isles often delivered its political muscle into the same camp as that of the Catholics.[13] The ambiguities and paradoxes inherent in such transactions frequently enliven and confuse the Victorian political landscape. It was, for example, the Anglican Protestant establishmentarians who most vigorously upheld the principle of a confessional state so beloved by conservative continental Catholics, while British and Irish Catholics frequently appealed to liberal principles of legal equality at the same time as Catholicism was

[11]   M. A. G. O'Tuathaigh, 'The Irish in Nineteenth-Century Britain: Problems of Integration', *Transactions of the Royal Historical Society*, 5th ser., 31 (1981), 149–73.

[12]   G. F. A. Best, 'Popular Protestantism in Victorian Britain', in R. Robson (ed.), *Ideas and Institutions of Victorian Britain* (London, 1967), pp. 115–42; W. L. Arnstein, 'The Murphy Riots: A Victorian Dilemma', *Victorian Studies*, 19 (1975–6), 51–71.

[13]   G. F. A. Best, 'The Religious Difficulties of National Education in England, 1800–70', *Cambridge Historical Journal*, 12 (1956), 155–73; D. Hempton, *Methodism and Politics in British Society 1750–1850* (London, 1984), pp. 149–78.

at war with political liberals in most of the rest of Europe. Still more confusing is the fact that although British Catholics appealed to liberal principles against Anglican exclusivity, they were not, like the Dissenters, dogmatic voluntaryists, and they repeatedly appealed for state support for Catholic education and other social policies they thought desirable, but could not themselves afford. Indeed, the ecclesiastical scramble for state favours to meet the social needs of a growing population not only opened up the sectarian conflicts with which we are familiar, but also brought into prominence a set of issues which paradoxically gave a kind of public homogeneity to religio-political conflicts in the century from the Napoleonic Wars to the Great War. Contests over the privileges of religious establishments, the extent of toleration, the respective powers of the State and the churches in the control of social policy, and the nature of the relationship between religion and public morality, gave a kind of ecclesiastical consensus to what the key issues in fact were, even if different churches in different parts of the British Isles displayed mutually conflicting self-interests in trying to fight their corners. In this way conflict operated within a certain ideological consensus about the social significance of religion in the British State.

Before leaving the subject of Protestantism and anti-Catholicism there are two issues that bear particularly hard on the theme of religion and identity. The first has to do with the immense impact on national life of the growth of Anglo-Catholicism and ritualism within the Church of England, and the second arises from the fact that anti-Catholicism did not decline at the same pace in all parts of the British Isles. Paz has confirmed that the effects of tractarianism hit English parishes earlier and harder than many suppose. It is difficult to exaggerate the psychological impact of the alleged Romeward advance of a church which for three centuries had stood out in British consciousness as the chief defender of Protestant liberties. The growth of Anglo-Catholicism not only damaged the credibility of those who defended Established Churches as bastions of confessional Protestantism, but supplied the means by which havering Dissenters could cut the apron strings of mother church. The vigorous Protestantism of the Wesleyans and Welsh Calvinistic Methodists, for example, was particularly offended by tractarianism. A mixture of fear, incomprehension and a sense of betrayal led some to see it all as a great conspiracy 'to exasperate the Wesleyan societies against the Church of England, and thus weaken the Protestant interest; ... so the Church of Rome may regain her lost ascendancy'.[14] After the 1840s it became increasingly difficult to defend the Established Church in England, Ireland or Wales in terms of its undiluted opposition to popery in all its forms. As a result, the Oxford Movement ironically gave a boost to Welsh Nonconformist Liberalism, Irish ultra-Protestantism and English voluntaryism. Ecclesiastical politics are nothing if not engagingly eclectic.

The speed and extent of the decline of anti-Catholicism in the British Isles has brought forth the same kind of disagreement as exists over the linked process of secularisation. Paz's not altogether convincing explanation is that anti-Catholicism declined with the religious world-view that occasioned it in the first place, so that by the end of the century the most extravagant claims of anti-Catholic orators were no more plausible than belief in hell itself. Moreover, the twentieth-century public seemed to have less taste for anti-Catholic orators as a form of popular amusement than its nineteenth-century predecessor, and had belatedly come to see that popery alone seemed a less serious threat to British interests than the growth of European belligerence. But the decline of anti-Catholicism, as with secularisation, did not proceed at the same pace among all social classes in all parts of the British Isles. During the Home Rule episode, for example, Ulster Protestants were bewildered by the apparent lack of a vigorous British anti-Catholicism which they had been able to take for granted a quarter of a century before.[15] Moreover, by the end of the century anti-Catholic orators from Ulster had to resort to more sophisticated tactics to please British audiences than had once been the case. Anti-Catholicism was far from dead in British society at the turn of the century, but its social significance outside cites such as Liverpool and Glasgow, and parts of south Wales and south-west Scotland, was beginning to decline. Ulster's rebellious loyalism was made all the more rebellious by the feeling that the rest of Britain no longer understood the kind of religious peril it was faced with on its own doorstep. In a sense the decline of anti-Catholicism as a major force in the construction of British identity was replaced by the more immediate problems of empire, European warfare and post-war depression. Perhaps the strength of anti-Catholicism is therefore as good a measure as any of the social significance of religion in the British State.

[14]  T. Jackson, *A Letter to the Rev. Edward B. Pusey* (London, 1842), p. 109.
[15]  D. Hempton and M. Hill, *Evangelical Protestantism in Ulster Society 1740–1890* (London, 1992), pp. 161–87.

## EVANGELICALISM

The hotter sort of Protestantism was given an unexpected boost in the British Isles in the eighteenth century by the evangelical revival, which had dramatic consequences for religious identities in all four countries. While many have demonstrated that evangelicalism in general and Methodism in particular had roots in the old High Church tradition, in Puritanism and in the Anglican religious societies that were common in London and provincial market towns at the beginning of the eighteenth century; and while others have interpreted the growth of evangelical religion as a reaction against erastianism, latitudinarianism, deism and economic disorder, much of the recent work has taken a rather different approach. Most striking has been the renewed emphasis on the international dimensions of pietism and revivalism which has shown that the British experience was neither unique nor isolated from wider currents in European and American Protestantism.[16] The irony of this subject is, therefore, that perhaps this most distinctively British form of religious enthusiasm had some of its origins in the heart of Europe, and was later exported, through a vigorous foreign missionary movement, to all parts of the earth. Religious identities in the British Isles are not as hermetically sealed as they at first appear.

The roots of the great religious revivals of the eighteenth century – from eastern and central Europe to the middle colonies of America – have been located in the resistance of confessional minorities to the real or perceived threat of assimilation by powerful states and established churches.[17] Such a perspective inevitably shifts the centre of gravity away from the conventional Anglo-American preoccupations of much revival scholarship to the displaced and persecuted Protestant minorities of Habsburg-dominated central Europe. In such communities a tangled web of circulating literature, itinerant revivalists and folk migrations combine to show that the great awakening of the eighteenth century was more of an international event than many have imagined, and cannot be reduced to the social and economic peculiarities of specific places, however much they may have shaped the distinctive local expression of revival enthusiasm.

[16]   M. Noll, D. W. Bebbington and G. A. Rawlyk (eds.), *Evangelicalism: Comparative Studies of Popular Protestantism in North America, The British Isles, and Beyond, 1700–1990* (Oxford, 1994); G. A. Rawlyk and M. A. Noll, *Amazing Grace: Evangelicalism in Australia, Britain, Canada and the United States* (Montreal and Kingston, 1994).

[17]   W. R. Ward, *The Protestant Evangelical Awakening* (Cambridge, 1992).

The seeds of future revivals in the eighteenth century are to be found deep within the Protestant frame of mind which was a compound of low morale, fear of vicious confessional conflict, eschatological neuroses and pious devotion – all serviced by an astonishing array of devotional publications. The spiritual life of Europe was quite simply breaking free from confessional control at precisely the time when such control was being pursued with renewed vigour. As a result the pietism of Halle and Herrnhut was fanned into revivals in various Protestant corners of the Habsburg Empire and was then carried to the British Isles and North America by sweeping population movements and by a remarkable collection of revivalists who knew of each others' labours and who believed themselves to be part of a world-wide movement of grace. Here was no epiphenomenon, but a powerful religious movement which did much to shape the cultural mores of societies from the Bernese Oberland to the Scottish Highlands and from Wales to New England.

Turning from the origins of evangelicalism to its progress and development during the eighteenth century, one of the difficulties in assessing its strength is the fact that it flowed through so many denominational tributaries apart from Methodism itself. The Church of England had an influential coterie of evangelicals who employed Methodist forms but repudiated what they considered to be Wesley's separatist tendencies. English orthodox Dissent, which had grown slowly but steadily from its nadir in the 1730s, was influenced by Whitefield's Calvinistic Methodism and Doddridge's patient mediation, but it was not until the last two decades of the century with the employment of itinerant preachers and the formation of county associations that evangelicalism made substantial headway.[18] Thereafter the speed of evangelical Nonconformist growth in England and Wales in the early nineteenth century is one of the most remarkable features of British social history. In Scotland, as in the Presbyterian settlements of Ulster, Methodism, despite some early gains in the 1740s and 1750s, did not make much of an impression. There was, however, a strong evangelical presence in the Established Church of Scotland which led to conflict between the so-called Moderate and Popular parties and resulted in a stream of secessions in the late eighteenth century. The growth of evangelicalism in Scotland was 'simultaneous in timing to the rise of evangelicalism and Methodism in England and

---

[18]   D. W. Lovegrove, *Established Church, Sectarian People: Itinerancy and the Transformation of English Dissent, 1780–1830* (Cambridge, 1988).

bore strong similarities in social appeal and religious temper'.[19] Thus, most of the support for evangelicalism seems to have come from the new entrepreneurial classes and from the lower orders who were experiencing profound social changes as a result of structural instability in the Scottish economy. By the end of the eighteenth century, therefore, a predominantly evangelical Presbyterian Dissent had established a firm foothold in many Scottish towns and cities.[20]

In Ireland a different pattern emerged in the eighteenth century. Those who have followed the course of the Methodist revival in both England and Ireland in the eighteenth century have been struck by a remarkable difference of strategy and tactics employed by Wesley in the two countries. Whereas in England Wesley saw himself as having a special – but not exclusive – ministry to the poor, and frequently made barbed criticisms of the worldliness of the English Church and its gentry patrons, 'in Ireland his mission worked downward from the gentry class and outward from the garrison in a way that would have been unthinkable in England'. The editors of Wesley's *Journal* state that the total number of his contacts among the Irish gentry was 'so great as to make it clear that Wesley's self-consciously asserted English mission to the poor was in Ireland refracted through the Protestant gentry class'. Similarly, Wesley devoted a considerable amount of his preaching time to military garrisons, court-houses and other places resonant of Ascendancy control, thereby guaranteeing that 'he could reap no great Catholic harvest'.[21] This helps explain why popular evangelicalism was unable to take more advantage of the ramshackle state of the Roman Catholic Church in the eighteenth century and why, unlike Wales in the nineteenth century, evangelicalism was never able to help the Irish express a mass cultural identity outside the province of Ulster. Moreover, Wesley was also better received by the bishops and clergy of the Church of Ireland than by their equivalents in the Church of England, and was consequently a good deal less critical of the Irish Church which in some respects he thought was superior to its English counterpart.[22] Hence Irish Methodism derived almost no benefit from the tide of anti-establishment sentiment which

[19]   C. G. Brown, *The Social History of Religion in Scotland since 1730* (London, 1987), pp. 12–18.
[20]   C. G. Brown, *The People in the Pews: Religion and Society in Scotland since 1780* (Dundee, 1993), pp. 9–33.
[21]   W. R. Ward and R. P. Heitzenrater (eds.), *The Works of John Wesley*, vol. XVIII, *Journals and Diaries*, I (1735–1738) (Nashville, Tenn., 1988), pp. 56–77.
[22]   T. E. Warner, 'The Impact of Wesley on Ireland', PhD dissertation, University of London, 1954, pp. 323–4.

did so much to help English and Welsh Methodism get established in the aftermath of the French Revolution.

The pattern in Wales was quite different. Notwithstanding traditional explanations of evangelical growth as a product of Anglican abuses and a heroic new gospel age, it now seems clear that the roots of the Welsh revival are to be found in the religious improvements within the Established and Dissenting Churches in the first third of the eighteenth century. In this period there was a remarkable growth in the dissemination of popular religious literature with an accompanying improvement in literacy rates. Within the Established Church there was a devotional revival of sorts based on the 'sober piety and strong moral emphasis of the Prayer Book and Church Catechism' which 'served to instil the basic fundamentals of Protestantism'.[23] It was only much later than is conventionally assumed that Welsh evangelicalism acted as a solvent of the old denominational order in Wales. It was in the nineteenth century that evangelical religion laid the foundations for a broadly based attack on the Established Church and episcopalian landowners in Wales, while in Ireland evangelicalism was patronised by landlords and established interests as part of a wider, and increasingly desperate, defence of Irish Protestantism.

What this brief survey of the roots of evangelical revival in the British Isles has tried to show, therefore, is that evangelicalism is an eclectic and variegated species which took different shapes in different parts of the British Isles within a broadly consensual tradition of conversionism, biblicism and religious activism.[24] As with many of the most powerful religious movements in British history, it gained a foothold initially in London and the universities before establishing its most durable cultural expressions in the peripheries of the British Isles which then served as religious bastions against further encroachments of metropolitan values. It was in the half century after the shock of the French Revolution that this vigorous religious tradition did most to shape the religious life of the four nations within the greater British State. Its most substantial gains were at the manifold frontier zones of the British Isles: the geographical and cultural frontier of Protestantism and Catholicism in the border counties of Ulster; the klondike frontier of fast-growing mining and industrial towns in south Wales and parts of England; the ideological frontier of old Scottish loyalty to the ideal of

---

[23]   G. H. Jenkins, *The Foundations of Modern Wales: Wales 1642–1780* (Oxford, 1987), pp. 342–85.
[24]   D. W. Bebbington, *Evangelicalism in Modern Britain: A History from the 1730s to the 1980s* (London, 1989).

the godly commonwealth and the modernising dynamics of the British State; the frontier of traditional village life and the tensions engendered by class and modernisation in rural counties such as Lincolnshire; and the frontier between middle-class determination to keep control of the urban and industrial environment and the upward social aspirations of the respectable working class. The list is endless, for as Mark Noll has observed of popular Protestantism in North America in the same period, 'evangelicalism was at its most effective in revolutionary situations because, with unusual force, it communicated enduring personal stability in the face of disorder, long-lasting eagerness for discipline, and a nearly inexhaustible hope that the same personal dignity affirmed by the gospel could be communicated to the community as a whole'.[25]

Not only the community, but, as this book has sought to demonstrate, regions and nations as well. Perhaps the most vivid illustration of these processes at work is to be found in the middle decades of the nineteenth century. Just as a number of Marxist historians have emphasised the 1840s and 1850s as respectively decades of destabilisation and restabilisation in the social history of Britain, there were, revealingly, similar processes at work in the sphere of religion and identity.[26] In the 1840s the disruption of the Church of Scotland, the great repeal of the Union campaign in Ireland and the 'treason of the Blue Books in Wales' all seemed to show how religion could act simultaneously as a solvent of a greater British identity and a powerful focus of national identities.[27] One could add to this list the bitter conflicts in England over Graham's factory education proposals, the Maynooth crisis and the activities of the Liberation society which all seemed to show that religious divisions were so deep-seated that the State was increasingly being drawn into the uncomfortable position of acting as an ecclesiastical referee. The religious stability of the British Isles, and its dependent cultural identities, seemed to be in imminent danger of fracturing into different pieces. Yet, paradoxically, religion was also drawing the British nations together as evangelical enthusiasm, the rage of voluntary associations, Irish Catholic migration and shared discussions about the legitimate rights of Established Churches penetrated every corner of the British Isles. Moreover,

[25] M. A. Noll, 'Revolution and the Rise of Evangelical Social Influence in North Atlantic Societies', in *Evangelicalism*, pp. 113–36.

[26] J. Foster, *Class Struggle and the Industrial Revolution: Early Industrial Capitalism in Three English Towns* (London, 1974), pp. 161–250.

[27] J. Wolffe, *God and Greater Britain: Religion and National Life in Britain and Ireland 1843–1945* (London, 1994), pp. 98–122.

the 1850s offered splendid opportunities for a vigorous re-assertion of British Protestant and patriotic values in the shape of the remarkable outcry against 'Papal Aggression' in 1850–1, national expressions of grief in response to the death of Wellington in 1852, the outbreak of the Crimean War in 1854, the renewed vitality of anti-Catholicism and anti-ritualism, and virtually unlimited enthusiasm for the extension of British influence overseas through Palmerstonian diplomacy, foreign missions and the spread of empire. It is to the relationship between religious values in the British Isles and the development of notions of empire that we must now turn.

### EMPIRE

In her book *Britons* Linda Colley suggests that a 'cult of commerce' in the eighteenth century became an increasingly important part of being British. In 1718 the annual directory *The Present State of Great Britain* opened its chapter on trade with the opinion that 'next to the purity of our religion we are the most considerable nation in the world for the vastness and extensiveness of our trade'. In the eighteenth century the imperial sector was the most dynamic element in the growth of British trade. 'In all, 95 per cent of the increase in Britain's commodity exports that occurred in the six decades after the Act of Union was sold to captive and colonial markets outside Europe.'

Colley suggests that after the Seven Years War, the most successful in Britain's history, Britain acquired too much power too quickly over too many people. Among the beneficiaries, however, were those in the Celtic fringes of the British State, especially the Scots, who had opened to them a formidable number of new posts and new opportunities for the creation of wealth. As many old Jacobite families were absorbed into imperial service, and as the Scottish universities churned out a seemingly endless supply of educated talent, the Scots made a particularly important contribution to the administration and military defence of empire. Indeed, it was the Scottish hunger for places that explains much of the anti-Scottish rhetoric of Wilkes and his supporters. Empire thus played a major part in the expansion of trade, the growth of the British economy, the reward of talent and the development of a distinctively British chauvinism, which all contributed to a genuinely *British* enthusiasm for empire.[28]

[28] Colley, *Britons*, pp. 55–145.

To the cult of commerce was added an unparalleled enthusiasm for foreign missions. The period 1780–1914, in which the map of the world came in large part to be painted red, was also, according to Porter, a period of unprecedented religious expansion and conflict.

Britain's varied Protestant communities led the way throughout in the global expansion of Christian missionary enterprise and church extension, intended not only to salvage expatriate souls and to convert or evangelise the heathen but to check the spreading corruptions of Roman Catholicism and Islam. International conflict, major social and political transformations, the creation of empires on an immense scale, were threaded through with religious strife, upheld by religious institutions, stimulated and embittered by the widespread and explicit intention to inculcate in different peoples many dominant British beliefs.[29]

Porter's supporting data remind us of the scale of this enterprise. In the 120 years after the founding of the first Anglican dioceses outside the United Kingdom (Nova Scotia, 1787 and Quebec, 1793) well over one hundred more colonial and missionary bishoprics were created. As ecclesiastical hierarchies multiplied so too did the numbers of British missionaries and the amount of money raised by the missionary societies. By 1899 some 10,000 missionaries, supported by £2 million of voluntary subscriptions, were promoting Christianity and, of necessity, British values in all parts of the globe. In the onward march of Christianity, commerce and civilisation the respective elements were not always in close harmony either in means or in ends, but the vital ingredient of religion is a fact to be reckoned with both for colonial governors at the time and for historians ever since. Porter has done more than anyone to show not only that 'Britain's religion and Britain's empire were obviously and inextricably linked', but also that a proper investigation of the relationship between religion and empire should be firmly rooted in the religious history of Britain itself. Thus the formation of voluntary societies in the 1790s, the growth of interdenominational competition in the period 1800–50, the conflict between Church and Dissent and between Protestantism and Roman Catholicism in the Victorian period, and the growth of millennialism and Keswick holiness teaching at different times in the nineteenth century, all had their effects at the vital ideological and cultural interface of missionary values and native responses.

Of most relevance to our theme is the suggestion that from 1750 to

[29]  A. N. Porter, 'Religion and Empire: British Expansion in the Long 19th Century, 1780–1914', Inaugural Lecture, King's College London (1991), pp. 2–3.

around 1820 the evangelical missionary movement, in line with the domestic history of popular evangelicalism in the same period, expanded without state support and often in confrontation with secular objectives. 'Nonconformists in particular were anxious to distance themselves from government, to secure greater freedom and toleration for their activities, and to eschew politics ... Just as religious enthusiasts were represented as a serious threat to domestic order, so the extension of their activities overseas was widely seen as likely to undermine empire.'[30] Moreover, a combination of millennial urgency and the sheer internationalism of popular evangelicalism seemed to clothe the missionary movement in more exotic garments than anything on offer from mere colonial bureaucrats.[31] In terms of identity, therefore, the early growth of the British missionary movement owed more to the voluntaryist and internationalist characteristics of early evangelicalism than to the deliberate extension of British values on the coat-tails of British imperialism.

Over the course of the nineteenth century, however, a different pattern emerges. The perceived need to counteract the ecclesiastical power of Rome and the entrenched religions of native cultures nurtured a greater reliance on state regulation, or, if necessary, state compulsion to disadvantage competitors. Anglicans and Nonconformists even appealed to the State against one another on grounds similar to those they employed in British towns and cities, despite the fact that religious establishments went out of business more quickly in the imperial fringes than in their British heartland. In the complicated jungle of missionary one-upmanship, churches, colonial administrators and traders all paraded their virtues one to another. Although older romantic notions of unaided missionary zeal lived on into the later nineteenth century, missionary concerns became increasingly bound up with wider themes of imperial security and commercial opportunities. Missions were too important to be left alone by colonial administrators, and the business of saving souls was too urgent to pass up the advantages which the power of the State seemed to confer.

One reason for this closer connexion between missionary enthusiasm and informal imperialism was the increased importance of evangelical middle-class values at home and overseas. By the early Victorian

---

[30]   Ibid., pp. 9–10.
[31]   D. Hempton, 'Evangelicalism and Eschatology', *Journal of Ecclesiastical History*, 31 no. 2 (1980), 179–94; R. H. Martin, *Evangelicals United: Ecumenical Stirrings in Pre-Victorian Britain, 1795–1830* (London, 1983).

period the emphasis on enterprise, sobriety and thrift, which had operated mostly in British towns and cities, was exported to the distant corners of the empire. The drunkenness, licentiousness and lack of enterprise of the British working classes in Victorian cities was paralleled by similar vices among Black Africans. The solution to both problems, in the evangelical mind, was to be found in a mixture of moral discipline, enterprise and free trade.[32] The latter came to be regarded not only as an important component of Britain's commercial well-being, but as desirable for its own sake. John Bowring, the governor of Hong Kong, stated bluntly that 'Jesus Christ is Free Trade and Free Trade is Jesus Christ'.[33] In short, free trade was regarded as a reflection of Britain's Protestant values. It was the secret of Britain's greatness, and properly applied, it could do the same for Africans and Indians as it had done for Britons. The Victorian religious enthusiasm for foreign missions was therefore in harmony with what the British government was seeking to do for reasons of economic self-interest. This shift in attitude had important effects in the empire. Before 1833, for example, missionaries in India were strictly licensed by the East India Company to service company employees only, but after that date they were given considerably more freedom to reach the masses.

By the late Victorian period, therefore, the gap between evangelical opinion in provincial Britain and those who ran the empire was much closer than it had been half a century earlier. Ironically, just when it seemed that the structure of empire could be used as a fast conductor for evangelical missions, the shift from informal to formal imperial control made it impossible for colonial administrators to run the empire as a tract distribution agency. The need for responsible government to protect native culture on the one hand, and the increasing opposition of indigenous churches to missionary colonialism on the other, combined to persuade the leaders of the international missionary movement that state support for missions was an attractive, but poisonous, potion. By 1910 when the World Missionary Conference was held in Edinburgh, 'something of the interdenominational co-operation, the genuinely global perspective, the detachment from government and the relative absence of condescension which had

---

[32]  B. Stanley, '"Commerce and Christianity": Providence Theory, the Missionary Movement, and the Imperialism of Free Trade, 1842–1860', *Historical Journal*, 26 no. 1 (1983), 71–94; A. Porter, '"Commerce and Christianity": the Rise and Fall of a Nineteenth-Century Missionary Slogan', *Historical Journal*, 28 no. 3 (1985), 597–621.

[33]  R. Hyam, *Britain's Imperial Century 1815–1914* (London, 1976), p. 58.

characterised late-eighteenth-century attitudes towards converts was beginning to be recovered'.[34]

The religious foundations of imperial sentiments were thus not without their complexities, but they were no less powerful for that. The economic benefits of empire, the national prestige it conferred, the religious enthusiasm it nurtured and the propaganda it distributed all combined to make empire a genuinely popular cause in Victorian and Edwardian Britain.[35] Churches throughout the British Isles supported missionaries in the field and were entertained by them on furlough; they offered homes to increasingly militaristic youth organisations and sang increasingly militaristic hymns; they revelled in the heroic adventures of David Livingstone and were outraged by the heroic death of General Gordon; they gloried in the defence of small nations and railed against the rival imperialism of larger nations, especially if they were Islamic or Roman Catholic; above all they supplied a vigorous religious defence of the whole notion of empire itself. In the words of Livingstone they were 'co-operators with God' forwarding 'the renovation of the world'.[36] Such a dramatic external vision acted as a powerful solvent of the national, denominational and class tensions in British society before the First World War. Although old hatchets were never fully buried, as Nonconformists became inexorably more imperialist in the thirty years before the Boer War and as the British working classes were fed a rich diet of imperial propaganda, the radical anti-imperialist ground was increasingly occupied by a spirited minority of old style Chartist radicals, pacifists, humanitarians and internationalists, who came to be as much fed up with the beer-swilling, sport-playing and money-grabbing predilections of some of their working-class constituents as they were with the politics of imperialism. Moreover, whether pro or anti, Britain's imperial commitments offered an available focus for a genuinely national debate, across all social classes and among all religious denominations, about the rights and wrongs of Britain's influence in the wider world. Although it took the Boer War to bring home the unpleasant truth that empire would have to be fought for, and that white Protestants could be just as serious an enemy as anyone else, enthusiasm for empire survived the war. There were, of

[34]   A. Porter (ed.), *Atlas of British Overseas Expansion* (London, 1991), p. 137; B. Stanley, *The Bible and the Flag: Protestant Missions and British Imperialism in the Nineteenth and Twentieth Centuries* (Leicester, 1990).

[35]   J. M. McKenzie, *Propaganda and Empire: The Manipulation of British Public Opinion 1880–1960* (Manchester, 1984); idem (ed.), *Imperialism and Popular Culture* (Manchester, 1986).

[36]   McKenzie, *Propaganda and Empire*, p. 59.

course, voices against the war, but the fault lines of support and opposition did not always line up in convenient ranks. Lloyd George, for example, took a predictably uncompromising line against Anglican expansionism, but Welsh Nonconformist Liberalism was not as pro-Boer as is conventionally assumed and, ironically, one of Lloyd George's most trenchant critics was a fellow Welsh Nonconformist, Hugh Price Hughes, who moulded the influential *Methodist Times* into an organ of 'benevolent' imperialism.[37] He defended the empire as a providential institution for the protection of weak races and accused the Boers of peddling liquor and slavery. It was the subsequent revelations about British concentration camps and brutal military tactics in the Transvaal that delivered Welsh Liberals and many others into the camp of the anti-war radicals, not the issue of imperialism itself.[38]

Empire and its dilemmas had a curious effect on British national identity. On the one hand, the smaller nations that made up the greater British State empathised with the fate of small nations everywhere in their resistance to the alleged cruelties of the Turkish, Spanish and German empires. This partly accounts for the disproportionately high military commitment of Ulster and Wales to the British forces in the Great War. On the other hand, pride in the British empire and allegiance to the religious and cultural values it represented were expressed in the most jingoistic of language, from the Welsh valleys to the Scottish highlands. As Colley has perceptively noted, the British empire was indeed the *British* empire while Britain itself was effectively *England*.

The one part of the British Isles which had little enthusiasm for the British empire was Catholic Ireland which often regarded itself as one of the small nations victimised by British imperialism. The outbreak of the Boer War and then the European war in 1914 radicalised Irish politics, boosted membership of the Gaelic League and laid the foundation for Sinn Féin. Anti-imperialism ultimately fanned the flames of Irish nationalism and yet there was unmistakable enthusiasm in Ireland for an alternative sort of world imperialism borne by the successive waves of Catholic Irish emigration to all corners of the globe. The respective adherents of the British and Irish empires fought

[37] J. H. S. Kent, 'Hugh Price Hughes and the Nonconformist Conscience', in G. V. Bennett and J. D. Walsh (eds.), *Essays in Modern English Church History* (London, 1966), pp. 181–205; S. Koss, 'Wesleyanism and Empire', *Historical Journal*, 18 no. 1 (1975), 105–18.

[38] K. O. Morgan, *Rebirth of a Nation: Wales 1880–1980* (Oxford, 1981), p. 45.

out their battles in mission-fields from Canada to Australia. Thus 'the Irish created in their nationalist organisations and in the Roman Catholic Church a spiritual empire both in Ireland and across the seas' which traded both on opposition to the British Empire and on the opportunities afforded by it.[39] What Ireland and the Irish diaspora signalled for the British State at the end of the nineteenth century was that there was a profound and disturbing ambiguity at the heart of the empire. As Viscount Bryce noted in 1889, in India, 'not a dog wags its tail against us among these 260 millions of people', yet Britain could not successfully govern a mere four million Irishmen even with the aid of 'the loyal garrison of one million'.[40] It was maddening and frustrating at the end of the nineteenth century, and turned out to be yet more serious in the twentieth, when Ireland, north and south, was as much divided in its view of empire as it was on other matters.

Ulster Protestants, in facing up to the threat of Home Rule at the end of the nineteenth century, feared losing their share of 'all the past glories and all the present greatness of the freest and mightiest nation the civilised world has ever seen', and of losing their shared identity 'with a kingdom on whose territory the sun never sets'.[41] More specifically, Edward Saunderson, the leader of the Irish Unionists, drew a parallel between the plight of the minority in Ireland and that of the British minority in the Boer republics. 'Given this hibernico-centric rationalisation of South African politics', states Saunderson's biographer, 'it was perhaps inevitable that Saunderson should view the war of 1899 almost as a holy crusade; and his defence of the British cause was all the more furious because Irish nationalists had begun to articulate the plight of the Boers.'[42]

The attitude of Irish nationalists to empire was more ambivalent than is sometimes assumed, but issues were forced into the open by the First World War and the part that Irishmen were to play in the British war effort. Redmond's support for Britain in the war was informed as

[39]    S. W. Gilley, 'Irish Catholicism in Britain' in D. A. Kerr (ed.), *Comparative Studies on Governments and Non-Dominant Ethnic Groups in Europe, 1850–1940*, vol. II (Dartmouth, N.Y., 1993), p. 254.
[40]    Hyam, *Imperial Century*, p. 87.
[41]    *Belfast News Letter*, 6 Jan. 1886; T. Hennessey, 'Ulster Unionist Territorial and National Identities 1886–1893: Province, Island, Kingdom and Empire', *Irish Political Studies*, 8 (1993), 21–36; D. Hempton and M. Hill, *Evangelical Protestantism in Ulster Society 1740–1890* (London, 1992), pp. 161–87; and J. Loughlin, *Gladstone, Home Rule and the Ulster Question 1882–93*, p. 296.
[42]    A. Jackson, *Colonel Edward Saunderson: Land and Loyalty in Victorian Ireland* (Oxford, 1995), pp. 132–3.

much by political calculation as imperial enthusiasm, but even that was challenged by opinion within the Irish volunteers.

England's relations with Germany are a matter of indifference to us. England's war is not our war, except in so far as it offers Ireland a unique opportunity to achieve freedom. In our unthinking past we helped England to starve and slay the peoples of half the world. Without Irish arms the Boer Republics would still be in existence and the people of India free. Irish arms painted the map of the world in the interests of English commerce, and the Judas price of it all was the patronising contempt of a few cockneys. We have no empire to defend. We have no colonies for our foreign trade.

We pay our share for a Dreadnought to protect English trade, but the money that builds it is spent in England . . . Volunteers our Empire is Ireland; our flag is Ireland's. Salute the colours![43]

According to this view the British empire was assuredly an English empire and vigorous Irish nationalists regarded the war as yet another bloody attempt to protect English interests throughout the world.

Irish separation and eventual withdrawal from the Commonwealth not only disturbed the integrity of the empire, but effectively ended the political homogeneity of the British Isles. Moreover, the survival of a partitioned and violent Ulster is a sad reminder that the complex interaction of imperial aspirations and religious identities threw up as many tragedies as it did dazzling glories. The problem remains to haunt the British State and the great British political parties, who are so confused by it all that they still seem undecided whether or not to organise support in the province they have assumed responsibility for governing. What does seem clear is that British people are at least united in frustration with the Irish problem, and that there has been a dangerous separation of Ulster's British identity from that regarded as acceptable by the other British nations.

The decline of anti-Catholicism, evangelical Protestantism and imperialism in the twentieth century has helped erode the powerful links between religion and national identity in the British Isles. All three had the capacity to promote national integration *and* separation in the British Isles. Yet, in terms of the erosion of religion as an important element in the affirmation of national and regional identities, none has been as influential as the inexorable decline of religious influence in the construction and implementation of social policy. Ironically, religion, which did much to supply the British State with an agreed legitimacy in the eighteenth century, was the main casualty of

[43] *Irish Volunteer*, 29 Aug. 1914.

the increased power of the State in the twentieth century. Except in Ireland, the inability of the churches to construct a social policy, either in harness with the State or in opposition to it, has done as much as anything to erode religion as a major component of national identity.

SOCIAL POLICY

In the eighteenth century, Established Churches, for all their structural weaknesses, were the main instruments not only of Christianising the people, but also of looking after their welfare. However inadequately this task was carried out in practice, it was still a fact that the religious identities of Britons were bound up not only with a shared Protestantism and anti-Catholicism, but with a shared assumption that education, poor relief, crime and punishment, rites of passage and local government were all closely bound up with the social function of religious establishments. The complex forces at work in the period 1780–1830, under the shadow of the French and industrial revolutions, altered forever that old pattern and set formidable new hurdles for churchmen all over the British Isles in their attempts to create a new one.

In the first place it was evident that Established Churches throughout the British Isles were in a much weaker position in 1830 than they had been fifty years earlier. Greater religious pluralism in England, the astonishing numerical growth of Nonconformity in Wales, the growth of voluntaryism and evangelicalism in Scotland and the resurgence of Catholic self-confidence in Ireland collectively eroded both the principle and the practice of established religion. At the same time the gradual triumph of a free market economy exposed a gaping hole in the old moral economy of the British countryside which was grounded in paternalism, deference, mutual responsibility and notions of natural justice. Even allowing for the fact that this moral economy never worked as well as rural romantics supposed, it nevertheless offered a rough regulator of mutual responsibilities beyond which everyone knew it was not wise to go.[44] The market posed new problems for all, but especially for the churches. In the accompanying growth of towns and cities Asa Briggs has stated that the central problem of the nineteenth-century city was how to combine economic individualism with a common civic purpose.[45] For churchmen of all denominations

[44]    E. P. Thompson, 'The Moral Economy of the English Crowd in the Eighteenth Century', *Past & Present*, no. 50 (1971), 76–136.
[45]    A. Briggs, *Victorian Cities* (London, 1963), p. 18.

the issue was how to bring an acceptable moral and religious dimension to highly impersonal classical market economics. In the same way that the stresses and strains of the French revolutionary period effectively ushered in a new and more eclectic denominational order in Britain, the industrial revolution led to a whole host of conflicting approaches to the formation of Christian social policy.

Tory radical paternalists tried to use the State to regulate the excesses of factory entrepreneurs and hoped to carry the world of labour with them. Christian socialists and social Christians from Maurice to Temple hoped that the co-operative principle of socialism could be yoked to the co-operative principles of the Christian faith to restore human dignity and fellowship in a world overrun with competitiveness and the profit motive.[46] Indeed, the problems faced by social Christians from the 1840s to the present have not changed all that much. The combination of working-class preoccupation with the realisation of tangible objectives and the Christian middle-class sanctification of thrift and self-improvement has not proved a happy one for Christian socialist aspirations. Yet another approach was to make the establishment principle work in new circumstances. In England, Bishop Blomfield pinned his faith on a vigorous church-building programme and on maintaining Anglican control over the education of the nation's children. Both strategies resulted in a fearful battle with Nonconformity which resulted ultimately in a disastrous over-supply of churches and an increased role for the State in supplying a more secular education. Thus, Callum Brown states that 'the secularisation of social policy in the mid- and late-nineteenth century resulted from a rising fervour for democratic ecclesiastical influence in public policy – and not from religious decline'.[47] The most comprehensive and intellectually coherent attempt to adapt Established Churches to new conditions was the revival of the ideal of the godly commonwealth in Scotland. Central to Chalmers's entire social philosophy was the view that economic self-interest had to be subordinated to the communal spirit if Christian social ethics were to stand a chance of mass realisation. Moreover, he continued to believe, against formidable evidence to the contrary, that the ecclesiastical parish could continue to service the spiritual, moral, educational and

---

[46] W. R. Ward, 'The Way of the World: The Rise and Decline of Protestant Social Christianity in Britain', *Kirchliche Zeitgeschichte*, 1. Jahrgang Heft 2 (1988), 293–305.

[47] C. G. Brown, 'A Revisionist Approach to Religious Change', in S. Bruce (ed.), *Religion and Modernization: Sociologists and Historians Debate the Secularization Thesis* (Oxford, 1992), p. 52.

welfare needs of the British population if only the State would play its part. There was in Chalmers more than a whiff of the Puritan godly magistrate in his desire to get control of state resources on the one hand and vigorously to Christianise the population on the other. One of the most revealing episodes in Chalmers's career was his opposition to the Reform Bill in 1831–2. 'He particularly feared that the enlarged electorate would soon encroach upon the privileges and endowments of the national religious establishments', and that the Reform Bill would encourage 'the British population to view the secular State, rather than the Established Churches, as the focus for national aspirations and the hope for national prosperity and happiness'.[48] As always with Chalmers his diagnosis of what was likely to happen was more impressive than his strategy for stopping it.

In Ireland and Wales the Established Churches employed different, but equally unsuccessful strategies. In Ireland the Established Church pursued a mixture of evangelical enthusiasm to convert the nation and utilitarian reform to remove the scandals of ecclesiastical abuses. The former did more to arouse Catholic hostility than convert them to the Protestant faith and the latter as much drew attention to the absurdity of the Church's position in Ireland as it did to make it less unpalatable. In truth, it is not easy to see how any strategy could have saved the Church of Ireland once the British State abandoned the principle of the Protestant Constitution in 1829. In Wales the State Church valiantly tried to make itself the bearer of Welsh cultural aspirations, but its association with an Anglicised and landowning elite did for it what a similar conjunction did for the Irish Church. As with the Catholic democratic movement in Ireland, Welsh Nonconformity built its edifice first with numbers and then with a sense of exclusion from the inflexions of power and influence.

Throughout the British Isles, therefore, the ability of the Established Churches to construct social policy was undermined by the very forces that were threatening the principle of religious establishments *per se*. Some of those forces were unleashed by the evangelical revival which seemed to offer yet another avenue for the construction of social policy. The creation of the ubiquitous voluntary associations for promoting virtue and opposing vice together with a powerful emphasis on individual salvation and self-help made an enormous impact on the social mores of British life before the First World War.[49] Evangelicals

[48]   S. J. Brown, *Thomas Chalmers and the Godly Commonwealth* (Oxford, 1982), p. 194.
[49]   F. K. Brown, *Fathers of the Victorians* (Cambridge, 1961).

lacked nothing in energy or political pragmatism, but evangelical ideology imposed its own limits on the extent to which it could supply a genuinely national social policy. Professor Ward has observed that 'innumerable evangelicals were equally possessed of a personal Christian ethic of love and a highly impersonal classical market economics; individuals and those executing church discipline in congregations can be shown trying to hold the two together, but there was never any satisfactory theory explaining how it was to be done'.[50] Moreover, Ward is persuaded that 'neither in England nor America is the case made out that evangelicalism was capable of rising from the conception of charity to that of policy'. One of the advantages of the plethora of good works societies was that it enabled some bridges to be built across some of the deepest chasms of British society – those of class, culture, denomination and identity – but it militated against a coherent theological and social programme. Perhaps even more damaging to the long-term success of evangelical social ethics is the way in which its chief concerns – temperance, sabbatarianism, sexual purity and thrift – were all associated with values of middle-class religious respectability throughout the British Isles. Moreover, there was a censorious majoritarianism in the evangelical mind which was not content with mere moral persuasion, but which insisted upon compliance to the will of the pious middle-class majority. A recent study of Hull, England's most evangelical city, has exposed the ambiguities and limitations of evangelical social policy.[51] In the first place, ecclesiastical rivalry between evangelical Anglicans and Dissenters undermined religious co-operation on the big issues of education and ecclesiastical provision for the masses. Secondly, temperance, sabbatarianism and the campaigns against vice and prostitution were regarded by opponents as having as much to do with class control as religious piety. To take the sabbath as an example, Hull was probably the most sabbatarian large city in England at the end of the nineteenth century, but the achievement was costly in social terms. Not only did sabbatarianism expose the rich to allegations of hypocrisy and self-interest, but the mechanisms for enforcing sabbath observance led to a good deal of unpleasant informing on neighbours and legal coercion. This was good business for the churches and for the corporation which raked in £1,000 a year in fines, but it did little to

50   Ward, 'The Way of the World', p. 297.
51   P. D. Stubley, 'Serious Religion and the Improvement of Public Manners: The Scope and Limitations of Evangelicalism in Hull 1770–1914', PhD dissertation, University of Durham, 1991.

sustain a genuinely co-operative social ideal among all sections of the population. In Dickens's words, the people could not be made Christian by 'main force'.

None of this is meant to deny the power and popularity of many of the crusades associated with the Nonconformist Conscience nor to diminish the importance of the religious foundations of Lib–Labism in the early twentieth century when it seemed that Christian radicalism could indeed create a durable political culture for twentieth-century conditions. The argument is rather that new conditions thrown up at the turn of the eighteenth century posed virtually insurmountable problems for churches that had customarily relied upon the principles and practices of religious establishments to sustain an effective social policy. Tory radicalism, Christian socialism, evangelical individualism and associationalism, the Nonconformist Conscience and revived visions of the parochial ideal all offered different ways of securing a place for religion as the central component of British identity in a modern state. Not only were these visions antithetical one to another, but they were unable to command the right levels of support in the areas that mattered most. In both the corridors of government and the world of labour, Christianity came increasingly to be seen as a private matter for the individual and as a community matter for the churches, but the real power and political influence lay elsewhere. The rather tame and incoherent response to social issues by churchmen in post-war Britain is therefore a consequence not only of intellectual feeble-ness, but of effective exclusion from parts of society they once controlled. It is not that churches have been unaware of the difficulties facing them, the problem has been to offer convincing solutions, given their lack of resources in comparison to those possessed by the modern State.

Efforts were made nevertheless. In my view the four most compelling and influential attempts to bring together religious values and social policy since the mid-Victorian period have been the Nonconformist Conscience, Anglican social Christianity as articulated by William Temple, the revival of the godly commonwealth ideal in Scotland in the inter-war period and the social policies of the Irish Catholic Church. Each offers salutary lessons.

Richard Helmstadter has suggested that from the 1820s to the 1880s British Nonconformity had a coherent social and political vision based on an increasingly evangelical theology, manifold grievances against established interests and a profound distrust of the State, which, after all, buttressed those very interests.[52] In politics the chapels championed the freedom of the individual against Anglican privileges and state support for the Established Church. Thus Nonconformists, in their various campaigns against the remnants of Britain's confessional state, seemed to be on the side of progressive democracy and assertive individualism. Their causes were free trade, freedom from compulsory church rates and tithes, free access to Oxford and Cambridge, freedom from slavery and freedom from the consequences of state support for Anglican social policy, especially in the sphere of elementary education. This progressive liberalism was underpinned by a vigorous emphasis on temperance, sabbatarianism, philanthropy and sexual purity. Nonconformist freedom was based not on licence but on self-help and social responsibility, and there is in all this an attempt to roll back the power of the State, the Established Church and urban vice and irreligion.

By the end of the century, however, many Nonconformists had lost confidence in evangelical individualism in the sphere of social policy and, ironically, had come to place more reliance on the State to enforce moral principles over matters such as alcohol, sexual ethics and gambling. Moreover, by the end of the century Nonconformists were as much divided over the big issues of the day as any other sector of the population. Irish Home Rule, imperialism and the Boer War, and the respective rights of capital and labour all drove great wedges into Nonconformist solidarity.[53] Only a vigorous campaign against Anglican educational privileges and a conviction that the Liberal Party, for all its weaknesses, would deliver more than the Conservatives, offered Nonconformist politics a degree of homogeneity. Although Helmstadter has exaggerated the ideological and political shifts of Nonconformity over the course of the nineteenth century, there can be little doubt that early libertarian crusades were more compelling than the positions adopted by the last Nonconformist generation before the First World War. By then Nonconformist membership as a proportion of the wider population was in terminal decline and the Free Churches were in no position to shape the social policy of the post-war world.

[52]  R. J. Helmstadter, 'The Nonconformist Conscience', in P. Marsh (ed.), *The Conscience of the Victorian State* (Hassocks, Sussex, 1979), reprinted in G. Parsons (ed.), *Religion in Victorian Britain*, vol. IV (Manchester, 1988), pp. 61–95; D. Bebbington, *Victorian Nonconformity* (Bangor, Gwynedd, 1992), pp. 58–71.
[53]  D. W. Bebbington, *The Nonconformist Conscience: Chapel and Politics 1870–1914* (London, 1982).

Anglicanism fared little better, despite the efforts of William Temple, who has been described by John Kent as 'the last great articulate exponent of Anglicanism', and the author of perhaps the last intellectually coherent attempt to bring the Church back into the centre of the construction of social policy.[54] At the heart of Temple's convictions was a strong belief in an organic humanity 'linked together with bonds of mutual sympathy and influence'. Social well-being thus required a common set of values shaped by the Christian tradition. In addition, the State must be given a spiritual and moral character even in its most material and secular functions. Here was the intellectual and theological foundation for a strong commitment to social justice and a repudiation of Victorian individualism. Temple was sufficiently realistic to know that the Established Church would have to be modernised for it to have a chance of recapturing its central role in Christianising the nation and influencing the political evolution of the State. Although Temple was also a committed internationalist and ecumenist he retained a warm appreciation of the Englishness of Anglicanism. 'The Church of England', he wrote, 'like other churches, has often failed to be completely Christian – always, indeed, if we take those words in all their proper depth of meaning; but it has never failed to be utterly, completely, provokingly, adorably English.'[55] Temple was not only clear about what he was for, but also what he was against. He described economic competition as 'organised selfishness' and disliked the Victorian emphasis of extending 'charity' only to the deserving poor. For Temple, 'charity' to be genuinely Christian had to be indiscriminate and impartial. In that sense his social philosophy was far closer to the ideals of the welfare state than to the practice of the Victorian churches. Temple also recognised that the Christian tendency to fall back into single issue politics was an inappropriate strategy for Christianising the social order.

Though admirably coherent in theory, Temple's vision of social Christianity was full of problems. Not only had pluralism and secularism combined to erode the national Christian consensus that Temple wished to reconstruct, but neither a political party nor the Established Church was in much of a position to implement it. The Church of England was after all an English church, while the State it wished to influence was British. Moreover, as the General Strike of

---

[54]  J. Kent, *William Temple: Church, State and Society in Britain, 1880–1950* (Cambridge, 1992); W. Temple, *Christianity and Social Order* (London, 1942).
[55]  Kent, *Temple*, p. 35.

1926 showed, the Established Church cut almost no ice in the world of labour. Thus Temple's vision of a Christian social order, however intellectually coherent, could not overcome the powerful forces ranged against it nor gain a foothold in areas of British society that really counted. It is perhaps wise not to dismiss too sweepingly the benign influence of Temple's views on the conscience of a nation increasingly committed to materialism and the profit motive, but it is hard to disagree with Kent's conclusion that by the 1970s and 1980s 'Temple's vision of a single Christian ideological movement working through the establishment to bring national pressure to bear on the lawmakers had been lost', probably forever.[56]

In the inter-war period many church leaders in the Church of Scotland were equally appalled by the consequences of laissez-faire individualism and class conflict on domestic living conditions and the world order. Although there was much to admire in their attempts to revive the faith and moral discipline of the Scottish people, it is hard to ignore the evidence that by the 1930s the godly commonwealth ideal was in danger of capitulating to an exclusive Presbyterian nationalism against Irish Catholic migrants on the one hand and to an insensitive appreciation of the social miseries occasioned by economic depression on the other.[57] Only in Ireland, it seemed, was the church able to secure a strong influence over state social policy. The Roman Catholic Church's success was built on its numerical strength, its remarkable control over education and its influence with Irish politicians who could not easily ignore the electoral consequences of alienating the church.[58]

What these brief case studies reveal is that churches had little opportunity to shape social policy once they had lost the affection of the people and the ear of politicians. They could still act as the moral conscience of the State, and give rise to bursts of intellectual and social enthusiasm, but, without either numerical strength or political clout, the danger for churchmen was that they could be easily lionised as the utterers of moral platitudes and pious good intentions.[59] Politicians, it

---

[56] Ibid., p. 190.
[57] S. J. Brown, '"Outside the Covenant": the Scottish Presbyterian Churches and Irish Immigration, 1922–1938', *Innes Review*, 42 (1991); idem, 'The Social Vision of Scottish Presbyterianism and the Union of 1929', *Records of the Scottish Church History Society*, 24 (1990).
[58] J. H. Whyte, *Church and State in Modern Ireland 1923–1970* (Dublin, 1971); idem, *Interpreting Northern Ireland* (Oxford, 1991); J. Lee, *Ireland 1912–1985: Politics and Society* (Cambridge, 1989), pp. 1157–67.
[59] J. Garnett, 'Hastings Rashdall and the Renewal of Christian Social Ethics, c. 1890–1920', in J. Garnett and C. Matthew (eds.), *Revival and Religion since 1700* (London, 1993), pp. 297–316.

seems, have become weary of churchmen who can neither fill their own pews nor offer a convincing social policy for the operation of a modern state. The future for religion as a central part of the identity of the British is not altogether promising. Even cemeteries, once the earthiest of all representations of the religious utility of the parish units into which the British Isles were divided, succumbed to capitalism and the market economy during the course of the nineteenth century as a thousand-year-old tradition of churchyard burials gave way to the economics of private enterprise and municipal management.[60] Death has not yet lost its sting, but it has suffered spatial dislocation.

[60]   T. W. Laqueur, 'Cemeteries, Religion and the Culture of Capitalism', in *Revival and Religion*, pp. 183–200.

## CHAPTER 8

# *Conclusions*

The complex relationship between religion and identity in the modern history of the British Isles is not reducible to tidy conceptual frameworks. Professor Robbins, in the most authoritative work on the subject so far, states that

churches have been, in some instances and at some periods vehicles for the cultivation of a 'British' identity corresponding to the political framework of Great Britain and Ireland. They have also been instrumental, in part at least, in perpetuating and recreating an English, Irish, Scottish or Welsh identity distinct from and perhaps in conflict with 'British' identity, both culturally and politically. Sometimes this role has been quite unconscious, but in other instances it has been explicit and deliberate.[1]

The essence of the problem is that the British Isles is a religious patchwork quilt of immense complexity in which national, cultural, economic and denominational boundaries rarely achieve an exact correlation one with another. Moreover, the pattern alters over time and according to historical circumstances. Only in Ireland, it seems, is there a clear division, based on Reformation polarities, between an overwhelmingly Roman Catholic state and the rest of the British archipelago. This division, according to the Dutch geographer M. W. Heslinga, is essentially religious and represents the real frontier of the British Isles.[2] The fact that there is a political border approximating to this division gives the argument a greater degree of plausibility. There is need for care, however, even in this apparently self-evident division. Not only is there a substantial Roman Catholic minority in Northern Ireland, but there has been a considerable Irish Catholic migration to other parts of Britain. Moreover, the alleged coherence of Ulster's

---

[1]   K. Robbins, 'Religion and Identity in Modern British History', in S. Mews (ed.), *Religion and National Identity, Studies in Church History*, 18 (1982), 465–6; idem, *Nineteenth-Century Britain: Integration and Diversity* (Oxford, 1988).

[2]   M. W. Heslinga, *The Irish Border as a Cultural Divide* (Assen, 1971).

Protestant identity has evaporated under the heat of recent historical and sociological analysis. Not only are there deeply felt denominational differences among Ulster Protestants, but their degrees of attachment to British, Ulster and Irish identities vary enormously according to circumstances.[3] Indeed, they seem more united in their dislikes, principally of Roman Catholic nationalism, than in their preferences.[4] Thus the relationship between religion and identity, even in the part of the British Isles where it is regarded as most important, is extremely complicated and varies over time and in response to external pressures. The same is true of other parts of the British Isles in the past, but historians and other commentators have not been deterred by the apparent difficulties of the subject.

Linda Colley has boldly stated that throughout the long eighteenth century a shared Protestantism, with all the associated values of cultural chauvinism, was the most important component in the formation of a British identity. This is especially true when identity was pressed into service as a cultural weapon against other European states or against threats to Britain's dynastic or social stability. As an explanation for the divine origins of Britain's essential superiority over the rest of Europe, Protestantism held formidable explanatory power and was ruthlessly exploited by propagandists. There is, however, a danger of falling victim to the success of state or ecclesiastical propaganda. Even in its shared Protestantism eighteenth- and nineteenth-century Britain was deeply divided over matters of religion: divisions between the orthodox and the heterodox, between episcopalians and Presbyterians, between Churchmen and Dissenters, between evangelicals and High Churchmen, between clergymen and anticlericals and between adherents of the political status quo and those who wanted to change it. Even within a single denomination such as Methodism, a vigorous Protestantism and anti-Catholicism was not sufficient to maintain internal discipline nor to override other religious issues which many saw to be more important to their daily lives.[5] Protestantism certainly offered an important organising principle for the expression of identity, but it did not always deliver on its own propaganda. Its limitations as well as its power need to be recognised.

---

[3]    The various shades of opinion are carefully set out by J. Whyte, *Interpreting Northern Ireland* (Oxford, 1991).

[4]    F. W. Boal and D. Livingstone, 'Protestants in Belfast: A View from the Inside', *Contemporary Review*, 246 (Apr., 1986), 169–75.

[5]    D. Hempton, *Methodism and Politics in British Society 1750–1850* (London, 1984).

Another stimulating attempt to relate religious identities to other social and economic frameworks in the development of British nationhood is to be found in the work of the American sociologist Michael Hechter. In his book *Internal Colonialism*, Hechter suggests that since the Reformation the British Isles has operated as an internal empire with the core exercising a degree of economic, political and cultural power over the periphery.[6] This helps explain the persistence of differentials in the economic and demographic growth of different parts of the British Isles. During the industrial revolution, for example, the English economy diversified more quickly and became more powerful than those on the Celtic periphery of the British State. The economic dominance of the English economy had cultural ramifications. Most notably there was an accompanying Anglicisation in the linguistic development of the British Isles which saw Gaelic languages in retreat everywhere, except in southern Ireland after 1920 when the British no longer exercised control. The political dominance of England has been equally marked; but as a free and relatively open society it has imported and exported talent from the Celtic fringes at all social levels. The one area in which Anglicisation has been conspicuously unsuccessful, according to Hechter, is religion and culture. Both Anglicanism and English Nonconformity made little headway in Scotland, while the episcopal Established Churches of Ireland and Wales were first eroded and then disestablished – though in Wales it has to be said that Nonconformity with English roots was appropriated by the Welsh to express a cultural identity against an anglicised establishment. The processes of cultural exchange are infinitely complicated.

Nevertheless, Hechter's main argument is that in the period of the industrial revolution, and beyond, religion was a better conservator of cultural values and identities in the Celtic peripheries than even language itself. The reason for this is that language was clearly seen to be a barrier against economic progress while religion was not. Representatives of disadvantaged groups, from Irish Roman Catholics to English Nonconformists, were effectively excluded from the higher echelons of economic and cultural power, but only for as long as land and patronage remained the chief engines of economic success. The problem with Hechter's otherwise persuasive analysis is that his treatment of religion is based solely on denominational affiliations and takes no account of the theological and cultural assumptions shared by the

[6]    M. Hechter, *Internal Colonialism: The Celtic Fringe in British National Development, 1536–1966* (London, 1975).

different denominations. For example, it is possible to argue that during the industrial revolution the expansion of evangelicalism in many different denominations throughout the British Isles acted both as a way of binding the periphery to the core and as a means of regional differentiation. This combination probably eased the stresses and strains occasioned by the industrial revolution and enabled the regions to express an identity without recourse to aggressively separatist movements. The exception once again was southern Ireland where evangelical proselytism helped foster an Irish Catholic nationalism rather than diminish it.

In the post-Reformation period, and more particularly during the industrial revolution, a combination of theological diffusion, population migrations, improved transport facilities and religious secessions from older churches made the British Isles more religiously pluralistic and more religiously homogeneous at the same time. Anglicans, Presbyterians, Methodists and Nonconformists ended up in Ireland, mostly in Ulster, while Irish Catholics and some Protestants crossed the Irish Sea in the opposite direction. Similarly, large numbers of English labourers migrated to Wales in the nineteenth century. This pattern was happening even within religious denominations as English Nonconformity recruited disproportionately from the Celtic fringes for its ministry, and the two Anglican Archbishops of Canterbury and York on the eve of the First World War were Scots. The existence of such lines of communication, together with the ubiquitous interdenominational religious societies of the nineteenth century, helped prevent the formation of hermetically sealed denominational islands in the peripheries of the British State. When such islands were created, they were as likely to emerge as discrete religious cultures within the more general fragmentation of urban life as they were to have any clearly defined regional pattern.

Three other issues have struck me with particular force from this examination of religious and political cultures in the British Isles over a quarter of a millennium. The first is the importance of ecclesiastical propaganda and the invention of tradition in the re-creation of the religious history of these islands. The power of living religious traditions to shape the past according to its current preoccupations is virtually inexhaustible. Welsh Nonconformity, Scottish Presbyterianism, the Oxford Movement, evangelical individualism, Irish Catholicism and Ulster Protestantism, to name but a few, have all given rise to powerful historiographical traditions of dubious reliability. Perhaps this problem is particularly evident in writings on faith and identity in which the very souls of nations seem to be at stake. Roy Porter suggested recently that

those who appeal to bygone ages for the way, the truth and the life, are often those who know least about them. The past thus seems to be up for grabs, a chest of props and togs ready-to-wear in almost any costume drama, available to fulfil all manner of fantasies; and it is no accident that a crop of books has been appearing with titles like *The Invention of Tradition* ... – explorations of what Raphael Samuel and Paul Thompson have elsewhere dubbed *The Myths We Live By*. If the present can invent the past according to its own preferences, the past also has the capacity to shape the fears and aspirations of future generations.[7]

Examples of both litter the pages of works on religious history dealing with religion and identity. What is unnerving about this is how much we are still the unconscious prisoners of ecclesiastical traditions in shaping the questions we ask of the past. Whoever tells the story of God's dealings with his people, as the Moravians recognised with particular clarity in the eighteenth century, is in a position of formidable power.

A second issue raised by the theme of religion and identity is the way in which churches in both Britain and Ireland either facilitated or retarded the growth of political citizenship among their adherents. Far more than they recognised at the time, they were dependent for their future fortunes on being appropriate vehicles for wider social and political aspirations. From the Catholic Association in Ireland to chapel culture in Wales, and from Chalmers's penny-a-week church-building auxiliaries in Scotland to the robust encounters between Church and Dissent in England, the churches made an immense contribution to organising, articulating and mobilising support for a wide variety of campaigns. In the process organisational and oratorical abilities were nurtured and religio-political issues were given a much wider currency. Some religious traditions benefited from their association with their adherents' social and political objectives while others were marginalised. Churches or religious traditions which set themselves against the economic, social or political aspirations of their potential recruits were unlikely to thrive and the reverse was generally the case. Nevertheless, the fact that the religious fragmentation and diversity of the British Isles was reflected in manifold competing claims probably contributed as much as anything to the preservation of certain freedoms and the

[7]    R. Porter (ed.), *Myths of the English* (Cambridge, 1992), p.1.

right to dissent. More homogeneous religious societies are, generally speaking, less tolerant of deviance.

Finally, it is difficult to resist the conclusion that the French revolutionary period is the most important in the modern religious history of the British Isles. Established Churches without either a genuinely popular appeal or vigorous state support were unlikely to prosper, while on the other hand voluntaryism and pluralism opened up the way for enthusiasm in the short term and apathy in the long term. In that respect the words penned by Professor Ward almost a quarter of a century ago are as relevant now as when they were first written.

> The generation about which I wish to speak was, I make no doubt, the most important single generation in the modern history not merely of English religion but of the whole Christian world ... The great crisis of the French Revolution altered for ever the terms on which religious establishments must work, and in doing so it intensified everywhere a long-felt need for private action in the world of religion.[8]

What this study has sought to demonstrate is that in the generation after the French and industrial revolutions, the churches in the British Isles found themselves in competition with one another, and often with the State as well, over the best ways to Christianise the masses and then assimilate them into their religious traditions. In that competition, access to power and the resources of the State proved to be a less vital ingredient than it had been in the past, when religion was sufficiently important for established interests to make it a matter of coercion. As religious coercion in the British Isles became a less acceptable proposition by the end of the eighteenth century, the future lay elsewhere. Of much more significance was the ability, or otherwise, of churches to reflect and propagate the social, political and cultural aspirations of their members. The spoils invariably went to those who could fuse religious zeal with important cultural identities. In that respect a sense of exclusion or disadvantage offered even greater rewards than did control over the inflexions of power. To say that is not to capitulate to a reductionist interpretation of religion. The reverse, if anything, is closer to the mark. The fact that churches in the long eighteenth and nineteenth centuries were closely bound up with the lives of their adherents is after all the main reason why the theme of national, regional and urban identities cannot be properly investigated without reference to religion.

---

[8]   W. R. Ward, 'The Religion of the People and the Problem of Control, 1790–1830', in idem, *Faith and Faction* (London, 1993), pp. 264–84.

# Select bibliography

What follows is a personal selection of the most important books bearing on the theme of religion and identity in Britain and Ireland since 1700. More assiduous enquirers should make use of the more detailed guidance on primary material, periodical literature and unpublished dissertations supplied in the notes for each chapter.

Akenson, D. H., *Small Differences: Irish Catholics and Irish Protestants 1815–1922*, Montreal and Kingston, 1988.

    *God's Peoples: Covenant and Land in South Africa, Israel and Ulster*, Montreal and Kingston, 1991.

Bartlett, Thomas, *The Fall and Rise of the Irish Nation: The Catholic Question 1690–1830*, Dublin, 1992.

Bebbington, D. W., *The Nonconformist Conscience: Chapel and Politics 1870–1914*, London, 1982.

    *Evangelicalism in Modern Britain: A History from the 1730s to the 1980s*, London, 1989.

    *Victorian Nonconformity*, Bangor, Gwynedd, 1992.

Binfield, Clyde, *So Down to Prayers*, London, 1977.

Bossy, John, *The English Catholic Community*, London, 1975.

Bowen, Desmond, *The Protestant Crusade in Ireland 1800–70*, Dublin, 1978.

Boyce, D. G., *The Revolution in Ireland, 1870–1923*, London, 1988.

Bradley, J. E., *Religion, Revolution and English Radicalism: Nonconformity in Eighteenth-Century Politics and Society*, Cambridge, 1990.

Brooke, Peter, *Ulster Presbyterianism: The Historical Perspective*, Dublin, 1987.

Brown, C. G., *The Social History of Religion in Scotland since 1730*, London, 1987.

    *The People in the Pews: Religion and Society in Scotland since 1780*, Dundee, 1993.

Brown, K. D., *A Social History of the Nonconformist Ministry in England and Wales 1800–1930*, Oxford, 1988.

Brown, S. J., *Thomas Chalmers and the Godly Commonwealth*, Oxford, 1982.

Brown, S. J. and Fry, M., eds., *Scotland in the Age of Disruption*, Edinburgh, 1993.

Bruce, Steve, *God Save Ulster!: The Religion and Politics of Paisleyism*, Oxford, 1986.

Bruce, Steve, ed., *Religion and Secularization: Historians and Sociologists Debate Modernization Theory*, Oxford, 1992.

Bushaway, Bob, *By Rite: Custom, Ceremony and Community in England 1700–1880*, London, 1982.

Chadwick, Owen, *The Victorian Church*, 2 vols., London, 1966, 1970.

Cheyne, A. C., *The Transforming of the Kirk: Victorian Scotland's Religious Revolution*, Edinburgh, 1983.

Coleman, B. I., *The Church of England in the Mid-Nineteenth Century: A Social Geography*, London, 1980.

Colley, Linda, *Britons: Forging the Nation 1707–1837*, New Haven and London, 1992.

Colls, Robert, *The Collier's Rant: Song and Culture in the Industrial Village*, London, 1977.

Colls, Robert and Dodd, Philip, *Englishness: Politics and Culture 1880–1920*, Beckenham, 1986.

Connolly, S. J., *Priests and People in Pre-Famine Ireland 1780–1845*, Dublin, 1982.
  *Religion and Society in Nineteenth-Century Ireland*, Dundalk, 1985.
  *Religion, Law and Power: The Making of Protestant Ireland 1660–1760*, Oxford, 1992.

Corish, P. J., ed., *Radicals, Rebels and Establishments*, Belfast, 1985.
  *The Irish Catholic Experience: A Historical Survey*, Dublin, 1985.

Cox, Jeffrey, *The English Churches in a Secular Society: Lambeth 1870–1930*, Oxford, 1982.

Cullen, L. M., *The Emergence of Modern Ireland 1600–1900*, London, 1981.

Cunningham, Valentine, *Everywhere Spoken Against: Dissent in the Victorian Novel*, Oxford, 1975.

Currie, Robert, Gilbert, Alan and Horsley, Lee, *Churches and Churchgoers: Patterns of Church Growth in the British Isles Since 1700*, Oxford, 1977.

Davies, E. T., *Religion in the Industrial Revolution in South Wales*, Cardiff, 1965.
  *A New History of Wales: Religion and Society in the Nineteenth Century*, Llandybie, Dyfed, 1981.

Davies, Rupert, George, A. R., and Rupp, Gordon, eds., *A History of the Methodist Church in Great Britain*, 4 vols., London, 1963–88.

Devine, T. M., ed., *Irish Immigrants and Scottish Society in the Nineteenth and Twentieth Centuries*, Edinburgh, 1991.

Devine, T. M. and Dickson, David, ed., *Ireland and Scotland 1600–1850: Parallels and Contrasts in Economic and Social Development*, Edinburgh, 1983.

Drummond, A. L. and Bulloch, J., *The Scottish Church 1688–1843: The Age of the Moderates*, Edinburgh, 1973.
  *The Church in Victorian Scotland 1843–1874*, Edinburgh, 1975.
  *The Church in Late Victorian Scotland 1874–1900*, Edinburgh, 1978.

Dyos, H. J. and Wolff, Michael, eds., *The Victorian City*, 2 vols., London, 1973.

Elliott, Marianne, *Partners in Revolution: The United Irishmen and France*, New Haven, 1982.

Evans, D. G., *A History of Wales 1815–1906*, Cardiff, 1989.

Evans, E. D., *A History of Wales 1660–1815*, Cardiff, 1976.

Fitzpatrick, David, *Politics and Irish Life, 1913–21: Provincial Experience of War and Revolution*, Dublin, 1977.

Foster, John, *Class Struggle and the Industrial Revolution: Early Industrial Capitalism in Three English Towns*, London, 1974.

Foster, R. F., *Modern Ireland, 1600–1972*, London, 1988.

Garnett, Jane and Matthew, Colin, *Revival and Religion Since 1700*, London, 1993.

Gash, Norman, *Pillars of Government*, London, 1986.

Gay, J. D., *The Geography of Religion in England*, London, 1971.

Gibbon, Peter, *The Origins of Ulster Unionism: The Formation of Popular Protestant Politics and Ideology in Nineteenth-Century Ireland*, Manchester, 1975.

Gilbert, A. D., *Religion and Society in Industrial England: Church, Chapel and Social Change 1740–1914*, London, 1976.

Gill, Robin, *The Myth of the Empty Church*, London, 1993.

Gilley, Sheridan and Sheils, W. J., eds., *A History of Religion in Britain: Practice and Belief from Pre-Roman Times to the Present*, Oxford, 1994.

Harvie, Christopher, *Scotland and Nationalism: Scottish Society and Politics, 1707–1977*, London, 1977.

Haydon, Colin, *Anti-Catholicism in Eighteenth-Century England: A Political and Social Study*, Manchester, 1993.

Hechter, Michael, *Internal Colonialism: The Celtic Fringe in British National Development, 1536–1966*, London, 1975.

Hempton, David, *Methodism and Politics in British Society 1750–1850*, London, 1984.

Hempton, David and Hill, Myrtle, *Evangelical Protestantism in Ulster Society 1740–1890*, London, 1992.

Herbert, Trevor and Jones, G. E., *People and Protest: Wales 1815–1880*, Cardiff, 1988.

Hilton, Boyd, *The Age of Atonement: The Influence of Evangelicalism on Social and Economic Thought, 1795–1865*, Oxford, 1988.

Hobsbawm, E. J., *Nations and Nationalism Since 1780: Programme, Myth, Reality*, Cambridge, 1990.

Hobsbawm, E. J. and Ranger, Terence, *The Invention of Tradition*, Cambridge, 1983.

Holmes, R. F., *Henry Cooke*, Belfast, 1981.
  *Our Irish Presbyterian Heritage*, Belfast, 1985.

Hoppen, T. K., *Ireland since 1800: Conflict and Conformity*, London, 1989.

Hyam, Ronald, *Britain's Imperial Century 1815–1914*, London, 1976.

Jackson, Alvin, *Colonel Edward Saunderson: Land and Loyalty in Victorian Ireland*, Oxford, 1995.

Jenkins, G. H., *The Foundations of Modern Wales 1642–1780*, Oxford, 1987.

Jenkins, G. H. and Smith, J. B., *Politics and Society in Wales, 1840–1922*, Cardiff, 1988.

Jones, I. G., *Communities: Essays in the Social History of Victorian Wales*, Llandysul, Dyfed, 1987.

Jones, I. G. and Williams, David, *The Religious Census of 1851: A Calendar of the Returns Relating to Wales*, 2 vols., Cardiff, 1976.

*Bibliography*

Keenan, Desmond, *The Catholic Church in Nineteenth-Century Ireland: A Sociological Study*, Dublin, 1983.

Kent, John, *William Temple: Church, State and Society in Britain, 1880–1950*, Cambridge, 1992.

Koditschek, Theodore, *Class Formation and Urban Industrial Society: Bradford, 1750–1850*, Cambridge, 1990.

Laqueur, T. W., *Religion and Respectability: Sunday Schools and Working Class Culture 1780–1850*, New Haven, 1976.

Larkin, Emmet, *The Roman Catholic Church and the Creation of the Modern Irish State 1878–86*, Dublin, 1975.

*The Historical Dimensions of Irish Catholicism*, New York, 1981.

Lovegrove, D. W., *Established Church, Sectarian People: Itinerancy and the Transformation of English Dissent, 1780–1830*, Cambridge, 1988.

Machin, G. I. T., *Politics and the Churches in Great Britain 1832 to 1868*, Oxford, 1977.

*Politics and the Churches in Great Britain 1869 to 1921*, Oxford, 1987.

Mackenzie, J. M., *Propaganda and Empire: The Manipulation of British Public Opinion 1880–1960*, Manchester, 1984.

Mackenzie, J. M., ed., *Imperialism and Popular Culture*, Manchester, 1986.

MacLaren, A. A., *Religion and Social Class: The Disruption Years in Aberdeen*, London, 1974.

McLeod, Hugh, *Class and Religion in the late Victorian City*, London, 1974.

*Religion and the Working Class in Nineteenth-Century Britain*, London, 1984.

*Religion and Irreligion in Victorian England*, Bangor, Gwynedd, 1993.

McLeod, Hugh, ed., *European Religion in the Age of Great Cities 1830–1930*, London, 1995.

Mews, Stuart, ed., *Religion and National Identity: Studies in Church History*, XVIII, Oxford, 1982.

Miller, D. W., *Queen's Rebels: Ulster Loyalism in Historical Perspective*, Dublin, 1978.

Mitchison, Rosalind, *Life in Scotland*, London, 1978.

Mitchison, Rosalind, ed., *The Roots of Nationalism: Studies in Northern Europe*, Edinburgh, 1980.

Morgan, K. O., *Wales in British Politics 1868–1922*, Cardiff, 1980.

*Rebirth of a Nation: Wales 1880–1980*, Oxford, 1981.

Morris, Jeremy, *Religion and Urban Change*, London, 1992.

Nicholls, David, *Deity and Domination: Images of God and the State in the Nineteenth and Twentieth Centuries*, London, 1989.

Noll, M. A., Bebbington, D. W., and Rawlyk, G. A., eds., *Evangelicalism: Comparative Studies of Popular Protestantism in North America, the British Isles, and Beyond, 1700–1990*, New York and Oxford, 1994.

Norman, Edward, *Anti-Catholicism in Victorian England*, London, 1968.

*The English Catholic Church in the Nineteenth Century*, Oxford, 1984.

O'Brien, Gerard, *Catholic Ireland in the Eighteenth Century: Collected Essays of Maureen Wall*, Dublin, 1989.

O'Ferrall, Fergus, *Catholic Emancipation: Daniel O'Connell and the Birth of Irish Democracy 1820–30*, Dublin, 1985.

Obelkevich, James, *Religion and Rural Society: South Lindsey 1825–1875*, Oxford, 1976.

Obelkevich, James, Roper, Lyndal and Samuel, Raphael, eds., *Disciplines of Faith: Studies in Religion, Politics and Patriarchy*, London, 1987.

Olsen, G. W., ed., *Religion and Revolution in Early Industrial England: The Halévy Thesis and its Critics*, Lanham, Md., 1990.

Parsons, Gerald, ed., *Religion in Victorian Britain*, 4 vols., Manchester, 1988.

Paz, D. G. *Popular Anti-Catholicism in Mid-Victorian England*, Stanford, Calif., 1992.

Porter, A. N., *Religion and Empire: British Expansion in the Long 19th Century, 1780–1914*, London, 1991.

Porter, Bernard, *The Lion's Share: A Short History of British Imperialism 1850–1983*, London, 1984.

Power, T. P. and Whelan, Kevin, eds., *Endurance and Emergence: Catholics in Ireland in the Eighteenth Century*, Dublin, 1990.

Prochaska, F. K., *Women and Philanthropy in Nineteenth-Century England*, Oxford, 1980.

Rees, D. B., *Chapels in the Valley: A Study in the Sociology of Welsh Nonconformity*, Upton, Wirral, 1975.

Robbins, Keith, *Nineteenth-Century Britain: Integration and Diversity*, Oxford, 1988.

Robson, R., ed., *Ideas and Institutions of Victorian Britain*, London, 1967.

Rosman, Doreen, *Evangelicals and Culture*, London, 1984.

Samuel, Raphael, ed., *Patriotism: The Making and Unmaking of British National Identity*, 3 vols., London, 1989.

Smith, Mark, *Religion in Industrial Society: Oldham and Saddleworth 1740–1865*, Oxford, 1994.

Smout, T. C., *A History of the Scottish People 1560–1830*, Glasgow, 1972.

*A Century of the Scottish People, 1830–1950*, Glasgow, 1986.

Soloway, R. S., *Prelates and People: Ecclesiastical Social Thought in England 1783–1852*, London, 1969.

Stanley, Brian, *The Bible and the Flag: Protestant Missions and British Imperialism in the Nineteenth and Twentieth Centuries*, Leicester, 1990.

Stewart, A. T. Q., *The Ulster Crisis: Resistance to Home Rule, 1912–14*, London, 1967.

*The Narrow Ground: Aspects of Ulster 1609–1969*, London, 1977.

Storch, R. D., *Popular Culture and Custom in Nineteenth-Century England*, London, 1982.

Swift, Roger and Gilley, Sheridan, eds., *The Irish in the Victorian City*, London, 1985.

*The Irish in Britain 1815–1939*, London, 1989.

Thomas, Terence, ed., *The British: Their Religious Beliefs and Practices 1800–1986*, London, 1988.

Thompson, David, *Nonconformity in the Nineteenth Century*, London, 1972.

Thompson, E. P., *The Making of the English Working Class*, Harmondsworth, 1968.

Virgin, Peter, *The Church in an Age of Negligence: Ecclesiastical Structure and Problems of Church Reform 1700–1840*, Cambridge, 1989.

Wallace, Ryland, *'Organise! Organise! Organise!': A History of Reform Agitations in Wales, 1840–1886*, Cardiff, 1991.

Waller, P. J., *Democracy and Sectarianism: A Social and Political History of Liverpool 1868–1939*, Liverpool, 1981.

Walsh, John, Haydon, Colin and Taylor, Stephen, eds., *The Church of England c. 1689–1833: From Toleration to Tractarianism*, Cambridge, 1993.

Ward, W. R., *Religion and Society in England 1790–1850*, London, 1972.

*The Protestant Evangelical Awakening*, Cambridge, 1992.

*Faith and Faction*, London, 1993.

Watts, Michael, *The Dissenters: From the Reformation to the French Revolution*, Oxford, 1978.

Whyte, J. H., *Church and State in Modern Ireland 1923–1970*, Dublin, 1971.

*Interpreting Northern Ireland*, Oxford, 1991.

Williamson, J. G., *Coping with City Growth During the British Industrial Revolution*, Cambridge, 1990.

Wolffe, John, *The Protestant Crusade in Great Britain, 1829–60*, Oxford, 1991.

*God and Greater Britain: Religion and National Life in Britain and Ireland 1843–1945*, London, 1994.

Yeo, Stephen, *Religion and Voluntary Organisations in Crisis*, London, 1976.

Young, Kenneth, *Chapel*, London, 1972.

# Index